Incom

Intern

Also by the same authors

Protectionism, by Jagdish Bhagwati, 1988

International Trade: Selected Readings, second edition, edited by Jagdish N. Bhagwati, 1987

Wealth and Poverty, Essays in Development Economics, volume 1, by Jagdish N. Bhagwati, edited by Gene M. Grossman, 1985

Dependence and Interdependence, Essays in Development Economics, volume 2, by Jagdish N. Bhagwati, edited by Gene M. Grossman, 1985

Power, Passions, and Purpose: Prospects for North-South Negotiations, edited by Jagdish N. Bhagwati and John Gerard Ruggie, 1984

The Theory of Commercial Policy, Essays in International Economic Theory, volume 1, by Jagdish N. Bhagwati, edited by Robert C. Feenstra, 1983

International Factor Mobility, Essays in International Economic Theory, volume 2, by Jagdish N. Bhagwati, edited by Robert C. Feenstra, 1983

Lectures on International Trade, by Jagdish N. Bhagwati and T. N. Srinivasan, 1983

The New International Economic Order: The North-South Debate, edited by Jagdish N. Bhagwati, 1977

Income Taxation and International Mobility

edited by

Jagdish N. Bhagwati
and
John Douglas Wilson

foreword by
Richard A. Musgrave

The MIT Press
Cambridge, Massachusetts
London, England

This book was set in Palatino by Asco Trade Typesetting Ltd., Hong Kong, and printed and bound in the United States.

Permission to reprint articles has been granted as follows:
Elsevier Science Publishers B.V. (North-Holland) for:
John Douglas Wilson. 1980. The effect of potential emigration on the optimal linear income tax. *Journal of Public Economics* 14: 339–353.
Jagdish Bhagwati and Koichi Hamada. 1982. Tax policy in the presence of emigration. *Journal of Public Economics* 18: 291–317.
John Douglas Wilson. 1982. Optimal linear income taxation in the presence of emigration. *Journal of Public Economics* 18: 363–379.
William J. Baumol. 1982. The income distribution frontier and the taxation of migrants. *Journal of Public Economics* 18: 343–361.
James A. Mirrlees. 1982. Migration and optimal income taxes. *Journal of Public Economics* 18: 319–341.
John Douglas Wilson. 1982. Optimal income taxation and migration: A world welfare point of view. *Journal of Public Economics* 18: 381–397.
New York University Journal of International Law and Politics (New York University) for:
Richard D. Pomp. 1985. The experience of the Philippines in taxing its nonresident citizens. 17: 245–286.

Library of Congress Cataloging-in-Publication Data

Income taxation and international mobility / edited by Jagdish Bhagwati and John Douglas Wilson.
    p. cm.
Some papers first presented at a conference held 1/81 in New Delhi.
Bibliography: p.
Includes index.
    Contents: Income taxation in the presence of international personal mobility / Jagdish N. Bhagwati and John Douglas Wilson—The experience of the Philippines in taxing its nonresident citizens / Richard D. Pomp—The state, the individual, and the taxation of economic migration / Gary Clyde Hufbauer—The effect of potential emigration on the optimal linear income tax / John Douglas Wilson—Tax policy in the presence of emigration / Jagdish N. Bhagwati and Koichi Hamada—Optimal linear income taxation in the presence of emigration / John Douglas Wilson—The income distribution frontier and the taxation of migrants / William J. Baumol—Migration and optimal income taxes / James A. Mirrlees—Optimal income taxation and migration / John Douglas Wilson.
    ISBN 978-0-262-02292-7(hc.:alk.paper) 978-0-262-51211-4(pb.:alk.paper)
    1. Income tax—Foreign income—Congresses.   I. Bhagwati, Jagdish N., 1934–
II. Wilson, John D. (John Douglas)
K4536.C56A55   1989
343.05′248—dc 19
[342.35248]   89-2512
                                                                          CIP

To the senior John D. Wilson
and to
Peter Diamond

Contents

Contributors

William J. Baumol
Professor of Economics, Princeton University, Princeton, New Jersey, and
New York University, New York, New York

Jagdish N. Bhagwati
Arthur Lehman Professor of Economics and Professor of Political Science,
Columbia University, New York, New York

Koichi Hamada
Professor of Economics, Yale University, New Haven, Connecticut

Gary Clyde Hufbauer
Wallenberg Professor of International Economics, Georgetown
University, Washington, D.C.

James A. Mirrlees
Henry Sidgwick Professor of Economics, Oxford University, Oxford,
England

Richard D. Pomp
Professor of Law, University of Connecticut, Storrs, Connecticut

John Douglas Wilson
Associate Professor of Economics, Indiana University, Bloomington,
Indiana

Foreword

This volume builds on and explores in depth Bhagwati's earlier call for a citizen's tax, a tax that would enable a developing country to share in the tax base provided by the income of its citizens who reside abroad. In part I Bhagwati and Wilson explore the rationale for such a tax. Part II includes examination of the experience with global taxation by the Philippines, one of two countries (the other being the United States) now practicing it. Part III deals with the development of an analytical framework for global taxation, based on the theoretical model of optimal income tax. The volume thus opens a new and exciting perspective on international income taxation, similar in some but different in other respects from the more familiar issues of international coordination under the corporation tax. Although the difficulties of a citizen's tax are substantial, the idea is challenging and well worth pursuing.

Under traditional tax theory the requirements for a good tax system are viewed within the borders of a set jurisdiction. Adam Smith's canons of taxation did not prescribe how His Majesty's taxes should apply to British traders residing in France or in the West Indies. Discriminatory product taxes on trade, to be sure, were debated since mercantilist days, but concern with the open-economy aspects of direct taxation is of recent vintage. Here primary focus to date has been on capital income and the *corporation tax*.[1] This is not surprising, since such coordination has been necessitated by the rapid expansion of international capital flows. The tax base created by the earnings of international capital can be reached by more than one jurisdiction, so that coordination is needed lest combined rates become arbitrary and excessive. The solution as formulated in tax practices and treaties has been designed to satisfy two conditions, one relating to the equity and the other to the efficiency aspects of the problem.

Beginning with the equity aspects, the requirement is to provide for a fair distribution of the tax base among concerned jurisdictions.[2] Coordination thus raises a problem of internation equity, parallel to but different from the closed-jurisdiction concept of interindividual tax equity. Internation equity has been interpreted to recognize two legitimate claimants, including the country of source (where the income originates) and the country of incorporation (or in some cases of head office), also referred to as the country of residence. The source country's claim may be taken to reflect its entitlement to impose a benefit charge for public services rendered, as well as to charge a "rental fee" for the opportunity to earn income in its borders. Because business operations may extend across various countries, several countries of source may be involved. This requires a complex procedure by which to allocate the total profit base among them, be it a rule of arm's length pricing or unitary taxation based on a formula approach. The claim extended by the country of incorporation may be derived from the proposition that incorporation in a particular jurisdiction also involves acceptance of that jurisdiction's fiscal system and its obligations.

There remains the question of what weight should be assigned to the two claims, a question that is not answered directly, but in relation to the second, or efficiency, condition. That condition calls for noninterference by taxation in the direction of capital flow, that is, for capital export neutrality.[3] It requires that investors find themselves subject to the same tax law, wherever they choose to invest. This requirement may be satisfied in various ways. Taxation may be by the country of incorporation only, while permitting tax rates to differ across countries; or it may be by the country of income source only, with rates equalized across countries. Finally, taxation may be by both the residence and source countries, but to assure neutrality the residency country must then permit the source country's tax to be credited against its own. Reverse crediting will not do.[4] There are thus various solutions that will yield export neutrality, but they differ sharply in how access to the base is divided. Because neutrality requires the credit to be given by the country of residence, the primary claim to the tax base is yielded to the country of source, and the country of residence is limited to the excess of its tax rate above that of the source country. This may or may not offer a fair solution, and complete freedom to satisfy both efficiency and equity considerations may require a further policy instrument, such as transfers between the treasuries of both countries.

Turning now to the *individual income tax*, the problem is similar in some respects but different in others. Once more typical practice is for two claimants to be recognized, including again the country of source and (in lieu of incorporation) the country of the taxpayer's residence. The reason underlying these two claims may be viewed in terms similar to those noted previously for the corporation tax. For labor income, source and residence tend to coincide, so that only one tax is involved. Assuming equal work options in two countries, a person may choose to file with the one with the lower tax. Thus tax factors are no longer neutral with regard to factor flow. Such is not the case, however, for capital income when two taxes apply and crediting again occurs. The crediting is again undertaken by the country of residence, but the surrender of tax base to the country of source is more limited than in the case of the corporation tax. This comes about because the source tax is typically restricted to a relatively low withholding rate, without attempting to match the individual income tax schedule of the source country. Because of this the rate of tax in the country of residence may become a decisive factor in residency choice. Although this does not distort the efficiency of capital flow, it may well interfere with internation equity in revenue distribution.

This points to an additional dimension of the individual income tax, a dimension that arises from a basic distinction between individuals and corporations. Whereas for the corporation there are only two claimants (country of source and country of incorporation or residence), the individual income tax may well recognize the country of citizenship as a third party of entitlement to the tax base.[5] Most individuals, to be sure, will reside in their country of citizenship so that this distinction does not matter, but there are important exceptions. Citizen X of country A may choose to migrate to B, where potential net earnings are higher. It may now be argued that this does not relieve X of fiscal responsibility to A. Citizenship in A may be viewed as involving membership in A's fiscal community with its resulting fiscal obligations to A. Whereas the claim of the country of residence applies to individual taxpayers in line with their current residence only, that of the country of citizenship is independent thereof and relates to the country of residence before migration. Individuals may escape (or swap) the former claim by choosing a new place of residence whereas the latter may not be dropped in this fashion. Does this mean that imposition of a fiscal obligation to the country of citizenship chains individual taxpayers to their past, a fate that typically was determined by others? Does this not involve undue interference with freedom to arrange one's own life? The answer is clearly no. A citizen tax, distinct from taxation by country of birth, leaves individuals free to remove this obligation by renunciation of citizenship. The problem therefore is not one of bondage to the past but of how the meaning of citizenship should be interpreted.

In future years developments may lead to a disappearance of nation-states, with individuals holding world citizenship only. In such a setting there would still be "local" (that is, geographically limited) fiscal units, just as local fiscs are needed now in a unitary state. Such would be needed simply because the spatial benefit incidence of various public services differs. But residents of all these units would then carry obligations to the world fisc, with concern for fiscal provision needed on a worldwide basis. But this is far off, and before such a state is reached, rival jurisdictions may yet appear in the form of unknown planets, thus beginning a new cycle. As long as the institution of nation-states exists, with individuals holding citizenship in one nation-state only, allegiance to the jurisdication of citizenship is a natural by-product of that institution. Such allegiance moreover involves privileges (for example, protection and right to vote) as well as obligations (for example, military service and fiscal responsibility), and it seems unreasonable to let the latter lapse with emigration while retaining the former.

Retention of fiscal allegiance to the country of citizenship (or recognition of that country's claim to a share of the tax base) is of particular importance, especially to developing countries where the lure of higher earnings abroad results in a costly drain of talented labor and loss of tax base.[6] The gap between earnings at home and abroad is typically large, as is the gap between the fiscal capacities of the home and guest country. All this renders the country of citizenship as a third claimant of special significance for developing countries, and this is the appropriate context in which this book presents the issue of global taxation.

At the same time a claim to global taxation by the country of citizenship is only half the solution. A number of further aspects need be considered. To begin with, there again remains the problem of how the claim is to be coordinated with the other claims. If the country of citizenship taxes its citizens abroad without crediting their residency tax, the total burden may well be so high as to invite revocation of citizenship or to forestall immigration. Crediting the foreign tax in turn may deprive the country of citizenship of most of its revenue gain. In-between solutions might be found by giving a partial credit, or the country of residence (reversing the direction of credit and yielding its prior claim by source) might credit the tax paid to the country of citizenship.[7] As far as the taxpayer is concerned, the direction of credit may not matter, but the pattern of base sharing again depends greatly on what arrangements are made. A credit given by the residency country might offer a novel means of support to the developing country, with the latter's gain depending on its own rate of tax. In fiscal terms such crediting might be viewed as a matching grant to the developing country's own tax on its citizens residing abroad.

Next there is the question of whether the country of citizenship can in fact reach its citizens abroad. The U.S. experience as detailed in chapter 1 has not been encouraging. The aim of global taxation as also shown in Chapter 3 has been controversial, and its pursuit has been half-hearted. For one thing opposition to the global rule has recently succeeded in providing legislation that grants an additional deduction of $80,000 for expenses of living abroad, so that the taxation of foreign residents is now limited to those earning higher incomes. For another the attempt at global taxation is effectively pursued only when foreign residence is limited, as in the case of temporary employment by U.S. companies abroad. About half of U.S. nationals residing abroad are said to fall into this group. Although the filing requirement also applies to long-term foreign residents, the compliance rate is said to be as low as 10 percent. This, however, is difficult to interpret as it may be taken to reflect unwillingness to enforce the provision, as well as difficulties in doing so. Retention of citizenship after all requires passports to be renewed every ten years, and tax compliance may be enforced in that context. The experience of the Philippines, as documented in chapter 2, has encountered similar or even greater difficulties. In the absence of an international tax authority, administrative cooperation by the country of residence would seem essential for successful implementation of the global rule by developing countries. This might not require outright collection with intergovernmental revenue transfer, but the availability of tax returns from the residency country to the country of nationality would seem essential. Such cooperation, however, is difficult to obtain. U.S. tax treaties, for instance, provide for quite limited cooperation in specific cases of fraud, but there is no general availability of foreign returns.

Although these practical issues may prove decisive in the end, there remains the analytical problem of what a global claim by developing countries would accomplish if it could be applied. This is examined in part III. Turning to the framework of optimal income taxation, the role of migration is introduced as an additional variable and earlier conclusions regarding optimal tax rates are reexamined in this broader context. Thereby a pioneering contribution is made to the theory of optimal taxation and important insights are gained into the potentials of a global or citizenship-based income tax. The analysis in large part makes use of a social welfare function that allows for the welfare of stay-at-homes only, rather than for the welfare of all nationals or even for world welfare. This limitation seems appropriate for the purpose of giving aid to the developing countries. Using a linear income tax model, the analysis first examines how introduction of migration will affect the optimal marginal rate of tax. Assuming that migrants cannot be taxed, opening the border is shown to lower the marginal rate, at least unless the social welfare function exhibits a very high degree of inequality aversion.

Introduction of migration without taxation of migrants, moreover, reduces revenue and depresses the welfare of those who remain behind. This loss is cushioned as the foreign income of émigrés comes to be included in the base. Indeed opening the border to emigration might now increase tax revenue and raise the welfare of those remaining behind. Such is the case especially if earning opportunities abroad are considerably greater than those at home.

Similar conclusions are likely to apply for more limited formulations of the problem. Thus the budget might be taken as given by its actual setting rather than be defined in terms of optimal redistribution; the gains may then be defined as those that would result if the income of nationals living abroad could be included in the base and domestic taxes were reduced accordingly. Substantial gains might still be achieved and the conclusions reached by the theoretical explorations of this book are indeed encouraging. But the difficulties of implementation remain substantial. To reach its citizens abroad, the country of citizenship will need administrative cooperation by the country of residence, which in turn will have to be willing to accept a crediting arrangement that leaves the country of citizenship with a significant share of the tax base.

Richard A. Musgrave

H. H. Burbank Professor of Economics, Emeritus, Harvard University

Adjunct Professor of Economics, University of California at Santa Cruz

Notes

1. For a recent discussion of these issues, see S. Cnossen, ed., *Tax Coordination in the Common Market*, 1986. The volume contains papers presented at a conference of the International Seminar in Public Economics, Erasmus University, Rotterdam, August, 1985.

2. See R. A. Musgrave and P. B. Musgrave, "Internation Equity," in R. Bird and J. Head, eds., *Modern Fiscal Issues*, Toronto, University of Toronto Press, 1977.

3. This concept of export neutrality should not be confused with an alternative quest for so-called import neutrality. Export neutrality by removing tax factors in choosing the location of investment is an efficiency requirement. The proposition that investors residing in different countries also should be subject to the same tax when competing in a third country is *not* an efficiency rule. Investors from high-tax countries may feel that such treatment is unfair when they are forced to compete against investors from a low-tax country, but this situation will be the same wherever they invest.

4. Crediting will ensure neutrality when the residence country's tax exceeds that of the source country. If the foreign tax is higher, neutrality would call for a refund to be given by the country of residence. But no refunds are in fact paid, so that the credit approach will be neutral only when the credited foreign tax falls short of the domestic tax.

5. Here as in many other instances of tax analysis it need be noted that all taxes in the end are paid by people, so that the corporation tax (assuming it falls on capital) is in the end simply a tax on individual recipients of capital income. This poses additional problems of interindividual equity (among people receiving income from different factors) and has further implications for application of the global rule. If a citizen of country A holds shares in a corporation incorporated in B and operating in C, the global (citizen tax principle) may again be applied, now giving A a claim to part of the corporation tax revenue. This, however, would be extremely difficult to implement. Further complexities—enough to boggle the observer's imagination—arise when some corporation taxes are integrated with the personal income tax, but others are not. It is thus prudent that this book's analysis is limited to the personal income tax only.

6. It should be added that emigration may involve low- as well as high-income recipients. Whereas emigration of the latter burdens the fiscal position of the developing country, emigration of the former may strengthen it. This raises another dimension of fiscal allegiance in relation to citizenship. If high-income migrants retain fiscal responsibility to their country of citizenship, does it also follow that the country of citizenship retains a fiscal responsibility to its low-income émigrés? This raises the further question of whether differential treatment of the two aspects is justified by reference to associated differences in the residents' average capacity to pay in the two countries.

7. In the case of labor income in which residence and source coincide, this may be said to interfere with labor export neutrality, an objection less serious than in the context of capital flow.

Preface

As our introduction (chapter 1) makes clear, this book is a product of interest in this question: If citizens can work or reside abroad, that is, if there is international mobility of people, how should the income tax jurisdiction of a country be exercised over the subset that is mobile? That is, should the income tax be extended to citizens abroad on a citizenship nexus, or should it be levied on the basis of residence, thereby effectively exempting from its scope those citizens who are abroad?

This issue belongs to the wider, and indeed increasing, interface of economics with law, sociology, politics, and moral philosophy. To deal with the issue, we must wrestle with questions such as which society does the mobile citizen "belong to" for the purpose of the welfare economist's delineation of the group over which social welfare is to be defined, and would it violate "natural" rights or received international law to have residents of the same nation with different nationalities taxed in effect at different rates? The economic theorist must, at each step, tread on these and other complex issues that the narrower discipline of technical economics does not confront in its normal preoccupations. The subject therefore is par excellence complex and rich, offering an intellectual feast where a gourmet's culinary craftsmanship and a subtle palate are called for.

It is also a subject of increasing relevance and concern. This is because people have now begun to move across borders in increasing numbers, legally and illegally. For both legal and illegal migrants, questions of their rights and obligations are increasingly coming to the forefront. This book can then be seen as making a contribution to the analysis of legal migrants' rights and obligations in the specific and inescapable area of income taxation.

The problem of appropriate income tax jurisdiction is novel; it is noteworthy that it was not even recognized in the recent comprehensive Meade report on direct taxation in the United Kingdom. Practices in this area have been largely matters of historical evolution, with little explicit thought being given to possible systemic alternatives. Drawing its inspiration from different sources, chiefly concerned with an appropriate response to the "brain drain" (see chapter 1), this book poses the problem sharply and in a fashion that fundamentally reorients the modern public-finance-theoretic analysis of income taxation to account for potential emigration of citizens.

In preparing this book, we have incurred several debts. In particular, acknowledgment must be made to the German Marshall Fund for supporting the research of Bhagwati and to the Guggenheim Foundation for the award of a fellowship to him for research on international migration. The Ford Foundation financed the conference Exercise of Income Tax Jurisdiction Over Citizens Abroad, held in New Delhi during January, 1981, jointly with the National Institute of Public Finance and Policy (India), where several papers in this volume were first presented. The comments of Nick Stern, Peter Diamond, Jesus Seade, and Joe Pechman on one or more chapters have led to improvements in the final shape of the book.

I Introduction

1

Income Taxation in the Presence of International Personal Mobility: An Overview

Jagdish N. Bhagwati and John Douglas Wilson

Introduction

When international personal mobility is recognized, new problems arise for the design of a country's income tax system. To begin with, a decision must be made about whom should be subject to the income tax. Most countries follow a residence-based system, described by lawyers as a "schedular" system, in which only residents pay domestic income taxes. But a few countries (the United States, the Philippines, and theoretically also Mexico) tax individuals according to their citizenship, so that citizens abroad are also subject to income tax. Furthermore the use of such citizenship-based taxation, described legally as a "global" system, has been recommended by Bhagwati (1977, 1979, 1980) as a means by which an LDC (less developed country) can augment tax revenues collected from its citizens, and might even be compensated for any losses that may follow when skilled citizens emigrate to a DC (developed country).

If the home government does tax citizens who are abroad, it must determine how these citizens' tax burdens should differ from those of citizens who are residents. Calling residents abroad "emigrants" throughout for simplicity (even though we do not wish thereby to exclude those who have not migrated in any legal sense and mean instead to include all citizens abroad regardless of their legal status or intentions regarding the length of their foreign stay), we must recognize that this problem arises even if emigrants are not taxed by home governments. This is because the potential for emigration still poses special problems for the design of the home country's income tax system. In particular the revenue losses resulting from the emigration of highly skilled citizens with correspondingly high incomes must be considered when the government determines whether to increase the progressivity of its tax structure. The government must also consider how much weight to give to emigrants relative to residents in the evaluation of its objectives.

The theoretical papers in this book address precisely this question of how to design an income tax system in the presence of international personal mobility. This work has been stimulated by the considerable interest aroused by Bhagwati's proposal that LDCs exercise their income tax jurisdiction on citizens abroad, and indeed several of the papers in this book were presented originally at a 1981 New Delhi conference to discuss this proposal.[1]

But the work has also been stimulated, as in Wilson's chapter 4, by the closed-economy models of optimal income taxation originally developed by Mirrlees (1971) and Atkinson (1973).[2] The focus of these original models was on the use of income taxation to achieve a more equitable distribution of income. Indeed this focus is largely retained by the theoretical work in this book (and distinguishes therefore the precise manner in which the analytics of the Bhagwati proposal should then be discussed by those who wish to examine its merits and demerits).[3]

This book therefore can be regarded as primarily an examination of the issue of the appropriate exercise of (international law–sanctioned) income tax jurisdiction on citizens abroad, building on the modern theory of optimal income taxation.

In view of the policy-related origins of this problem, as already outlined, the book also contains an invaluable examination by Richard Pomp (chapter 2) of the Philippines's experience with the exercise of income tax jurisdiction on citizens abroad (with a sketch of the evolution of the practice in the United States of such jurisdiction treated in an appendix to this chapter). Pomp's analysis is important in defining the administrative, legal, and political realities within which the exercise of such income tax jurisdiction on citizens abroad must be considered and its theoretical analysis situated.

The policy background and objectives in fact explain also some of the assumptions underlying the theoretical analysis in this volume. Thus the original motivation included, as already discussed, the policy problems created by the migration of highly skilled workers from the developing to the developed countries. Consequently some (but not all) of the models assume that the citizens living abroad possess relatively high incomes, and most of the models ignore the issue of how a country should tax the incomes of noncitizen residents. These are among the many issues that will need to be addressed in subsequent research.[4]

In view of the different approaches taken in the theoretical chapters in this book, despite the common thread provided by the theory of optimal income taxation, there is a compelling need to describe and synthesize their major analytical approaches and conclusions. The remainder of this chapter therefore addresses this task.

We start by discussing the various criteria used in the papers to compare the relative desirability of alternative income tax systems. In the section following we discuss how the incomes of a country's residents should be taxed when the country is unable to tax emigrants' incomes. Then we deal with the case in which emigrant incomes can be taxed. The main question dealt with here is how heavily these incomes should be taxed relative to resident incomes.

In the next three sections we describe some directions in which the theoretical analysis reviewed in the two preceding sections can be usefully extended. In particular we consider one important extension, namely, the issue of how to evaluate the desirability of the global, citizenship-based tax system when the goals of the home government differ in undesirable ways from those of the populace. This problem is emphasized by Hufbauer's chapter, but largely ignored in the theoretical models. By treating it here, we hope to emphasize the need for further research on the "political economy" of international tax issues. Finally, we summarize the main theoretical results in a nontechnical manner.

The Social Welfare Criteria

If a government is to choose among alternative tax systems, it must have a criterion for evaluating the relative desirability of these tax systems. Two separate approaches to tax design have been used for instance to justify the proposal that LDC citizens living abroad continue to pay domestic income taxes.

According to the "benefit approach," each citizen's tax burden should reflect the benefits that he or she receives from the goods and services provided by the government. An important benefit often received by LDC citizens before they emigrate is state-subsidized educational services. Some proponents of a tax on the "brain drain" have therefore argued that such a tax should be imposed to compensate LDCs for the loss of human capital that they experience as a result of emigraton. Interestingly opponents of taxes on emigrants have also used the benefit approach to partially justify their stand. Thus Hufbauer argues against such taxes by noting that "the assertion of these taxes amounts to assertion of a quasi-property claim by the state, a claim not balanced by public goods or cultural associations offered by the state to the citizen living abroad."[5] Clearly the difference of opinion here involves critically a matter of timing: Should tax payments be received only when the benefits are received, or should we take a wider view that "lifetime benefits," appropriately discounted over time, should equal discounted liftime payments?

A proponent of the "ability-to-pay approach" would perhaps argue that this controversy is largely irrelevant because it ignores equity considerations. According to this approach, everyone's tax burden should in some sense reflect his or her ability to pay. It can then be argued that most LDC emigrants should pay taxes to the home government because their level of economic well-being is generally significantly higher than that of those citizens remaining in the home country.

Both approaches represent only partial guides to tax policy, however, because they ignore efficiency considerations. Taxes that are both administratively feasible and equitable invariably distort economic decision making, and some taxes are better than others simply because the efficiency losses that they create are less severe.

The theoretical papers in this book explicitly attempt to incorporate the tradeoff between efficiency and equity into the design of income tax systems for open economies. They do so by taking what we call the *social welfare approach*. This approach treats tax policy as a problem in applied welfare economics, thereby allowing the modern tools of economic theory to be brought to bear on tax policy issues.

Under the social welfare approach the objective of a tax planner is to maximize a social welfare function that has as arguments the utilities of individuals.[6] Assumptions must be made about both the form of this function and the cardinal properties of utility functions, and these assumptions essentially represent value judgments about the relative desirability of different distributions of economic well-being. For closed economies a widely supported value judgment is that all individuals in the economy should be treated equally in the measurement of social welfare. In other words any two individuals with identical utilities should contribute equally to the measurement of social welfare. When an economy is open, however, the question arises as to how to treat those individuals who either emigrate from the home country or have no past association with the home country. Perhaps the most morally attractive approach is to evaluate tax systems according to their contribution to "world welfare," where all are treated equally in the measurement of social welfare. But as Mirrlees states in chapter 8 this criterion "may be thought not to be what an advisor to a democratic state is expected to be guided by." The alternative is "national welfare," in which the social welfare function includes only nationals, that is, citizens as defined by past and present association with the home country. If this latter criterion is accepted, there is still the further decision of how to treat citizens working abroad relative to residents in the measurement of social welfare.

The theoretical work in the book focuses mostly on various forms of the national or home-country welfare criterion. Correspondingly it does not address questions of host-country or DC welfare or of world welfare. The only exception is the analysis of Wilson (chapter 9), which takes explicitly a world welfare point of view, maximizing the social welfare of the world population, where social welfare is a function of the utilities of individual members of the world population and this function is increasing in each utility.

As Wilson notes, however, if a country's income tax system maximizes national welfare, then it is likely to be inefficient from the viewpoint of world welfare. By "inefficient" we mean that there exists a change in the tax system, accompanied by lump-sum transfers of income between countries, that raises every country's national welfare. The problem here is that it is difficult to imagine the correct international income transfers being implemented in the actual world economy.[7]

In any case because a fully efficient income tax system for the world economy is apparently not feasible, research should focus on the potentially "second-best" alternatives. Such alternatives undoubtedly must rely to a large extent on decentralized (uncoordinated) decision making by national governments. One way to model this decision making is to assume that each government attempts to maximize the welfare of the nation. The theoretical research in this book can be viewed therefore as describing some of the implications of this behavior.

Some economists would object to this characterization of government behavior, arguing instead that the objectives of government officials have little in common with traditional measures of social welfare. For example, Niskanen (1971) models government decision making as the outcome of the expenditure-maximizing behavior of government bureaucrats, whereas Brennan and Buchanan (1980) assume that the government attempts to maximize its surplus, defined as the excess of tax revenue over public expenditures. Again, even if governments are largely concerned with the welfare of the populace, they may be greatly constrained by the "directly unproductive profit seeking" (DUP) activities of political pressure groups (see Bhagwati 1982).

Hufbauer's argument in chapter 3 against citizenship-based tax systems clearly reflects his fear that governments will abuse the power to tax citizens abroad. Although this is certainly a legitimate concern, it may be that the possible government abuses of their ability to tax emigrants are outweighed by the potential efficiency and equity gains. We shall return to this issue later in this chapter. First, however, we discuss the theoretical research in this book.

Income Taxation with No Taxes on Emigrant Incomes

Several chapters deal with the design of an income tax system for a country that faces potential emigration but cannot tax citizens abroad. This issue is important because the difficulties involved in administering a tax on emigrants, or political preferences or constraints, may force governments to rely almost completely on resident-based taxes. Pomp in chapter 2, for instance, argues that the successful administration of a tax on LDC citizens living in DCs will require significantly more cooperation between LDC and DC tax authorities than presently exists. Whether such cooperation should be forthcoming could depend in part on the problems experienced by LDCs as a result of their inability to tax emigrants.

To isolate the redistributive role of income taxation, the chapters in this book consider the use of an income tax to raise national welfare by redistributing income between people with different productivities in work. Intuitively the existence of a high propensity to migrate, if appropriately defined, should imply that the income tax creates a sizable distortion of migration decisions. Thus a high propensity should significantly reduce the extent to which it is desirable to use income taxation as a tool for income redistribution. Surprisingly a common implication in the chapters is that this intuition is not always valid.

Consider first chapter 8 by Mirrlees. In it he constructs a simple model in which the income tax distorts only migration decisions. The migration propensity of a given type of worker is defined as the elasticity of the supply of nonmigrants with respect to after-tax income in the home country. The main implication of the model is that "rather high tax rates are justifiable even if the propensity to migrate is quite large."

Chapter 5 by Bhagwati and Hamada and chapters 4 and 6 by Wilson take the standard closed-economy optimal income tax models, in which education decisions or labor-leisure decisions are the focus, and extend them by including migration decisions. Unlike Mirrlees they constrain the tax system to be linear, in which case the tax schedule can be completely described by two parameters, a constant marginal tax on income and a uniform poll subsidy. The particular way in which these chapters characterize the impact of potential emigration on the optimal income tax is by asking how the optimal marginal tax depends on whether the home country is open or closed to migration. Intuitively, opening the country should lower the optimal marginal tax by introducing an additional cost associated with income redistribution; namely, the distortion of migration decisions. In Bhagwati and Hamada's model, where only high-income individuals are potential emigrants, the marginal migration distortion is measured by the revenue loss that occurs when these individuals emigrate in response to a rise in the marginal tax. Yet Bhagwati and Hamada demonstrate that opening the borders to migration may actually raise the optimal marginal tax (see their proposition 3). Wilson in chapter 6 explains this possibility in terms of the "income effects" created by opening the borders, and then he shows that it depends on Bhagwati and Hamada's particular definition of a "closed country." Under the alternative definition introduced by Wilson in chapter 4, closing the country must raise the optimal marginal tax.[8] In any case, an important message of Bhagwati and Hamada's result is that one cannot unambiguously state that the potential for emigration makes the optimal tax structure less egalitarian.

This message appears in a different form in chapter 4. By not restricting the innate "ability" levels possessed by potential emigrants, Wilson is able to demonstrate that the effect of potential emigration on the optimal income tax depends on the distribution of ability levels among potential emigrants. Closing the country to migration will raise the optimal marginal tax if the people who migrate in response to a tax change possess sufficiently high or low ability levels. If these potential emigrants possess ability levels in some intermediate range, however, then closing the country will lower the optimal marginal tax. The basic argument is that with potential emigrants in this range, increasing the marginal tax produces migration flows that generate additional revenue. Either additional individuals who face a positive tax burden are induced to remain in the home country, or additional individuals with a negative tax burden are induced to leave. In either case closing the economy cuts off these revenue gains, thereby reducing the benefits of a tax increase.

The issue of how *tax rates* differ between closed and open regimes should be distinguished from the issue of how *welfare* differs between these regimes. Whereas Bhagwati and Hamada find that a country's marginal tax may rise or fall when the borders are opened to migration, they conclude unambiguously that national welfare, which is determined in their model by the utilities of the low-income workers remaining in the home country, must fall (see their Proposition 1). The basic reasoning is that opening the borders allows high-income individuals to escape taxation and thereby worsens the tradeoff between equity and efficiency as viewed by the home country. Baumol, in chapter 7, fully develops this reasoning with the aid of ingenious graphical techniques.

It is worth noting that a common feature of the social welfare functions considered in these chapters (except for chapter 5) is that the contribution of each individual's utility to social welfare does not depend on whether he or she emigrates or remains at home.[9] On the other hand much of the early theoretical literature on the "brain drain," in particular the classic articles of Johnson (1960, 1965) and Grubel and Scott (1966), focused analysis on the welfare of the nonmigrants, the so-called TLBs (those left behind), and so does Bhagwati and Hamada's analysis.[10] Bhagwati (1976) has argued, however, that modern migrations are increasingly such that social welfare in the home country may have to be defined over emigrants as well since the emigrants retain ethnic ties to their home countries and are very much a part of the diaspora that ready transportation, increased tolerance for ethnic diversity and the like seem to encourage in such countries of immigration as the United States.

Both its moral attractiveness and also this sociological reality may then legitimize the practice of disregarding where an individual citizen is, whether at home or abroad, in defining the contribution of his or her utility to social welfare of the home country. On the other hand it is equally manifest that some governments and intellectuals exhibit little concern for the welfare of emigrants, regarding them in consequence as beyond the range of the country's social welfare function! In yet other cases the government's behavior may reflect a social welfare function in which the utilities of citizens who emigrate are simply weighted less than the utilities of otherwise similar citizens who stay home.

In the kind of analysis contained in this book, such discriminatory weighting of citizens abroad and at home has been embodied in the early work of Hamada (1975), who defined social welfare simply as the average utility of citizens residing at home. Compared with summing both resident and emigrant utilities, this criterion provides the home government with an additional incentive to lower marginal tax rates to encourage individuals with above-average utilities to remain in the home country. This is because social welfare falls if any such individual leaves the home country and the utilities of the remaining residents do not change. Evidently a useful task for future researchers will be to explore the implications of other social welfare functions in which residents and emigrants are treated differently.

Taxation of Emigrant Incomes: The Mirrlees Model

Taxing the incomes of citizens abroad clearly provides a domestic government both efficiency and equity gains. But it is not clear how much of a tax
burden emigrants should bear relative to residents.

Bhagwati and Hamada (chapter 5) investigate this issue using a model in
which the decisions facing an individual are how much education to obtain
and whether to emigrate. They show that emigrants and residents should
both be taxed nearly 100 percent with educational expenses being subsidized nearly 100 percent. Their analysis does not indicate, however, how
emigrants should be taxed relative to residents in more realistic models in
which (nearly) 100 percent taxation is undesirable.

The significant contribution of Mirrlees (chapter 8) is to investigate a
model in which incomes should be taxed significantly less than 100 percent
because individuals are able to engage in tax avoidance. One difficult
feature of the model is that differences between individuals are no longer
described by a single parameter ("ability"), as in the standard optimal
income tax model for closed economies. Instead there are three production
sectors: taxable work at home, taxable work abroad, and nontaxable work.
An individual possesses a separate productivity for performing each type
of work. Despite this apparent difficulty, Mirrlees manages to obtain conditions that characterize the optimal tax structure. We may now explain
certain key features of these conditions that may not be altogether evident
from Mirrlees's original analysis.

The home government in Mirrlees's model cannot alter the utilities
obtained by individuals in the nontaxable sector. But it can alter utilities in
taxable work by imposing taxes on income. The tax system is optimal if it
maximizes the sum of the utilities of all individuals.

The parameters n and m denote before-tax incomes in taxable work at
home and abroad, respectively (m is calculated net of foreign taxes), $t_h(n)$
and $t_f(m)$ are an (n, m)-person's total domestic tax payments at home
and abroad, and after-tax incomes are $z = n - t_h(n)$ at home and $y =
m - t_f(m)$ abroad. These net incomes provide utilities $u_h(z)$ and $u_f(y)$. The
location of nontaxable work is irrelevant for the formal analysis, but the
obvious interpretation is that (high n, low m)-people tend to perform
nontaxable work at home, whereas (low n, high m)-people tend to perform
this work abroad.

One method by which Mirrlees obtains some useful insights is to compare the home and foreign taxes faced by an (n, m)-person who is indifferent
to performing taxable work at home or abroad. Because this comparison

provides an important indication of how the tax system treats emigrants relative to residents, we shall discuss it at length. The key condition describing the difference between the optimal $t_h(n)$ and $t_f(m)$ is derived by combining Mirrlees's first-order conditions for optimal taxation (see eqs. (50) and (51) in chapter 8) and then reinterpreting the terms in the resulting expression as elasticities. We shall write this expression as

$$\frac{u_f}{mu_f} - \frac{u_h}{mu_h} = t_f(m)[E_{hf} + E_{fh} + E_{fe}] - t_h(n)[E_{hf} + E_{fh} + E_{he}], \tag{1}$$

where $u_h = u_f$ by assumption, mu_h and mu_f are the (n, m)-person's marginal utilities of income at home and abroad, and the E_{ij}'s are used to denote various elasticities:

$E_{hf} =$ flow of n-people from home taxable work to foreign taxable work in response to a one percent decline in their $u_h(z)$

$E_{fh} =$ flow of m-people from foreign taxable work to home taxable work in response to a one percent decline in their $u_f(y)$

$E_{he} =$ flow of n-people from home taxable work to nontaxable work in response to a one percent decline in their $u_h(z)$

$E_{fe} =$ flow of m-people from foreign taxable work to nontaxable work in response to a one percent decline in their $u_f(y)$

Each of these flows represents a first-order approximation and is defined in percentage terms as the number of workers moving from one sector to another, divided by the total number of workers in the sector from which this flow originates. It is perhaps useful to think of E_{hf} and E_{fh} as "migration elasticities," E_{he} as the "home evasion elasticity," and E_{fe} as the "foreign evasion elasticity." These elasticities depend on the cardinal properties of utility functions, but so does the left side of eq. (1). By multiplying both sides of eq. (1) by either mu_n/u_n or mu_f/u_f, an equality is obtained in which neither the left nor right side depends on these cardinal properties. We shall later return to the issue of how cardinal properties affect the optimal income tax.

Intuitively, setting $t_f(m)$ different from $t_h(n)$ distorts decisions about where to perform taxable work, and the size of this distortion should be positively related to E_{hf} and E_{fh} (given the other elasticities and the mu_i's). Consequently the magnitude of the optimal difference between $t_f(m)$ and $t_h(n)$ should be negatively related to E_{hf} and E_{fh}. In fact eq. (1) shows that this magnitude is directly related to the *sum* of these two elasticities: given one of these taxes, say $t_h(n)$, a fall in $E_{hf} + E_{fh}$ moves the optimal $t_f(m)$ further away from $t_h(n)$.

The tax rate $t_h(n)$ distorts the decisions by n-people about whether to perform taxable or nontaxable work, while $t_f(m)$ distorts the similar decision by m-people. The efficiency losses from these two distortions should be positively related to E_{he} and E_{fe}, respectively. Thus we should expect the optimal $t_h(n)$ to be negatively related to E_{he}, and the optimal $t_f(m)$ to be negatively related to E_{fe}. Again eq. (1) agrees with intuition: given $t_h(n)$, a rise in E_{fe} reduces the optimal $t_f(m)$, and this tax eventually converges to zero as E_{fe} goes to infinity. The same type of relation holds between the optimal $t_h(n)$ and E_{he}.

Perhaps the most reasonable empirical assumption to make about these elasticities is that the foreign evasion elasticity (E_{fe}) significantly exceeds the home evasion elasticity (E_{he}). This assumpion is suggested by Pomp's finding (see chapter 2) that the compliance levels of Philippine citizens living abroad with respect to their country's tax laws are quite low. It should be kept in mind, however, that *current* compliance levels and the *sensitivity* of these compliance levels to tax rate changes are two distinct issues. As our observations clearly show, it is the latter issue that is important for optimal tax design. And the model contains no theoretical argument that E_{fe} exceeds E_{he}. But the model does suggest that if developed countries such as the United States were to aid the Philippines in collecting taxes from citizens working abroad, then it would be desirable for the Philippines to increase its tax rates on these citizens significantly above the currently low levels.

Mirrlees refrains from using differences in evasion elasticities as a justification for high tax rates on emigrants. In fact he imposes an assumption that implies that the home and foreign evasion elasticities defined above are identical (his separability assumption), and then he presents another argument for high foreign tax rates. His crucial assumption is that given any taxed foreign worker and taxed home worker with identical utility levels, the home worker always possesses a marginal utility of income that is at least as great as that of the foreign worker. The idea here is that emigrants should be thought of as individuals who retain some type of attachment to the home country. As such they cannot obtain more enjoyment from consumption at the margin than similar workers at home. In symbols the asumption is written

$$mu_h \geq mu_f \quad \text{if} \quad u_f = u_h. \tag{2}$$

Having assumed that $E_{he} = E_{fe}$ at those (n, m) where $u_h = u_f$ (the separability assumption), Mirrlees is able to conclude that "the tax optimally paid by a person who earns taxed income at home is not greater than that paid by a person of equal utility who earns taxed income from abroad." This result follows directly from eqs. (1) and (2). Along with some less formal arguments, it provides his justification for substantial tax rates on foreign incomes.

It should be noted that the sign of the difference between mu_h and mu_f is independent of the cardinal properties of the utility functon. The (n, m)-person under consideration is indifferent to home and foreign taxable work, and mu_h/mu_f measures the amount of additional income that he or she must receive in foreign taxable work to remain indifferent following a dollar rise in income from home taxable work. Whether this ratio exceeds or falls short of unity clearly depends only on the ordinal properties of the utility function. Furthermore eq. (1) is completely unchanged if we assume that social welfare is measured by summing $G(u^i)$ over all individuals, where u^i is person i's utility and the function G is increasing in utility. (This is the generalized utilitarian criterion that includes the Rawlsian welfare function as a limiting case.) This is so because the ratio of the (n, m)-person's social marginal utilities of income, $(G'(u_h)mu_h)/(G'(u_f)mu_f)$, equals the ratio of corresponding private marginal utilities of income (because $u_f = u_h$).

Thus Mirrlees's argument for substantial tax rates on foreign incomes is essentially an *efficiency* argument, because it depends neither on how utilities are weighted in the social welfare function nor on the cardinal properties of utility functions.

So far we have discussed only the relative optimal domestic taxes faced by an emigrant and resident with identical *utilities*. An alternative comparison is between the domestic taxes paid by an emigrant and resident with identical before-tax *incomes* (calculated net of foreign taxes). The results from this second comparison are not implied by the first because an emigrant and resident with identical utilities need not possess the same before-tax incomes. In fact Mirrlees assumes that the emigrant's income is higher.

Unfortunately Mirrlees is able to obtain results for the second comparison only for a special case. His additional assumptions include those used in the first comparison plus an assumption that implies that eq. (2) holds with equality: emigrants and residents with identical utilities possess identical marginal utilities of income. Under these assumptions he shows that an emigrant should always pay a lower domestic tax than pays a resident with the same before-tax income.

Thus whether the tax paid by an emigrant to the home government should be lower or higher than that paid by a similar resident depends on how we define "similar." Both comparisons are useful, although the second is most directly concerned with the properties of the tax schedules faced by emigrants and residents. In any case the conclusion that Mirrlees sees in his analysis is that "it seems that it may well be desirable to institute substantial income taxes on foreign incomes, if only the narrowly economic considerations incorporated into our model are relevant."

Extensions

There are several directions in which the theoretical research discussed in the previous sections could be usefully extended.

Evasion

One important extension would be to model explicitly some of the more important mechanisms, both legal and illegal, by which residents and emigrants avoid paying taxes. Doing so should provide a better understanding of the relative magnitudes of the taxable work elasticities, which we have argued are central to the relative rates at which emigrants and residents should be taxed in the Mirrlees model.

Furthermore it would then be possible to model the enforcement methods that the home goverment might use to reduce illegal tax evasion among both residents and emigrants. Presumably such methods would be more effective at reducing tax evasion by residents rather than emigrants.[11] If so, the implementation of an optimal enforcement program might tend to raise the optimal rates at which residents should be taxed relative to emigrants.

Even for closed economies there has been almost no research on optimal income taxation in the presence of illegal tax evasion (see Sandmo 1981 for an exception). One problem with modeling tax evasion is that it inherently involves intertemporal decision making. An individual's present and future probabilities of getting caught, along with the various penalties, will normally depend on his or her past history of tax evasion. Consequently a present decision to evade taxes will partially depend on expectations about future work and leisure activities; this decision will also influence future choices among these activities.

These intertemporal aspects are especially evident in the open-economy context, as is nicely illustrated by Pomp (chapter 2) in his discussion of the "tax clearance system" used by the Philippines before 1973 to enforce its income tax on emigrant incomes. Without a "tax clearance certificate" a citizen could not leave the Philippines or, if already abroad, could be prevented from renewing his or her Philippine passport. Pomp observes that the tax clearance system was not viewed as a satisfactory device for dealing with tax delinquents. One problem is that it reduced the number of times the emigrants returned to the Philippines for visits, thereby diminishing the amount of revenue and foreign exchange generated by these visits. Furthermore it may have induced a sizable number of emigrants to obtain DC citizenship, in which case their tax liability to the Philippines was entirely eliminated. To appropriately analyze the problems created by the tax clearance program, it is clear therefore that we would need a model that recognized the possibility that emigrants could return to the home country either permanently or for temporary visits.

The absence of intertemporal considerations is an important limitation of the models presented in this volume. The model presented by Bhagwati and Hamada does contain an intertemporal utility maximization problem, whereby individuals must choose how many years of education to receive before they start earning income. But each individual earns all of his or her lifetime income in only one location, at home or abroad. This limitation, which is shared by the other theoretical models in this book, prevents consideration of many important legal and illegal tax avoidance methods.

One particularly important legal method by which emigrants may avoid paying taxes to the home government is to change their citizenship.[12] Presumably the emigrant's ability and willingness to do so are positively related to the number of years spent abroad. This relation would appear to provide a pure efficiency argument for a tax system in which the total tax burden faced by an emigrant declines with the number of years spent abroad.

Remittances

Another issue not addressed in this book concerns the income remittances that migrants make to relatives and friends remaining in the home country. If an emigrant's willingness to make these remittances is negatively related to his or her tax payments to the home country, a significant "remittance elasticity" may provide a justification for taxing emigrants at relatively low rates.

Such empirical estimates as are available, however, suggest that remittances are an important characteristic of low-income rather than high-income emigrants. If so, this may moderate in turn the remittance-based justification for taxing emigrants at relatively low rates because most remittances may then be from emigrants who are below the tax-exemption limit and because the propensity to remit may be declining with taxable income.

Political Economy: DUP Activities and Malign Governments

A major characteristic that all the theoretical contributions in this book share is that they assume, with conventional economics, a *benign* government. Such a government simply exists with a view to implementing the optimal or suboptimal tax policy whose consequences we analyze.

But a powerful new trend in economic theory rejects this view of the government and permits what are described variously as DUP (directly unproductive, profit-seeking) (Bhagwati 1982) activities. In this view lobbying activities are addressed to enacting policies that improve one's income or are triggered by such policies. For example, a tariff may be enacted by tariff seeking; the revenues from the tariff may trigger revenue seeking by lobbies. Again the bureaucrats or politicians who are cogs in the governmental machine may act as a malign force, using policies to garner rewards for themselves rather than the populace. They may divert revenues to personal accounts or selfish expenditures.

This latter viewpoint is expounded by Hufbauer in chapter 3. He claims that "malign states are far more commonplace than benign states." He argues that emigration may serve the important function of limiting the degree to which a government is able exploit its citizens. To support his argument, he recalls Tiebout's (1956) famous insight that local public goods could be efficiently provided by communities within a country if people could costlessly migrate between communities until they obtained their most preferred tax-expenditure packages.

Extensive research in recent years has uncovered many reasons why decentralized decision making by local governments is likely to be inefficient, even if there are no impediments to labor mobility (see Bewley 1981 for a survey). These negative results would seem to be applicable to the uncoordinated decision making by national governments in the world economy. Just as Tiebout's argument certainly contains an important grain of truth, however, so does the assertion that emigration opportunities between countries serve to make national governments more responsive to the preferences of the populace.

Presumably a malign LDC government could use its ability to tax citizens working abroad to further its own objectives at the expense of the populace. Consequently a DC government could appeal to the malign nature of most governments to justify not aiding LDCs in the collection of taxes on emigrant incomes. We shall argue, however, that the case against taxing emigrants is far less clear-cut than it may appear at first, even if the assertion that governments are malign is accepted at face value.

To illustrate the basic issues, we briefly sketch a simple general-equilibrium malign-government model. Consider an LDC that is ruled by a goverment that uses an income tax to transfer income from the LDC citizens to itself. In other words the government is controlled by individuals who raise more revenue than needed to finance public good expenditures, and then consume the surplus. Following Baumol (chapter 7), we treat "real income" as the single final consumption good in the economy. The public goods supplied by the government may then be viewed as intermediate inputs in the production of this single good. Whereas Baumol focuses on the allocation of real income between different groups of citizens, our focus is on the allocation of real income between the government and citizens.

S is used to denote the surplus of real income that the government consumes, and C denotes the total real income remaining for citizens. There are a fixed number of citizens, and they may work at home or in a DC. National income, $N = C + S$, includes the real incomes of citizens working abroad, calculated net of foreign taxes. We interpret C as including the "psychic income losses" that emigrants suffer upon leaving the home country. An emigrant's total income equals his or her money income minus psychic income loss, and an individual becomes an emigrant if and only if he or she can earn more real income abroad than at home, as calculated net of all taxes. Throughout the discussion we shall ignore the issue of how C is distributed across different citizens and interpret a rise in C as an improvement in the welfare of the populace.

Let us suppose that the government has preferences over allocations of real income between itself and the citizens, as represented by the utility function $U(C, S)$. This function may be interpreted as reflecting at least a small amount of benevolence on the part of the individuals controlling the government, or their belief that their ability to stay in power is positively related to the level of C.

Suppose first that the government is able to tax the money incomes of both residents and emigrants. Then it is able to implement a tax system in which each individual's tax payment to the LDC is independent of resi-

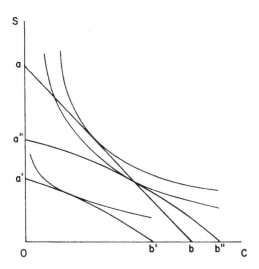

Figure 1.1

dence. Because such a tax system does not distort migration decisions, the government can use it to obtain an allocation (C, S) lying on or below the "first-best" production possibility frontier (PPF), which we label ab in figure 1.1. The government's chosen allocation is represented by the tangency between this PPF and one of its indifference curves. We have drawn the PPF with a slope equal to -1, reflecting the assumption that there are no other distortions in the economy when both residents and emigrants can be taxed. (Other distortions, such as those involving labor-versus-leisure choices, could be added without affecting the main conclusions.) The government can then be viewed as solving a two-step maximization problem whereby it first chooses its public production plan to maximize national income and then uses its income tax to divide the resulting income between itself and the populace.

Now suppose that the government is unable to tax emigrants, perhaps because the DCs do not cooperate in the collection of such a tax. Then the PPF facing the government becomes $a'b'$ in figure 1.1. This "second-best" PPF lies below the original PPF because the income tax on residents alone distorts migration decisions, causing an inefficiently large number of citizens to move abroad. And this distortion is present even when the government surplus equals zero, because tax rates must still be positive to finance public expenditures. Notice also that the slope of the PPF has declined in absolute value. When the government raises taxes to finance a unit increase in the surplus, the foreign work becomes more attractive, thereby further distorting migration decisions. Labor flows out of the country, and the efficiency loss may be measured by the lost tax revenue resulting from this migration. As a result of this revenue loss, the slope of the PPF now falls short of one in absolute value.

This decline in the slope represents a "substitution effect" that provides the government with an incentive to increase C. However, there is also an "income effect:" at any level of the surplus the maximum feasible level of C has declined. If C is treated as a normal good by the government, then this income effect gives it an incentive to reduce C. Consequently we cannot conclude that the elimination of taxes on emigrants necessarily raises the welfare of the populace, as measured by C. If, for example, the government always allocates national income in fixed proportions between itself and the citizens (i.e., L-shaped indifference curves), then its inability to tax emigrants must lower C. Thus it need not be desirable for DCs to deny a "malign" LDC government assistance to enable it to tax its citizens working in the DCs. Simply stated, the improvement in the incentives faced by the LDC government may not be worth the cost in terms of efficiency losses. In figure 1.1 we have illustrated the case in which C declines.

There is a policy, however, that improves incentives without creating any efficiency loss (that is; without moving the LDC below its first-best PPF). Let us assume that the LDC just described is one of many LDCs. The DCs agree to administer an "LDC tax" on the money incomes of each LDC's emigrants and return the revenue to the LDC government. They do not let the LDC government choose the tax rates, however, and they return the revenue as a lump sum payment. In other words although the income transfer to the LDC is set equal to the revenue obtained from the LDC tax, the LDC government is told that any changes in its behavior will not affect the transfer. Thus the LDC government, being one of many LDC governments, behaves like a "perfectly competitive consumer" by maximizing utility under the assumption that it has no effect on the taxes and income transfers that it faces.

Now suppose that the DCs design the LDC tax so that each emigrant's tax payment equals the total tax that he or she would pay while residing in the home country. The effect of this policy is to eliminate migration distortions and thereby place each LDC on its first-best PPF. However, the substitution effect described above still remains: because the LDC has no control over the LDC tax and accompanying income transfer, it still views as an efficiency loss the decline in tax revenue that occurs when its citizens leave the country in response to higher taxes. Thus it still faces a "perceived" PPF ($a"b"$ in figure 1.1) with a slope that is less than one in absolute value, and it maximizes its utility at an allocation where this PPF crosses the first-best PPF and is tangent to an indifference curve, as illustrated in figure 1.1. Given the higher perceived cost of raising the government surplus, the LDC government now decides to provide the populace with a higher level of real income than it would if it was directly choosing the taxes on emigrants.

Thus the model shows that the manner in which taxes are collected from emigrants becomes a crucial issue when governments are malign. It is never optimal for the LDCs to choose the tax rates and directly receive the tax revenue; the DCs can raise the real incomes of LDC citizens by taking over the decisions concerning tax rates and transferring the income back to LDC governments as a lump sum payment. In fact we have argued that these real incomes are higher when the DCs follow the LDC policy of taxing emigrants in a manner that does not distort migration decisions. (The DC and LDC policies will not be identical, because the LDCs will alter their taxes on residents when the DCs take control of the taxes on emigrants.) Of course this normally will not be the best policy for DCs to follow. A small deviation does not move an LDC's (C, S) significantly below the first-best PPF (by the usual argument that a small price distortion causes no first-order efficiency loss). But such a deviation almost always changes the slope of the perceived PPF facing the LDC, so that the LDC alters its choice of (C, S). Thus the DCs can obtain a further improvement in the incentives faced by the LDC government by taxing emigrants "inefficiently." Whether the policy that maximizes C involves emigrants being taxed more or less heavily than residents, or maybe even being subsidized, cannot be ascertained without adding more structure to the model, including restrictions on the properties of the LDC government's utility function.

To pursue these issues much further would naturally require a much more detailed model of government than we have provided. We hope to have convinced the reader however that such a model is needed before a well-informed judgment can be made about whether and how taxes should be collected from citizens abroad and returned to their home governments. The statement that governments are generally "malign" simply does not constitute a compelling argument against such taxes.

Finally, we may address a related concern about exercise of income tax jurisdiction on emigrants. It should be noted that under commonly accepted international law the income tax jurisidiction of the home country may be exercised by a malign government, but simply cannot be enforced in the host country courts. It is always open for citizens escaping malign countries to refuse to pay without legal harassment by the host country. The disturbing notion that somehow Picasso would have had to pay income taxes to Franco of Spain or that Idi Amin would chase Ugandans through the courts in New York is occasionally aired. But it has simply no foundation whatsoever.

Tax Harmonization

We now turn our attention to one further problem that is not modeled in the theoretical work in this book but becomes particularly important if only one country or subset of countries in the world economy proceeds to exercise tax jurisidiction on citizens abroad. This is the problem of harmonization implied by the coexistence of different income tax systems. It is best illustrated by reference to the questions raised in the concrete case of the United States. Recall that in the United States (and the Philippines) the global income tax system that extends the income tax to citizens abroad is practiced. Other countries are on the "schedular" income tax systems that do not tax citizens abroad.[13] For the United States, this has meant a two-fold problem, with consequent opposition to its global system from political lobbies preferring the schedular system.

1. Private U.S. citizens abroad, who are taxed on the basis of the global system, allege that they are unfairly taxed because nationals of other countries abroad (for example, French in Bangkok, alongside Americans) are not so taxed by their own governments and because nationals of the countries in which they reside (for example, Thais in Bangkok) are subject only to domestic taxes (for example, the Thai income tax), which are equally borne by the U.S. citizens in addition to any applicable U.S. income tax. Hence the *intranational (horizontal) equity* of the global system runs afoul of the *international (horizontal) equity* claims.

2. Also, once trade in goods and services is considered, the harmonization issue becomes one of otherwise distorting comparative advantage and hence efficiency, in turn. If U.S. firms have to pay U.S. income tax on U.S. citizens they employ abroad, whereas French firms employing French citizens abroad do not have to pay the French income tax, distortion of comparative advantage could easily follow. That is to say, French firms having to pay certain net-of-tax salaries for, say, Saudi construction contracts, would then have a smaller real cost, *ceteris paribus*, than U.S. firms competing for the same contracts. Of course this model assumes that the incidence of the global tax system, unlike in the models of personal income taxation in this book in the tradition of the classic papers of Mirrlees

(1971) and Atkinson (1973), does not fall on the taxed individuals. It also assumes, in the stark version outlined above, that the French firms must hire French and the U.S. firms must hire Americans; if the two were total substitutes, as they almost certainly are not for different reasons, the harmonization issue would disappear. This problem needs formal analysis, but has certainly played a major role in the political economy of American income taxation. People, such as Senator William Proxmire of Wisconsin, who accept the equity underlying the global system and argue that the "café-crawling" Americans in Paris ought to pay their share of U.S. taxes instead of leaving the burden to the workers in Detroit, have traditionally been pitted against pressure groups such as corporations handling construction works abroad.

Summary

Evidently the research reported in this book starts us on the road to an extension of the usual income tax theory to an open economy (in which the openness implies international personal mobility). The problems that potential emigration creates for income tax design in LDCs provide much of the motivation behind this research. Consequently the theoretical analysis has mostly concerned the welfare of the emigrants' home country. With the exception of chapter 9, in which Wilson takes explicitly a world-welfare viewpoint, host-country welfare has not been considered.

The following paragraphs summarize the theoretical results in a nontechnical manner.

1. If a country cannot tax emigrants, then opening its borders to emigration will usually lower social welfare, even if emigrants are not treated any differently from residents in the measurement of social welfare. The basic reasoning concerns the use of the income tax as a policy instrument for redistributing income. Opening the country's borders allows high-income individuals to escape taxation by emigrating, thereby reducing the government's ability to achieve a more equitable income distribution. Bhagwati and Hamada in chapter 5 formalize this reasoning within the context of their particular model, and Baumol in chapter 7 helps explain the result with the aid of ingenious graphical arguments.

2. It is *not* always true, however, that the ability of residents to escape home-country taxes by emigrating lowers the optimal marginal rate at which residents' incomes should be taxed. Two reasons are given for this possibility. First, opening the borders to emigration may raise the optimal tax rate in Bhagwati and Hamada's model (chapter 5), because of what

Wilson in chapter 6 refers to as "income effects." In particular the emigration of high-income individuals creates a revenue loss, and the government's optimal response to this loss may be to try to offset it by taxing residents' incomes more heavily. Second, Wilson shows in chapter 4 that the impact of potential emigration on the optimal tax rate depends on the incomes possessed by potential emigrants: potential emigration among individuals with relatively high or low incomes tends to lower the optimal tax rate, but potential emigration among residents with incomes in some intermediate range tends to raise the optimal tax rate. Although both chapters follow the usual practice of building models that relate individual incomes to a single innate attribute caled "ability" or "skill," future research needs to consider more complex and realistic reasons for income disparities.

3. Mirrlees in chapter 8 provides additional evidence that the existence of potential emigration need not significantly lower the optimal tax rate on residents' incomes. In particular, he finds that "rather high tax rates are justifiable even if the propensity to migrate is quite large."

4. Mirrlees also considers the case in which a country can tax the incomes of both residents and emigrants. His main conclusion is that "it seems that it may well be desirable to institute substantial income taxes on foreign incomes, if only the narrowly economic considerations incorporated in our model are relevant." His theoretical model includes both equity and efficiency goals, but we have argued above that his argument is based on *efficiency* considerations. In particular his conclusion holds regardless of the degree to which the country's social welfare criteria exhibit inequality aversion.

5. Finally, Wilson shows in chapter 9 that if countries individually choose their tax systems to maximize national welfare, rather than world welfare, the resulting collection of tax systems is likely to be inefficient from the viewpoint of world welfare. In other words there will exist a way of changing these tax systems that, combined with a system of income transfers between countries, raises national welfare in some countries without reducing it in any other country. Once political and administrative realities are recognized, however, the case for facilitating LDCs in the collection of taxes on emigrant incomes may become attractive as a feasible second-best policy. Unfortunately Pomp's chapter on the Philippines's experience with nonresident taxation serves to emphasize that such taxes also impose special political and administrative problems. Successful implementation of a tax on nonresidents will undoubtedly require the cooperation of the host countries.

Taken as a whole, the theoretical results in this book instruct us to be wary about arguments that use the openness of the economy as a reason for substantial reductions in income tax rates. But this research represents only a beginning. Many problems, such as those we have already sketched above, will need to be modeled.

Appendix: The Evolution of Alternative Practices on Income Tax Jurisdiction: United Kingdom and United States[14]

The United States has been unique, except for the Philippines and Mexico—both countries within the U.S. "sphere of influence"—in exercising its income tax jurisdiction quite explicitly on its citizens abroad to tax their global income. The U.S. practice stands in contrast to the European practice, which broadly exempts the taxation of income earned abroad by citizens abroad, a practice that is generally adopted worldwide today.

The U.S. citizenship-based practice is described as "global," and the Europe-originated rival practice is called "schedular," in legal analysis. The question as to why the two contrasting systems grew up in these two differing regions is intriguing. Although the United States has adopted its citizenship-based tax system ever since initiating the Federal Income Tax in 1913, equally it is true that the introduction of income taxation in the United Kingdom at the end of the eighteenth century was conceived at the outset more narrowly in terms of jurisdiction over those resident in the United Kingdom. A contrast in the evolution of the two systems in the United Kingdom and the United States is therefore instructive.

The United Kingdom: Schedular System

The British turned to income taxation when it was manifest that the Napoleonic War was the most expensive conflict that Britain had ever fought. With a national debt of over £200 million and difficulty of raising the Land Tax further, Prime Minister William Pitt had also exhausted the avenue of increased taxes on consumer goods and building materials, stamp duties and enhanced taxation of property. In 1799 he turned to a general income tax at 10 percent, charged in respect of all income originating in Britain, whether accruing to foreign residents of Britain or to British citizens resident at home or abroad. The key exemption related, from our perspective, to income earned abroad by British citizens in residence abroad.[15]

Repealed in 1802 with the end of the war and the Peace of Amiens, it was revived at a rate of 5 percent as the war recommenced in 1803. By pressure of public opinion, familiar again to advanced democracies today, the income tax was repealed once again in 1816. The credit for reenactment and perpetuation this time of this great innovation in public finance belongs to Prime Minister Robert Peel, whose other great achievement was the repeal of the Corn Laws in 1846 that ushered in the era of free trade. In fact Peel reintroduced the income tax in 1842 as a companion measure to offset the reduction in revenues that would result as he began experimenting with tariff reduction before ultimate repeal of the Corn Laws.[16] Imposed initially for four years, the income tax remained on the books and has become a permanent feature of the landscape.

Why did the exemption of citizens abroad from taxation (of their incomes there) become a natural and enduring feature of the British, and indeed the European, tax systems? Indeed a search through legal and economic commentaries reveals several supportive assertions and arguments, several citing the "injustice" of doing otherwise.

Thus Judge C. B. Kelley, in an 1876 Tax Court judgment, which he said was momentous because it involved "most important principles of great weight as affecting the law of England, and I may almost say as affecting the international law of the world," declared support for the principle of nontaxation of nonresidents in no uncertain terms: "I must say ... that in the first place the great principle of the law of England in relation to taxation is, that taxation shall only be imposed on persons or things actually within this country."[17]

A typical defense of this principle was the view of Charles Tennant (1872, p. 20): "... why should the subject contribute to the support of the Government out of a revenue derived from a foreign country? ... On no ground of policy or principle of justice can such a proposition be maintained."

As the noted economist C. F. Bastable (1892, pp. 303–304) also observed, "Where a citizen emigrates with all his property ... it is plain that he is only amenable to the laws of his adopted country; there is no power on the part of his native land to levy taxes on him and no justice in doing so," and "the income tax should be levied by the country of residence." The injustice was evidently by reference to the principle that taxation should reflect accrual of benefits rather than ability to pay, and the benefits, if you were abroad, were assumed to be negligible.[18] The inability to collect income taxes from nonresident citizens, although noted by Bastable, appears to have been a far lesser consideration than this sense of what was just.[19]

As it happens, it was precisely an opposed view of justice—that it was unjust to exclude from tax jurisdiction those citizens who were residing abroad, that it would violate the canons of "horizontal equity" among citizens who must all bear the burden of income taxation according to ability to pay rather than exclusively by benefits received—that made the United States embrace the global system of income taxation from the beginning.

The United States: Global System

The adoption of the income tax in the United States has been an even more complex task than in the United Kingdom. Although the first federal income tax was enacted in 1861 to pay for the Civil War expenses, it was supplanted by the 1862 Act, which levied a progressive tax at 3 percent and 5 percent. After the war ended, the income tax was abandoned in 1872. It was resurrected by the 1894 Income Tax, but oddly to be ruled unconstitutional by the Supreme Court in a bizarre judgment in the celebrated *Pollock v. Farmers' Loan and Trust Company* case, decided in 1895. But within two decades the situation had been reversed with the enactment of the 1913 Income Tax, its validation by the Supreme Court in the *Brushaber v. Union Pacific Railroad Company* case, and its subsequent permanence on the U.S. scene.

The income tax applied on a worldwide basis to citizens of the United States and to aliens resident in the United States (Surrey and Warren 1962, p. 203). The affirmation of the constitutional validity of the global character of the U.S. income tax would come in the classic case of *Cook v. Tait* in 1924. In this case the question explicitly at stake was whether Congress had the power to tax the income received by a native citizen of the United States domiciled abroad from property situated abroad. The plaintiff was permanently resident and domiciled in Mexico, and the U.S. tax under contention was levied on income derived from property permanently and solely within the territorial jurisdiction of the Republic of Mexico. Solicitor General Beck argued, "How can the duty of the citizen to support the government which protects him depend upon his place of residence? Wherein does the Constitution impose such a limitation upon the power of Congress to tax?" Mr. Justice Joseph McKenna, delivering the opinion of the court, concluded emphatically that[20]

... the basis of the power to tax was not and cannot be made dependent upon the situs of the property in all cases, it being in or out of the United States, and was not and cannot be made dependent upon the domicile of the citizen, that being in or out of the United States, but upon his relation as citizen to the United States and the relation of the latter to him as citizen. The consequence of the relations is that the native citizen who is taxed may have domicile, and the property from which his income is derived may have situs in a foreign country and the tax be legal—the government having power to impose the tax.

This judicial view as to the constitutionality and legitimacy of exercising tax jurisdiction over citizens domiciled abroad has enjoyed widespread legal support in the United States. Thus Hyde (1922, p. 205) wrote

It must be clear that the rights of the territorial sovereign to impose a personal tax upon an individual depends upon the intimacy and closeness of the relationship that has been established between itself and him. Internationally, a sufficient relationship always exists between the State and its national, and that regardless of his residence.

Again, Webster (1891, pp. 167–168), writing earlier on the law of citizenship in the United States, asserted plainly that

A state has the right to levy a tax on its citizens resident abroad. The collection of such a tax is difficult. The authorities of the foreign state in which the citizens reside cannot be called upon to make the collections, nor is there any power to enforce them. This, however, does not prevent notice to such citizens residing abroad that such a tax is due and is to be paid by them to the authorities of their country.

Quite aside from the constitutional legitimacy of exercising tax jurisdiction over citizens domiciled abroad for their global incomes, the view that it was also a just practice is evident from the early writings and precepts. The payment of the U.S. taxes, even when domiciled abroad, was itself regarded as a presumptive proof of continuing citizenship, through acceptance of obligations implied by citizenship itself, in deciding on questions as to the extension of the benefits of passports and U.S. protection to those domiciled abroad. Thus Bochard (1915, pp. 697–698), writing on the diplomatic protection of citizens abroad, stated,

The payment of the income tax under the Act of October 3, 1913, will also be "duly considered in deciding the question of the right to the continued protection of this government in cases of native citizens who have resided abroad for a period so long that the natural presumption may be held to have arisen that they have abandoned this country" [according to a Department of State Circular, dated March 18, 1914] ... during the administration of Secretary Fish and his immediate successors the payment of the income and excise taxes imposed on American citizens or the possession of property in this country were made tests in determining the intention to retain American citizenship. The question having been raised whether a naturalized citizen against whom the presumption of expatriation had arisen could overcome the presumption by showing that he had paid or was ready to pay the income tax provided for by the Act of October 3, 1913, the Department [of State] ... held that such rule had not been prescribed, but added that "if a person against whom the presumption ... has arisen presents ... evidence that he has paid the income tax, this fact will receive due consideration."

In the country that had made the phrase "no taxation without representation" famous, its obverse, "no representation [that is, citizenship] without taxation," was a manifest truth, a matter of simple "horizontal equity" among citizens. The theme would recur again and again in the evolution of the U.S. practice in this regard, up to the present.

This history shows evidence of a continuous tussle between the proponents of the U.S. view of horizontal equity and those who believed that, given the schedular tax system of others, the global system put American export industries (such as construction) at disadvantage in overseas competition with rivals who did not carry the burden of domestic income taxes on their employees overseas. Thus starting from a fairly full-fledged global system at its inception, the United States moved temporarily close to the schedular system in 1926 and then, prompted by long-standing horizontal-equity considerations, gradually wound its way back to the global system, alternating between exclusions and exemptions whose scope has varied with successive legislations. The following is a synoptic history.[21]

1913–1942

Up to 1925 extreme pressure was placed upon Congress by American industry to develop incentives for industrial expansion overseas. There was concern that many foreign companies doing business in the United States had unfair advantages, because foreign nationals generally were exempt from domestic taxes in their home countries. In 1926, as a result of these concerns, the first foreign-earned income exclusion law, Section 213(b)(14), was enacted by Congress. The law permitted U.S. overseas workers to exclude or subtract from their gross taxable income "amounts derived and received from sources (business conducted) without the United States"; that is, if a person had lived six months or more abroad, income earned while residing abroad was exempt from taxation. Up to that time overseas workers had only been allowed to credit against their U.S. tax bill their income taxes paid to foreign governments.

In 1928 Section 213(b)(14) was designated Section 116(a). Senator Reed of the Senate Finance Committee moved to repeal this section in 1932. He contended that although the intent of the law was to promote American business activity abroad, a foreign-income exclusion was not necessary to help foreign trade and was unfair to citizens resident in the United States, who received no similar privilege. Senator Reed further argued that the intent of Section 116(a) had been distorted. He cited cases in which American ambassadors, ministers, and officials of the foreign service had used the law to sidestep income taxes. After some debate and compromise, Section 116(a) was amended so that income paid by the U.S. government or its agencies could no longer be excluded or deducted.

1942–1951

Continued concern with abuses of the law led Congress to amend Section 116(a) again in 1942. As amended Section 116(a) applied only to "an individual citizen of the U.S. who established to the satisfaction of the Commissioner that he was a bonafide resident of a foreign country during the entire taxable year," not just six months.

1951–1962

Residency requirements were again changed in 1951. The amended law established that any income earned overseas by a U.S. citizen could be excluded if he or she resided abroad for 17 out of 18 months. This part of the law was designated Section 116(a)(2). The purpose of the change was to encourage citizens "to go abroad on a short-term basis to increase technical knowledge in backward areas."

At the same time another subtle addition to the law, Section 116(a)(1), clarified when certain foreign residents could actually start to claim income exclusion.

In 1953 the amount of excludable income under Section 116(a)(2) was limited to a $20,000 ceiling. In 1954 Section 116(a)(1) became Section 911(a)(1). Section 116(a)(2) was renumbered and subdivided: the residency portion of Section 116(a)(2) became Section 911(a)(2). The provision for a $20,000 ceiling became Section 911(c).

1962–1975

In 1963 Congress changed the ceiling to an income exclusion of $20,000 for the first three years of residence and $35,000 for each year thereafter. The $35,000 limit was lowered in 1965 to $25,000. By 1975 Section 911 provided for

1. A $20,000 income exclusion for those who had resided in a foreign country for 17 out of 18 months and a $25,000 exclusion for those with three or more years of bonafide residency.

2. Permission to subtract the exclusion off the top of earned income; the remainder was the income base for tax calculations. In effect this left the taxpayer in a lower rate bracket than would otherwise have been the case.

3. A tax credit on all foreign income taxes paid. Those claiming the U.S. standard deduction, however, could not claim the foreign tax credit. For example, a worker earning $50,000 paid $230 under the 1975 law.

Although the 1975 law was more stringent than earlier laws, many felt it still gave unfair tax advantages to a special class of Americans.

1976 Tax Reform Act
The sweeping Tax Reform Act of 1976, which changed several areas of U.S. tax laws, also altered Section 911 significantly. Among other things the amended section 911 provided that

1. A maximum of $15,000 could be excluded from earned income by a U.S. citizen who was present in a foreign country for at least 17 out of 18 months. An employee of a charity was allowed a $20,000 exclusion.

2. Taxable income remaining after the application of the earned income exclusion was subject to taxation at higher-bracket rates. Specifically the remaining income was to be taxed at the rate applicable before the exclusion.

3. Any foreign taxes paid on the $15,000 of excluded income could not be included as part of the foreign tax credit.

4. Individuals applying the standard deduction could also apply foreign tax credits.

Thus as a result of this legislation the exclusion was dropped to $15,000, and income was taxed at higher rates.

As originally enacted, the 1976 Act made the changes effective for the 1976 tax year. The sweeping changes in Section 911 brought about by the Tax Reform Act elicited such strong negative reaction, however, that Congress delayed the effect of the 1976 law for one year until January 1, 1977. Further delays were later effected to allow a thorough examination of opposing views of the law.

1978 Foreign Earned Income Act and 1981 Tax Reform Act
In the end the intention to tighten the law so as to tax Americans abroad more in the interest of horizontal equity was frustrated, and the 1978 legislation that follows moved somewhat in the opposite direction. This was a consequence of growing sentiment and organized lobbying that stressed not merely contrary views of equity but also the possibility that American exports may be jeopardized by greater taxation of Americans abroad.

But the 1978 legislation was nonetheless considered inadequately liberal toward Americans abroad, and a succession of studies and reports were written to move it yet further in that direction. Notable among these studies were those that sought to show that the U.S. taxation of citizens abroad discouraged U.S. exports: for example, the Report of the U.S. Comptroller General to the Congress (1978), the U.S. Treasury Department's study (1978), a study of Chase Econometrics for the American Chamber of Commerce (1980), a study by the General Accounting Office again (1981), and a study by Larkin (1983). None of these studies suffered from necessary sophistication, but their conclusions were consonant with prevalent preconceptions and found favor.

The different views of horizontal equity, which the opponents of the global system embraced, related not to equity between Americans at home and abroad but to equity between Americans abroad and others abroad. These views reflected sentiments long held and articulated. Thus Mr. Davis, representing the Foreign Trade Council in Hearings of the 69th Congress on this subject in 1925, had this to say:

Four or five years ago we collected, through the assistance of the Consular Service, the tax laws of pretty much all the world. We made a very elaborate study of those tax laws, and we reached the conclusion that the United States is the only country in the world which does follow this policy of taxing its nationals abroad upon income which they earn in the country of residence. *Now, our people who live abroad, and who are engaged in the promotion of our business in this way, naturally regard it as a discrimination against them. They feel it.* [p. 16, our italics]

Take, for instance, Mr. Whittemore ... He is the representative in the Argentine of the Singer Sewing Machine Company ... he is in competition with the representatives of British and German sewing-machine companies. Now, those men, the British and the Germans, pay no income tax to their own Government upon the amount which they earn in the conduct of that business in the Argentine Republic. Whittemore has to, and to that extent Whittemore is handicapped. *But more than the handicap is the feeling that it is an injustice: that it is a discrimination.* [p. 117, our italics]

The sense of inequity extended even to Americans abroad *versus* the local population. Thus Judge Williams (1921, p. 194) stated to the Eighth National Foreign Trade Convention of the American Chamber of Commerce:

The Philippines are domestic territory of the United States, and Americans enjoy no benefits and receive no protection from American sovereignty in the Islands which are not shared equally by Filipinos and resident aliens. The enforcement of this tax against one element of the community, therefore, to the exclusion of others engaged in the same business or calling, is class legislation of the rankest sort—something absolutely prohibited in the States by our Constitution.

The 1978 Act had replaced the previous foreign-income exclusionary rules with special deductions instead for cost-of-living differentials, housing and schooling expenses, home-leave travel expenses, and increased deductions for many expenses and for separate households. But the opponents felt that these deductions were insufficient, and the procedures for claiming them time-consuming and complex.

Backed by the cited studies of the adverse effects on exports, the construction and architect/engineering firms managed to spearhead successful lobbying efforts for new revisions in Section 911. Their efforts were crowned with success in the Tax Reform Act of 1981, as part of President Reagan's liberalization of tax benefits for industry.

The 1981 Act greatly liberalized different aspects of how American taxpayers overseas would be taxed. *First,* in terms of residency requirements the Tax Reform Act of 1981 required that the tax home be in the foreign country for 11 of 12 months (330 days) instead of the previous 510 days. Physical presence in more than one country during the period was allowed. If one could not satisfy the physical presence law, there was a stricter bonafide residency test incorporated. This was based on the criteria of

1. the taxpayer's intentions;

2. establishment of a home by the taxpayer for an indefinite period;

3. participation in the activities of the community where the taxpayer lives on a social and community level;

4. physical presence in the country consistent with the taxpayer's employment;

5. nature, extent, and reason for temporal absences from the temporary home;

6. assumptions of economic burdens and payment of taxes in the foreign country;

7. status of resident contrasted with sojourner;

8. taxpayer's marital status and residence of family;

9. nature and duration of assignment;

10. taxpayer's good faith.

Second, a generous exclusion was incorporated for foreign-earned income according to the progressive schedule:

$80,000 for 1982–1987;

$85,000 for 1988;

$90,000 for 1989;

$95,000 for 1990 and thereafter.

Except for this exclusion no other deductions, exclusions, or credits were allowable except an allowance for war, civil strife, and the like, and a "housing-cost" amount. Strongly supported by industries with large overseas operations, the 1981 Act easily passed both chambers of Congress and became law.

Congress would then leave Section 911 alone until the major 1986 Reform Act. Then, however, with the new emphasis on closing loopholes, the pendulum swung somewhat mildly back toward emphasizing equity through less benefits for overseas Americans.

Proposals contained in the Conference Agreement on the bill for the Tax Reform Act of 1986 would have lowered the exclusion for foreign-earned income of Americans working abroad from the present $80,000 to $70,000 for taxable years beginning after 1986. The provision that income greater than the exclusionary amount be taxed as the first dollars of income was retained. The Joint Committee on Taxation suggested that this income above the exclusionary amount be taxed at the marginal tax rate prevalent at the level of income if there was no exclusion.

Lobbying by special interests was less visible in 1986 than in 1981. The circumstances were different also. In the House tax bill overseas taxpayers would have been subject to a minimum tax on individuals. The Senate, on the other hand, offered to lower the exclusion amount. Because they realized that either way they would lose, the lobbyists concerned with Section 911 kept a low profile during conference negotiations. A compromise agreement emerged when the House accepted the Senate proposal for a lowering of the exclusion amount rather than being subject to a minimum tax: a better situation than the minimum tax, but still a loss to the overseas taxpayer.

It is not entirely clear which way the next legislation will turn. With the current preoccupation with U.S. exports, and obsession with fair trade and competitiveness, it is possible that next time around there will be a liberalization in favor of Americans abroad. But the concern with the budget deficit may lead the legislators in the other direction. Only time will tell.

Notes

Bhagwati's research was supported by the German Marshall Fund and the Guggenheim Foundation.

1. This specific version of Bhagwati's original proposal to "tax the brain drain" from LDCs to augment their tax revenues for developmental spending was the result of earlier economic, legal-philosophical, administrative, and human rights analyses that followed the preliminary statement of his ideas (Bhagwati 1976; Bhagwati and Dellalfar 1974). The evolution of these ideas and their eventual format, as stated by Bhagwati (1977, 1980) and discussed in the New Delhi conference, is traced by Bhagwati (1983).

2. The specific use of the Mirrlees-Atkinson type of framework to discuss Bhagwati's proposal, as distinct from simply extending it to the possibility of emigration as an intellectual exercise, however, should be attributed to Hamada (1975) and to Bhagwati and Hamada (chapter 5).

3. We might add that the Bhagwati proposal has been analyzed in several other analytical formats as well, for instance, as by Bhagwati and Hamada (1974) and McCulloch (1976).

4. Despite the emphasis on income taxation, readers should keep in mind the existence of other policy instruments for financing public expenditures and improving the distribution of economic well-being. In fact the optimal taxation literature has emphasized that it is almost always desirable to supplement income taxation with a system of excise taxes. Mirrlees (chapter 8) suggests that what is called a tax on earnings in these models should be thought of as corresponding to all taxes on incomes and expenditures in the real world. A task for future research should be to analyze some of these taxes separately rather than as a single aggregate variable.

5. Citizenship does provide assurance of having access to these benefits at will, so Hufbauer's argument is certainly overstated even if its premises are not challenged.

6. This approach may not be accepted, of course, as a decisive choice criterion by all. Thus within international trade theory, since the early work of Harry Johnson (1960, 1965) and Bhagwati and Srinivasan (1969), for instance, it has long been customary to put "noneconomic" objectives alongside goods and services into the social utility function as arguments. Recently such alternative approaches have

become even more fashionable, thanks to the impetus provided by Nozick's theory of rights.

7. But with the levels of economic well-being presently distributed quite unevenly between LDCs and DCs, national welfare maximization by LDCs may not significantly conflict with world welfare maximization.

8. Bhagwati and Hamada close the economy by allowing no individual to emigrate. Wilson on the other hand considers a closed economy to be formed by taking an open economy in which emigration occurs freely, with its tax set optimally, and then imposing the constraint that no individual may change his residence in response to changes in the tax (see chapters 4 and 6). This means of course that individuals who are emigrants (residents) in the optimal open economy remain so in the closed economy.

9. See, however, the discussion of this issue by Bhagwati and Hamada in sections 2 and 6 of chapter 5.

10. In Bhagwati and Hamada's analysis TLBs are defined as an invariant set of low-income individuals who remain residents through all relevant variations in tax parameters. Bhagwati and Hamada give a Rawlsian interpretation to justify the use of this analytically convenient criterion.

11. This need not be so, paradoxically, if bilateral cooperation on tax information makes evasion more difficult for emigrants although domestic tax enforcement continues, for political and administrative reasons, to be difficult.

12. Renunciation of citizenship or refusal to pay (thus making it extremely risky to return to one's home country in any way) are other alternatives to change of citizenship.

13. These contrasts are not wholly pure. Thus, for example, the United States does not extend several exemptions (other than double-tax avoidance) to citizens abroad, and there are certainly restrictions in European systems on the definition of foreign residence that justifies exclusion from tax liability. The central thrust and principles of the two tax systems are very clear and different, however, in both cases.

14. The contribution of John Wooton, now at University of Western Ontario, in tracking down several U.K. and U.S. sources here and in London was invaluable and went beyond the call of duty. Brian Wesol has helped to bring the story up to the present day.

15. The Act was passed on January 9, 1799, and explicitly exempted from its scope all nonresident citizens except those who had "gone abroad, for any temporary purpose." For details, see Dowell (1884). Other useful references are Sabine (1966) and Coffield (1970).

16. See the splendid discussion of the interplay of ideas (or "political economy") and interests in Peel's conversion to the repeal of the Corn Laws by Douglas Irwin (1989).

17. The judgment was delivered on February 2, 1876, in a case involving the Calcutta Jute Mills Company, Ltd., and the Surveyor of Taxes (Henry Nicholson), in the Exchequer. Compare *Exchequer Cases*, Act 37 Vict. C. 16, Part VI, pp. 92 and 101.

18. The dominance of the benefit principle of taxation at the time is beyond dispute. For instance, the tax historian Kennedy (1964, p. 89) has argued, "The state, instead of being conceived, as the Crown was in the sixteenth century, as an instrument for the general regulation and defense of the whole community, came to be though of rather as an instrument for protecting the rights of the members; and their duty to the state came to be limited in theory to the payment of their share of the cost of maintaining this protecting instrument." Except for maxims such as avoiding taxation of necessities and the poor, so as to avoid raising the real cost of labor, the principles of taxation seemed therefore to reflect the notion that taxes should broadly be commensurate with benefits, implicit and explicit.

19. Supplementary explanations have been advanced, as in Bhagwati (1982a): (1) that tax exemptions and loopholes reflect power structure; with Englishmen abroad usually wearing the same ties as the men in Parliament, it was unlikely that the British government would vote to exercise income tax jurisdiction over them; and (2) that if the assumption was that most Englishmen abroad were civil servants and managers of the British empire, they would have to be paid some "net-of-tax" salary to get them out to the tropics; if so, charging them the income tax would mean that their gross salaries would have to be adjusted upward, and no revenue benefit would accrue to the exchequer anyway.

There is however no evidence for either argument as an explanation of the origins of the British system. The former argument, however, may have played a role in the continuation of the system: it certainly plays a role in the unwillingness of developing country elites and policymakers to consider adopting the differing U.S. practice.

20. Extracts from the Opinion of the Court, October Term 1923, 265 U.S. 47, pp. 51, 56.

21. The account up to 1976 is from Bhagwati 1982b, which drew in turn on material compiled by Christine Heckman.

References

Atkinson, A. B. 1973. How progressive should income tax be? In *Essays in Modern Economics*, ed. M. Parkin. London: Longman.

Bastable, C. F. 1892. *Public Finance*. London: MacMillan & Co.

Bewley, T. 1981. A critique of Tiebout's theory of local public expenditures. *Econometrica* 49: 713–740.

Bhagwati, J. N. 1972. The United States in the Nixon era: The end of innocence. *Daedalus* (fall).

Bhagwati, J. N. 1976. Introduction. In *The Brain Drain and Taxation: Theory and Empirical Analysis*, ed. J. Bhagwati. Amsterdam: North Holland.

Bhagwati, J. N. 1977. The brain drain: International resource flow accounting, compensation, taxation and related proposals. Presented at the Intergovernmental Group of Experts Meeting, UNCTAD, Geneva. In *Essays in Development Economics: Dependence and Interdependence*, J. Bhagwati. Oxford: Basil Blackwell, vol. 1, 1985.

Bhagwati, J. N. 1979. (July) International migration of the highly skilled: Economic, ethics and taxes. *Third World Quarterly* 1, no. 3.

Bhagwati, J. N. 1980. North-South dialogue: An interview. *Third World Quarterly* 2 (April).

Bhagwati, J. N. 1982. Directly unproductive, profit-seeking (DUP) activities. *Journal of Political Economy* 90: 988–1002.

Bhagwati, J. 1982a. Introduction. *Journal of Public Economics* 18.

Bhagwati, J. 1982b. Taxation and international migration. In *The Gateway: U.S. Immigration Issues and Policies*, ed. B. Chiswick. Washington, DC: American Enterprise Institute.

Bhagwati, J. N., and W. Dellalfar. 1974. The brain drain and income taxation. *World Development* 1, nos. 1, 2: 94–101.

Bhagwati, J. N., and K. Hamada. 1974. The brain drain, international integration of markets for professionals and unemployment: A theoretical analysis. *Journal of Development Economics* 1, no. 1.

Bhagwati, J. N., and T. N. Srinivasan. 1969. Optimal intervertion to achieve non-economic objectives. *Review of Economic Studies* 36, no. 1.

Bochard, E. M. 1915. *The Diplomatic Protection of Citizens Abroad*. New York: Banks Law Publishing Co.

Brennan, G., and J. M. Buchanan. 1980. *The Power to Tax*. Cambridge, Engl.: Cambridge University Press.

Chase Econometric Associates, Inc. (for the American Chamber of Congress). 1980 (June). *Economic Impact of Changing Taxation of U.S. Workers Overseas*.

Coffield, J. 1970. *A Popular History of Taxation*. London: Longman.

Davis, O. K. 1925. Statement before Committee on Ways and Means: Hearings (Revenue Revision, 1925), 69th Congress, 1st Session. Washington, DC: U.S. Congress.

Dowell, S. 1884. *History of Taxation and Taxes in England*. London: Longmans, Green and Co.

Grubel, H., and A. D. Scott. 1966. The international flow of human capital. *American Economic Review* 56 (May).

Hamada, K. 1975. Efficiency, equity, income taxation, and the brain drain: A second best analysis. *Journal of Development Economics* 2: 281–287.

Hyde, C. C. 1922. *International Law, Chiefly as Interpreted and Applied by the United States.* Boston: Little, Brown and Co.

Irwin, D. 1989 (Mar.). Political economy and Peel's repeal of the Corn Laws. *Economics and Politics* 1, no. 1.

Johnson, H. G. 1965. The economics of the "brain drain:" The Canadian case. *Minerva.*

Johnson, H. G. 1960. Cost of protection and the scientific tariff. *Journal of Political Economy* 68 (October).

Joint Committee on Taxation, U.S. Congress. 1985 (June 18). *Tax Reform Proposals: Taxation of Foreign Income and Foreign Taxpayers*, Washington, DC.

Joint Committee on Taxation, U.S. Congress. 1986 (Aug. 29). *Summary of Conference Agreement on HR3838 (Tax Reform Act of 1986)*, Washington, DC.

Kennedy, W. 1966. *English Taxation 1640–1799.* London: Frank Cass & Co. Ltd.

Larkin, E. R. 1983. *The Impact of Taxes on U.S. Citizens Working Abroad.* Ann Arbor, MI: UMI Research Press.

McCulloch, R., and J. Yellen. 1976. Consequences of a tax on the brain drain for unemployment and income inequality in developed countries. In *The Brain Drain and Taxation: Theory and Empirical Analysis*, ed. J. Bhagwati. Amsterdam: North Holland.

Mirrlees, J. A. 1971. An exploration in the theory of optimal income taxation. *Review of Economic Studies* 38: 175–208.

Niskanen, W. 1971. *Bureaucracy and Representative Government.* Chicago: Aldine-Atherton.

Sabine, B. E. V. 1966. *A History of Income Tax.* London: Allen & Unwin Ltd.

Sandmo, A. 1981. Income tax evasion, labour supply, and the equity-efficiency tradeoff. *Journal of Public Economics* 16: 265–288.

Surrey, S. S., and W. C. Warren (eds.). 1962. *Federal Income Taxation: Cases and Materials.* Mineola, NY: New York Foundation Press.

Tennant, C. 1872. *The People's Blue Book: Taxation As It Is and As It Ought to Be*, London: Longmans, Green & Co.

Tiebout, C. M. 1956. A pure theory of local expenditures. *Journal of Political Economy* 64: 416–424.

Webster, P. 1891. *A Treatise on the Law of Citizenship in the United States.* Albany, NY: M. Bender.

Williams, D. 1921. The Effect of Double Taxation on our Foreign Trade. Eighth National Foreign Trade Convention Proceedings (Third General Session), National Foreign Trade Council. New York: J. J. Little & Ives Co.

II　　　　　　　　Taxing Citizens Abroad:
　　　　　　　　　　Current Experience and
　　　　　　　　　　Some Issues

2

The Experience of the Philippines in Taxing its Nonresident Citizens

Richard D. Pomp

Introduction

Whether a less developed country should tax the income of its citizens who reside abroad has been the subject of at least four international conferences since 1975.[1] This attention is attributable to Jagdish Bhagwati of Columbia University, who has written extensively about the "brain drain": the large-scale movement of skilled labor from less developed countries (LDCs) to developed countries (DCs).[2] Bhagwati has proposed a tax to transfer revenue to LDCs that experience a brain drain.[3] The Bhagwati proposal has generated considerable controversy because the brain drain raises fundamental moral and political questions about a citizen's right to self-realization and fulfillment.[4] The controversy is also fueled by a lack of consensus on the causes and effects of the brain drain.[5]

Initially three versions of the Bhagwati proposal were discussed: a tax levied by the United Nations, a tax levied by the country of immigration (the host DC), and a tax levied by the country of emigration (the LDC). An income tax levied by an LDC on its nonresident citizens emerged from international discussion as the most feasible version.[6] This form of the Bhagwati proposal is attractive because any LDC can adopt it unilaterally.[7] Moreover, precedent for taxing citizens and emigrants abroad already exists. For a number of years the United States,[8] the Philippines,[9] and (until recently) Mexico[10] have levied an income tax on the worldwide income of their citizens, both resident and nonresident. None of these countries, however, adopted this broad assertion of jurisdiction in response to the brain drain.

In contrast to the United States and the Philippines, most countries view citizenship as irrelevant for tax purposes. In these countries residency is the relevant jurisdictional nexus.[11] In other words residents are taxable on their worldwide income, but nonresidents are not taxable on their income from abroad even if they are citizens of the taxing country.[12] Although definitions of "resident" vary among countries and may include persons temporarily living and working abroad, persons who have emigrated—the group most likely to constitute the brain drain—do not fall within any of the traditional definitions.[13] An LDC that relies on residency jurisdiction is therefore unlikely to tax the income earned abroad by its emigrant citizens.

An LDC that desired to implement the Bhagwati proposal could follow the precedent of the United States, the Philippines, and Mexico and assert jurisdiction on the basis of citizenship.[14] Before adopting such an approach, however, an LDC would have to be confident that it could administer this broad assertion of tax jurisdiction effectively.

Problems that an LDC might encounter in implementing a tax on nonresident citizens have been predicted in the theoretical literature.[15] Empirical evidence does not exist, however, to indicate whether these administrative problems would actually materialize. Neither the Philippine nor the Mexican experience in enforcing a tax on nonresidents has been studied before. Although information on the U.S. experience is available, it is of limited value[16] and not helpful in predicting the problems that an LDC might encounter.[17]

Without information about the administrative feasibility of an LDC tax, international discussion of the Bhagwati proposal has reached an impasse. Debate continues over the fairness, political, and human rights issues posed by such a tax, but these issues are neither easily resolved nor susceptible to empirical inquiry.[18] Moreover, the debate will be moot if the administrative difficulties of implementing an LDC tax prove insurmountable.

To gain some insight into the administrative aspects of the Bhagwati proposal, the World Bank commissioned me to conduct a case study of the Philippine taxation of nonresident citizens. By documenting the Philippines's experience, the World Bank hoped to better predict problems that other LDCs might encounter in implementing a tax on nonresident citizens. This case study provides the focus for this chapter.

The next section describes the experiences of the Philippines in taxing its nonresident citizens during three time periods: before 1970, 1970–1972, and 1973 to the present. In each period the Philippines tried a different approach to the taxation of nonresident citizens.

Analysis of these three approaches illuminates two general sets of problems. The first involves the question whether an LDC should tax nonresidents in the same manner as residents or use special rules. Before 1970 the Philippines taxed resident and nonresident citizens identically; since that time, however, it has applied special rules to nonresidents.[19]

The second set of problems centers around the administrative difficulties of imposing a tax on persons abroad. The Philippines appears to have been markedly unsuccessful in enforcing its tax on emigrants. Noncompliance among this group is apparently widespread, and the Philippines lacks any effective response or sanctions.

The third section analyzes the implications of these problems for the Bhagwati proposal. That section proposes a possible resolution to the structural problem of designing an LDC tax suitable for nonresidents. The administrative problems of the Bhagwati proposal, by comparison, are less easily resolved. To enforce the tax equitably for all nonresidents, an LDC will need the cooperation of each host DC. The necessity of obtaining DC cooperation, however, undercuts one of the attractive features of an LDC tax—that it can be adopted unilaterally by an LDC.

The last section poses the dilemma that Bhagwati and his supporters face. If they are unable to convince the DCs to cooperate in policing an LDC tax on nonresidents, the tax will fall disproportionately on transient nonresidents. Because most of the transient nonresidents are unskilled workers, the LDCs would inevitably tax the "muscle drain" rather than the brain drain.

The Philippine Experience with the Taxation of Nonresident Citizens

Before 1970

The early Philippine reliance on citizenship as a basis for tax jurisdiction reflects more the country's colonial legacy from the United States than a carefully developed policy. Initially Philippine citizens were taxed under the U.S. Revenue Act of 1913.[20] This act, adopted shortly after ratification of the sixteenth amendment in the United States,[21] taxed the worldwide income of U.S. and Philippine citizens, regardless of where they lived.[22]

In 1918 the United States authorized the Philippines to adopt its own tax code.[23] Pursuant to this power and without extensive discussion or debate, the Philippines adopted a tax code based substantially upon then-existing U.S. tax law,[24] and taxed all citizens identically, regardless of their residence. Thus, early in its history, the Philippines incorporated citizenship jurisdiction into its own law following the U.S. model.

The Philippines taxed all citizens uniformly regardless of residence until 1970. Their worldwide net incomes were subject to progressive rates that started at 5 percent on net incomes of up to 2,000 pesos and reached 70 percent on net incomes exceeding 500,000 pesos.[25]

Philippine citizens could either deduct any income taxes paid to a foreign country from gross income or credit those taxes against their Philippine income tax.[26] This option was intended to mitigate the burden of multiple taxation that can result when a taxpayer or his or her income is subject to the tax jurisdiction of more than one country. For example, both the United States and the Philippines could tax Philippine citizens working in the United States.[27] These taxpayers would presumably choose to credit their U.S. taxes against their Philippine taxes rather than to deduct their U.S. taxes from gross income. A credit would produce a peso-for-peso offset against their Philippine taxes, whereas the benefit of a deduction would be limited to the product of their Philippine tax rates and the peso equivalent of their U.S. taxes.

Three sets of problems emerged from this pattern of taxation. The first arose around 1970, when the peso floated and the exchange rate of the peso to the U.S. dollar increased dramatically from 2:1 to 7.5:1.[28] Because of the devaluation, even modest foreign salaries made nonresident Philippine citizens living in the United States appear wealthy by Philippine standards. Consequently many nonresidents were thrust into the highest tax brackets of the progressive Philippine rate schedule.

For example, at a 2:1 exchange rate, the Philippine 70 percent marginal tax rate was applicable to incomes of $250,000 (500,000 pesos divided by 2) or more. At a 7.5:1 exchange rate, however, the highest tax rate was reached at incomes of $66,667 (500,000 pesos divided by 7.5). The effect of the devaluation was that Filipinos working in the United States were viewed for tax purposes as having incomes in pesos 3.75 times (7.5 divided by 2) larger than before. They consequently experienced a sharp increase in their tax burdens, even though in dollars their incomes had not changed.[29] It is not surprising that many nonresident Filipinos complained to their government about inequitable Philippine tax burdens and questioned the propriety of being subject to the same rate schedule that applied to residents.[30]

A second set of problems involved the determination of net income. Some nonresidents complained that Philippine tax law was unduly restrictive and therefore ill-suited to cope with conditions and practices abroad. They argued that the Philippine tax law did not allow deductions for certain types of expenditures incurred abroad.[31] Some of those expenditures were evidently allowed as deductions by the tax laws of the host

DCs, which suggested to nonresidents that Philippine tax law was too harsh.

The third and most severe set of problems centered around the administration of the Philippine tax. Measures that facilitated the administration of the income tax at home, such as the use of withholding, information returns, audits, the seizure and sale of assets, garnishment, and civil and criminal fines and penalties[32] were unavailable or ineffective abroad because the taxpayers, their assets, and the payors of their incomes were outside the jurisdiction of the Philippines. The national boundary was a formidable impediment to the enforcement of a tax on nonresident citizens.[33]

Three obstacles confronted the Bureau of Internal Revenue (BIR).[34] First, many nonresident citizens failed to file a return. The BIR did not have a master taxpayer roll that listed all nonresident citizens and thus could not determine the identities of those nonresidents who did not file.[35] Compiling an accurate master list would have been difficult, however, because detailed records of emigrants were not kept until recently.[36] Moreover, although these emigrant records specify the country of initial destination, they do not provide current addresses.[37] Without such addresses the BIR would have had difficulty contacting those nonresidents whom it identified as nonfilers.

In addition, the prolonged and expensive effort involved in determining a nonfiler's current address would not necessarily be productive, because the absence of a tax return might be due to such causes as death, marriage, change of citizenship, unemployment, retirement, or receipt of nontaxable income. For these reasons the BIR still has not attempted to generate a master roll of nonresident taxpayers.[38]

Second, the BIR had difficulty verifying the information contained in those returns of nonresidents that were filed.[39] The BIR did not have powers, beyond those held by private citizens, to conduct an investigation or an audit in a foreign country. As a result the BIR generally relied on correspondence to verify information.[40]

Audits by correspondence proved unsatisfactory, however.[41] The normal delays in the mail between the Philippines and the host DCs made these audits time-consuming. The problem was exacerbated by the ability of nonresidents to drag out these audits interminably, either by design or otherwise. They would ask for clarifications of BIR questions, raise diversionary issues, and request extensions of time to gather requested information.[42]

Even if the information was eventually supplied, the BIR often had trouble determining its authenticity. For example, nonresidents would sometimes be required to submit a copy of their DC tax returns so that the BIR could check the Philippine tax returns for consistency. The BIR suspects that some of the copies it received were bogus foreign tax returns specifically prepared for purposes of the audit.[43] Moreover, some nonresidents simply ignored BIR requests for supplementary information and documentation.[44]

Third, the BIR had difficulty collecting taxes due.[45] If the BIR knew of any assets held by nonresidents within the Philippines, it could seize and liquidate them. Otherwise the BIR was unable to compel payment through normal attachment or garnishment procedures.

Some of these problems also blunted one of the BIR's primary tools for dealing with recalcitrant taxpayers—the tax clearance certificate.[46] This certificate, issued by the BIR, is evidence that a taxpayer has no outstanding tax liabilities or delinquencies.[47] A citizen is prohibited from leaving the Philippines without obtaining a tax clearance certificate, and diplomatic and consular officers have the power to refuse to issue or to renew Philippine passports unless the applicant presents such a certificate.[48]

The tax clearance certificate was ineffective for dealing with certain delinquent nonresident taxpayers. First, nonresidents who did not renew their passports did not return to the Philippines, or returned but did not leave afterward so had no reason to apply for certificates. Second, some nonresidents became citizens of other countries and returned to the Philippines under foreign passports. As "tourists" in the Philippines, they were not required to obtain tax clearance certificates before departing (even for those years in which they had been citizens), provided they had not "engaged in commerce."[49]

The system of tax clearance certificates had a third weakness that reduced its effectiveness in the case of taxpayers abroad. Certain nonresidents filed returns that stated an incorrect amount of income, paid the tax owed on that amount, and therefore had no outstanding liability or delinquency. Unless the BIR had reason to suspect that the income reported on the return had been understated, it routinely issued a tax clearance certificate.[50] In some cases nonresidents visiting the Philippines and anticipating a challenge by the BIR brought specially prepared documentation with them that purported to corroborate their tax returns.[51]

Even when the BIR uncovered cases of nonfiling by nonresidents through the tax clearance certificate requirements, special problems still confronted the agency.[52] The absence of a tax return might become apparent when a nonresident's records were reviewed for outstanding liabilities and delinquencies, but the problem of determining tax liability remained. Some nonresidents would claim that they had no taxable incomes because they were unemployed, retired, or being supported by friends or relatives. Lacking an easy and inexpensive way of investigating the taxable status of these nonresidents, the BIR reluctantly accepted their explanations and usually issued the certificates requested.[53]

Because of the weaknesses in the system of tax clearance certificates, many embassies and consulates were less than vigilant in requiring nonresidents to produce such a certificate before renewing their passports.[54] Furthermore some embassy and consular personnel felt that the strict enforcement of the tax clearance requirement might be counterproductive in the case of emigrants who had applied for DC citizenship. The tax clearance certificate system may have induced these emigrants to postpone travel to the Philippines until they had obtained new citizenship and new passports, which would make it unnecessary for them to obtain a certificate and renew their Philippine passports. As a result the Philippines not only failed to collect delinquent taxes, but also forfeited the revenue and foreign exchange that would have been generated by their visits.[55] Thus rigorous enforcement of the tax clearance certificate system may have provided emigrants with an additional inducement to obtain DC citizenship.

To respond effectively to the administrative problems posed by nonresident citizens, the BIR would have needed the assistance of the host DCs. The tax administrations of the host countries might already have had information in their files on the income of Filipino taxpayers. Even if they did not, they could have conducted the necessary investigations.[56] In addition, the host DCs had jurisdiction not only over resident Filipinos, but also over their assets in the DCs. This authority could have facilitated a solution to the BIR's collection problems.

Most DCs, however, offered a limited amount of cooperation in assessing and collecting foreign taxes. The degree of assistance needed by the BIR greatly exceeded that available through normal DC practices,[57] and the BIR rarely approached the host DCs for additional help. Access to DC courts was also unavailable.[58]

The widespread lack of compliance by nonresidents, including their failure to file returns, is evidence of the administrative difficulties that confronted the BIR in attempting to follow the U.S. model of citizenship jurisdiction. The existing data do not provide a firm basis for evaluating the extent of noncompliance during this period. All BIR officials interviewed, however, felt that taxpayer noncompliance was rampant, especially among emigrant nonresidents.[59] The officials distinguished between emigrant nonresidents and transient nonresidents, such as contract workers, seamen, and other unskilled and semiskilled Filipinos who contracted to work abroad for a specific period of time. The migration of these transient nonresidents constitutes the so-called muscle drain, rather than the brain drain.[60]

Tax officials believed that emigrant nonresidents had a higher rate of noncompliance than transient nonresidents.[61] In some instances noncompliance may have been unintentional because emigrants may have been unaware that their Philippine tax obligations continued even after moving abroad. In other cases noncompliance may have been deliberate. Those who left the Philippines for political reasons may have refused to pay Philippine taxes. Those who left because of a lack of professional opportunities may have also resented any obligation to pay. The longer emigrants stayed abroad, the more they may have questioned the right of the Philippines, rather than the right of the host DC, to tax their incomes. Also physical distance from the Philippines could have bred a sense of security that encouraged emigrants to disregard their Philippine tax obligations. Emigrants would have easily justified their noncompliance if they considered their Philippine tax burden onerous or excessive. Finally, noncompliance may have been encouraged by the BIR's inability to discover and punish emigrants' noncompliance.[62]

In contrast to emigrants, transient nonresidents usually could be identified and the amount of their earned incomes ascertained, because their employment often was controlled and regulated by the Philippine government.[63] In addition, any assets owned by transient nonresidents were usually located in the Philippines and thus could be liquidated by the BIR to satisfy outstanding tax liabilities. Transients also knew that they would eventually return to the Philippines where they would be within close reach of the BIR. Such pressures probably induced transients to comply with their tax obligations.

As this section suggests, the Philippine tax regime before 1970 clearly was unsatisfactory. After the devaluation of the peso, the extension of the normal Philippine rate schedule to nonresidents produced harsh tax burdens. The BIR had difficulty policing the tax abroad, and noncompliance apparently was widespread. Complaints voiced both by taxpayers and by the BIR led to changes in 1970.

1970 and 1971

In 1970 the Philippine tax law was changed to distinguish between nonresident and resident citizens. Nonresident citizens were allowed three special deductions that were not available to residents.[64] In addition, the rules governing the credit for foreign taxes were liberalized.[65] Each of these changes was intended to alleviate special hardships suffered by nonresident citizens[66] and to increase compliance.

The first of the new deductions directly responded to the complaint that the Philippine tax law was too restrictive in that it did not allow nonresidents to deduct certain expenditures incurred abroad.[67] Nonresidents were now allowed to deduct on their Philippine tax returns those expenditures that were deductible in the country where they earned their income.[68] The second change introduced a deduction for transportation expenses incurred in obtaining employment abroad.[69] Last, nonresident citizens were allowed to deduct their housing costs, either in the amount of rent actually paid or the fair rental value of an owner-occupied residence.[70]

In addition, the scope of the foreign tax credit was broadened. Nonresidents were allowed to credit not only the income taxes they paid to a foreign country, but also the income taxes paid to the state, county, or city in which they earned their income.[71]

These new deductions and the expansion of the credit did not mollify the overseas community. Nonresidents complained that even after these changes, a modest foreign income, when converted into pesos, could still generate a large Philippine tax liability.[72] Apparently none of the 1970 changes was generous enough to offset completely the effects of allowing the peso to float.[73]

The 1970 changes not only failed to satisfy the overseas community, but also aggravated the verification and enforcement problems of the BIR. The BIR now faced two new problems. First, it had to verify deductions allowable under unfamiliar foreign tax laws. The BIR attempted to solve this problem by requiring nonresidents to attach copies of their foreign tax returns to their Philippine tax returns.[74] Nonresidents routinely frustrated this approach, however, by submitting copies of bogus foreign returns.[75]

An ambiguity in the Philippine tax law further compounded the difficulties of the BIR. The statute was unclear about whether a nonresident could claim the same deduction twice: once under domestic Philippine tax law and a second time because it was allowed under foreign law.[76] The BIR took the reasonable position that a double deduction for the same expenditure was not permitted. But it was not always obvious from a nonresident's return whether the same expenses were being deducted twice.[77]

The BIR's second new problem involved the near impossibility of verifying a nonresident's housing costs. Tenants could easily manufacture bogus rental receipts, and homeowners could exaggerate the fair rental value of their home to increase their deductions. Consequently the 1970 changes did little to eliminate the source of the problems that both taxpayers and the BIR were experiencing.[78]

1972 to the Present

Because of the general dissatisfaction of both the BIR and Philippine taxpayers with the pre-1972 regime,[79] the taxation of nonresidents was overhauled in 1972. Under the new scheme, which is still in effect, nonresident citizens are taxed under a special rate schedule. These rates are 1 percent on the first $6,000 of adjusted gross income,[80] 2 percent on amounts exceeding $6,000 but not over $20,000, and 3 percent on amounts exceeding $20,000.[81] Because of these rates the tax regime is known as the "1-2-3 system."

Since 1973 nonresident citizens have been allowed two deductions: a personal exemption of $2,000 for a single taxpayer or $4,000 for a married taxpayer or a head of household, and a deduction—but not a credit—for income taxes paid to the foreign country in which the taxpayer resides or for income taxes paid to the foreign country in which the income was derived.[82] The 1-2-3 system is tied to the U.S. dollar: the deductions and the brackets of the rate schedule are all stated in U.S. dollars, and nonresidents are required to report their incomes in U.S. dollars.[83]

Only Philippine citizens who qualify as nonresidents are subject to the 1-2-3 system. From 1972 to 1978 a citizen had to be physically abroad for an uninterrupted period that included an entire year to qualify as a nonresident.[84] The requirement that the period abroad be uninterrupted was not interpreted literally, however; home visits by a taxpayer employed abroad on a regular basis did not interrupt the required period.[85] The definition of a nonresident was broadened in 1978.[86]

The 1-2-3 system was designed to mitigate the problems that had plagued the earlier approaches.[87] First, by allowing almost no deductions, the Philippines tried to eliminate the BIR's administrative problems of auditing a wide range of expenditures. Second, the country kept its tax rates low to compensate for the small number of deductions and to induce taxpayer compliance.[88] Third, the Philippines intended the multiple rates, in combination with the personal exemption, to achieve a modest degree of progressivity. Fourth, the country provided a deduction for foreign taxes to alleviate the burden of multiple taxation.[89] Finally, by tying the tax system to the U.S. dollar, the Philippines hoped to avoid the pre-1972 problems caused by the floating of the peso.[90]

Although the tax imposed by the 1-2-3 system is in effect a tax on gross income, many of the policymakers viewed the system at the time of its inception as a proxy for a tax on net income.[91] A tax on gross income can serve as a proxy for a tax on net income if either of two conditions is satisfied. First, if the available deductions are a very small percentage of gross income for all taxpayers, the tax is almost a tax on net income. Second, even if the available deductions are not a very small percentage of gross income, but constitute nearly the same percentage of gross income for all taxpayers, then any set of tax rates that might be applied to net income can be translated into an equivalent, and lower, set of tax rates that could be applied to gross income.[92]

In 1972 BIR officials assumed that most nonresidents were employed and that deductions denied under the 1-2-3 system constituted either a small percentage of gross income or the same percentage of gross income, for most nonresidents.[93] Policymakers viewed the 1-2-3 approach as being roughly equivalent to a net income tax without any of the administrative problems caused by the need to scrutinize a panoply of deductions.[94]

Although the 1-2-3 system eliminated the need to audit a vast array of deductions, the BIR must still verify each nonresident's gross income and the amount of foreign taxes paid. Although the BIR requires nonresidents to submit copies of their foreign tax returns and evidence of payment of foreign taxes,[95] it suspects that it continues to receive copies of bogus tax returns.[96] Moreover, many nonresidents fail to submit any documentation at all. As one official stated, "If they fail to submit proof of their foreign taxes, we could deny them a deduction for their foreign taxes and increase their tax liability. But so what? We wouldn't be able to collect the increased taxes anyway."[97] This comment nicely captures the passivity and frustration that mark the BIR's administration of the 1-2-3 system. Most of the administrative problems that characterized the pre-1972 tax regimes continue to plague the BIR. Because the BIR still lacks any effective means of collecting delinquent taxes, it makes few attempts either to identify nonfilers or to conduct audits.

The extent of noncompliance by nonresidents is difficult to evaluate. Data regarding the 1-2-3 system are presented in table 2.1, which summarizes the number of returns filed by nonresident citizens and the amounts of revenue collected from 1973 to 1982. Data were not available for 1972, the first year of the system.[98] For purposes of comparison, data for 1971, the last year of the old system, are also included.

One technique for evaluating the success of the Philippines in administering the 1-2-3 system and the degree of voluntary compliance is to

Table 2.1
Number of Returns and Revenue Collected from Nonresident Citizens

Year	Returns	Increase (Decrease) over Prior Year (%)	Revenue Collected (millions of pesos)	Increase (Decrease) over Prior Year (%)
1982	184,053	23	44.2	53
1981	149,172	20	28.9	24
1980	119,338	42	22.0	12
1979	83,543	17	19.5	20
1978	71,625	24	16.2	100
1977	57,791	7	8.1	1
1976	54,055	29	8.0	(29)
1975	41,755	49	11.3	135
1974	27,956	(13)	4.8	(55)
1973	32,170	—	10.6	—
1972	N/A	—	N/A	—
1971	13,000	—	0.342	—

Source: Data for 1971–1979 were compiled by the author from the records of the Bureau of Internal Revenue. Data for 1980, 1981, and 1982 were provided to Bhagwati by the Bureau of Internal Revenue.

compare the total amount of income actually reported on tax declarations with macroeconomic data on the amount of income that would have been reported had there been full compliance by all nonresident citizens.[99] In the domestic situation an estimate of the amount of income that would be reported if taxpayers complied fully can be based on national income data, which often are assembled by government economists and statisticians. Data on national income in the Philippines are irrelevant, however, in estimating the amount of income that should be reported under the 1-2-3 system because the relevant taxpayers are abroad. Instead one needs an estimate of the amount of income earned abroad by nonresidents. Because no government agency has made this estimate,[100] no comparison can be made between the total amount of income reported under the 1-2-3 system and the amount of income that should have been reported.

Another technique for measuring noncompliance is to compare the number of taxpayers filing returns with an estimate of the number of taxpayers who should have filed returns.[101] The BIR has estimated that the number of nonresident citizens taxable under the 1-2-3 system was 800,000 in the late 1970s.[102] For 1979, the year during the period of the estimate in which the most returns were received, less than 11 percent of the estimated taxpaying population filed. BIR officials were not surprised by this low rate of filing; it simply reaffirmed their suspicion that noncompliance was pervasive among nonresident citizens.

Unless the BIR's estimate of the number of returns that should be filed under the 1-2-3 system is grossly inaccurate, a more rigorous analysis of the data in table 2.1 probably would not produce results contradicting the BIR's conclusion of widespread tax evasion. Nevertheless a detailed analysis could be useful for other purposes, such as comparing the degree of compliance between emigrants and transient nonresidents, between employees and self-employed nonresidents, and among the members of each group.

A rigorous analysis is hindered, however, by a number of weaknesses in the data. First, not all of the tax collections shown in table 2.1 are attributable to the 1-2-3 system. From 1972 to 1974 the Philippines issued a series of decrees granting amnesty for tax evasion on income realized before 1972 and 1973.[103] The BIR data used to generate table 2.1 aggregated all taxes collected from nonresident citizens, whether attributable to the amnesties or to the 1-2-3 system. The effects of the amnesties cannot be isolated. Drawing any meaningful inferences about the success of the 1-2-3 system is therefore difficult.[104]

A second obstacle results from the government's "Balikbayan" program, which was established to encourage Filipinos overseas to visit the Philippines.[105] This program appears to have at least two objectives: first, to obtain scarce foreign exchange and, second, to demonstrate the progress that has been made in the Philippines to encourage expatriates to return permanently.[106] As part of this program the use of tax clearance certificates was suspended in 1973.[107] The impact of these changes on the data presented in table 2.1 is unclear.[108]

Third, the data do not reveal how the operation of the 1-2-3 system has been affected by two important changes in the nonresident community. Both the numbers of self-employed Filipinos and contract workers abroad have increased. The first increase challenges the assumptions made when the 1-2-3 system was instituted that the overseas community consisted primarily of employees and that a tax on gross income was an adequate proxy for a tax on net income.

Although statistics are not available, BIR officials familiar with the overseas community believe that the number of self-employed Filipinos, such as doctors, engineers, restauranteurs, and importers is growing.[109] According to the BIR, self-employed nonresidents regard the 1-2-3 system as unfair because it does not allow deductions for the costs of doing business such as wages, rent, depreciation, advertising, materials, and supplies. In some cases these costs constitute a significant percentage of gross income. The impact of the low 1, 2, or 3 percent rate of tax can therefore be substantial.[110] The BIR acknowledges that it receives few returns from self-employed nonresidents. Apparently the self-employed overseas community simply ignores the tax.

The other major change in the composition of the overseas community— the increase in the number of contract workers—can be traced to the burgeoning demands for unskilled and semiskilled labor by the Organization of Petroleum Exporting Countries, which provides employment for a large number of Filipinos. In 1974 the Philippine government created the Overseas Employment Development Board (OEDB), partially in response to this new overseas demand.[111] From 1975 to 1979 the OEDB placed in the Middle East more than 40,000 of the 52,849 contract workers abroad.[112]

Private employment agencies also have been active; in 1979, for example, they placed over 75,000 contract workers abroad, the majority of them in Saudi Arabia.[113] The number of Filipino seamen working outside the Philippines also increased through the efforts of the National Seamen's Board. In 1979 approximately 45,000 Filipinos worked aboard foreign-bound ships.[114]

The percentage of the overseas community represented by transient nonresidents has increased because the number of emigrants from the Philippines has not increased rapidly[115] whereas the number of contract workers and seamen has grown dramatically.[116] It is unclear whether the increase in the number of nonresident filers from the years 1975 to 1979 supports the BIR view that transient nonresidents have a higher rate of compliance with the 1-2-3 system than emigrants do, because statistics are not kept on the occupations of 1-2-3 taxpayers. No breakdown is available on the number of returns received from employees, contract workers, seamen, or self-employed individuals; nor are there statistics showing whether filers were emigrants or were only temporarily outside the Philippines. It is therefore difficult to test empirically any suspected relationship between the increase in the number of transient nonresidents, the number of returns filed by nonresidents, and the amount of revenue collected under the 1-2-3 system.[117]

Many BIR officials thought that the large increase in the number of transient nonresidents introduced an inequity into the administration of the 1-2-3 system. They believed that compliance with the 1-2-3 system by emigrants was primarily voluntary. Officials thought that they could exhort, cajole, or coax the emigrant community into recognizing its tax obligations, but that they lacked effective tools for persuading recalcitrants to pay. Transient nonresidents, however, generally were believed to be paying the proper amount of taxes.

My interviews with BIR officials indicated overall support of the 1-2-3 system despite its problems. Although these BIR officials perceived that the enforcement of the 1-2-3 system could not be uniform, they did not recommend its elimination. Instead they emphasized that the revenue and foreign exchange raised by the system greatly outweighs the system's administrative cost and any inequity suffered by particular nonresidents. Their attitude was that the tax revenue collected, great or small, was a windfall.[118]

No reasonable estimate of the cost of administering the 1-2-3 system, however, was available. Because BIR officials did not spend a significant portion of their time working on the 1-2-3 system, any estimate would require an analysis of the officials' workday to determine how their time was actually allocated. Administrative costs were thought to be modest because personnel performing functions relating to the 1-2-3 system were lower-paid clerical workers who checked returns for completeness, processed payments, and filed the completed returns. The returns of 1-2-3 taxpayers received little nonclerical attention.

Occasionally the BIR's nonclerical staff lectured about the 1-2-3 system to groups who were preparing to leave the Philippines. BIR officials sometimes were sent abroad to lecture to the overseas Filipino community and to assist in the preparation of returns. These activities appeared to be minor, however, when compared with the other responsibilities of the BIR staff. Even personnel who were assigned to Philippine embassies or consulates as BIR attachés or representatives did not devote a significant portion of their time to the administration of the 1-2-3 system.[119] One official summarized the situation: "We don't waste much time going after emigrants because they won't pay us anyway if they don't want to. And contract workers pay us without our doing anything. So running 1-2-3 is cheap."[120]

Implications of the Philippine Experience

The present study identifies the serious problems encountered by the Philippines in asserting citizenship jurisdiction over nonresident Filipinos. The Philippine experience validates, to a great degree, problems that had been anticipated in earlier theoretical literature[121] and suggests that other

LDCs may face similar difficulties if they wish to adopt Bhagwati's proposed tax on nonresident citizens.

This study identifies two major groups of issues that an LDC must address if it seeks to implement an effective income tax for nonresident citizens. First, the country must develop rules or principles for defining items of income and deductible expenses, and a rate schedule appropriate for nonresidents. Second, it must develop administrative capabilities and resources needed to enforce a tax on its nonresidents, both emigrant and transient.

Designing a Tax for Nonresidents

The experience of the Philippines demonstrates that an LDC's domestic tax system may prove inadequate when extended to nonresident citizens. If a progressive rate schedule developed in the context of an LDC's cost of living, salary levels, and distribution of income is applied to nonresidents living in DCs, it may generate inappropriate tax burdens. The pre-1972 Philippine experience indicates that nonresidents who earn salaries that are modest by DC standards might appear wealthy by LDC standards when their DC incomes are converted into the LDC currency. The extension of an LDC's progressive rates to a nonresident may therefore produce a substantial LDC tax burden that many nonresidents may perceive as inequitable and harsh.[122]

The Philippines tried to cope with these structural problems in two very different ways. In 1970 and 1971 nonresidents were allowed special deductions not available to residents, but their income remained taxable at domestic rates. Since 1972 nonresidents generally have been denied all deductions available to residents, but have been taxed at low rates. Neither of these approaches has proved completely satisfactory.

The issue of designing an LDC tax suitable for nonresidents might be resolved by an approach not yet tried by the Philippines: the use of a surtax.[123] Under such an approach an LDC would levy its tax as a percentage, perhaps 5 percent, of the tax paid to the DC in which the nonresident citizen resided. To calculate the LDC tax payable, a nonresident citizen would compute the amount of income taxable under DC rules, apply the DC's rate schedule, and multiply the resulting tax by 5 percent.[124]

The surtax approach has a number of desirable features. First, it avoids the problem of defining a new tax base for nonresidents.[125] Because a nonresident would be taxed on the same amount of income by both the LDC and the DC of residence, an LDC would avoid the problems that the

Philippines encountered in modifying its domestic definition of taxable income.[126]

Second, the surtax approach would allow the LDC to benefit from the audit procedures of the DC tax administration, thus reducing the need for the LDC to conduct its own audits. Any DC enforcement activity would benefit the LDC, at least to the extent that it determined the nonresident citizen's DC tax liability, upon which the LDC surtax would be based.

Third, because the LDC surtax would be a percentage of the DC tax, the LDC tax burden would be related to the DC tax burden. Assuming that the DC uses a fair and equitable tax rate, a modest LDC surtax would also be reasonable. The burden of multiple taxation would be minimal, and resort to special relief mechanisms would be unnecessary.[127] Also, the problems caused by currency conversion, which troubled the Philippines before 1972, and the need to design a special rate schedule would be avoided. Demands for progressivity would be satisfied because the surtax would reflect the progressive nature of the DC tax rates.[128] A disadvantage of the surtax approach, however, is that it cannot be applied easily to nonresidents who are not subject to DC taxes, such as employees of international organizations and certain contract workers.[129]

Administrative Considerations

Although the surtax provides a pragmatic design for a tax on nonresidents, it would do little to overcome the second of the two major issues: enforcement of the tax. Voluntary compliance would of course be encouraged if nonresidents viewed the LDC tax as reasonable or equitable in amount and form. In comparison with many of the other approaches available to an LDC, some of which are illustrated by the Philippine experience, the surtax approach would be clearly preferable. Self-employed nonresidents certainly would be treated more fairly under a surtax than they would be under other approaches.

Yet an evaluation of the experience of the Philippines, though based more on impressionistic than on empirical analysis, suggests that certain nonresident citizens, especially emigrants, may choose to ignore all LDC attempts to tax their DC income, even at low rates. Is this behavior idiosyncratic to Filipino emigrants? Numerous factors affect the willingness of a nonresident citizen to comply with an LDC tax: the circumstances surrounding the departure from the LDC, the amount of loyalty felt toward the LDC of citizenship, the burden of the LDC tax, and the risk that evasion of the tax will be discovered and punished. Many commentators believe that of all of these factors, the possibility of discovery and punishment is the key to voluntary compliance.[130] The Philippine experience suggests, however, that most LDCs are unlikely to be capable of credibly exerting the threat of discovery and punishment against emigrants.

Moreover the experience of Mexico—the only other LDC that taxed nonresident citizens on their income earned abroad—appears to be similar to that of the Philippines. This explains in part why the foreign source income of Mexican nonresidents was exempted from taxation in 1981.[131]

Furthermore the growth of the untaxed underground economy in the United States demonstrates that no country has a monopoly on noncompliance once individuals perceive that their risk of discovery and punishment is minimal. Recent studies of the U.S. underground economy indicate that taxpayer noncompliance increases dramatically whenever income is not subject either to withholding or to a requirement that the payor file an informational return with the IRS notifying it of the amount paid.[132] The noncompliance of overseas Filipinos is entirely consistent with this finding because income received by nonresident citizens from persons abroad is not subject by the Philippines to either withholding or informational returns. If the host DC were willing, such an approach would be feasible, at least in theory.

If widespread noncompliance, at least among emigrants, is likely to be the rule and not the exception, the inability of the Philippines to respond effectively is obviously discouraging for other LDCs. Stated differently, unless LDC tax administrations can discover and punish cases of noncompliance, such behavior will not be deterred. Admittedly, the Philippines has not been overly aggressive in its attempts to enforce its tax, and the administration of the 1-2-3 system has been marked by passivity. This passivity, however, reflects the BIR's frustration at having few sanctions directed at the collection of delinquent taxes from emigrants. The BIR's resources are limited and must be concentrated where they are most productive. Unless the BIR actually can collect the taxes owed, efforts directed at identifying nonfilers or auditing taxpayers are not productive.

The BIR's lack of aggressiveness also may reflect an underlying conflict between vigorous tax collection and the government's policy of encouraging nonresidents to visit the Philippines. The dilemma was sharply focused by the now suspended requirement that a tax clearance certificate be presented before a passport is issued or renewed. The more strictly this requirement was enforced the more likely it was that certain emigrants would simply postpone trips home until they had obtained their new citizenship and new DC passports.[133] Even before the official suspension of tax clearance certificates as part of the Balikbayan program, some embassies and consulates stopped requiring a tax clearance certificate before renewing or issuing a passport. Because other LDCs usually encourage visits by their overseas community—if only to obtain scarce foreign exchange—this conflict is not limited to the Philippines.[134]

If this conflict is to be avoided, an LDC must collect its tax in a manner that does not discourage visits home. The quandary is that an LDC may have no other opportunities, or leverage, to collect a tax from nonresidents who, along with their assets, are safely beyond the reach of the LDC. Tying the renewal or issuance of a passport to a tax clearance certificate is a potentially effective solution because it forces nonresidents to identify themselves.[135] Although such identification enables the LDC to collect its tax, it may also undermine the competing government interest in encouraging trips home.

A different manifestation of the tension between rigorous enforcement of the tax and the undermining of a competing governmental interest is exemplified by a problem the Philippines never confronted: renunciation of citizenship to sever the jurisdictional basis upon which the LDC levies its tax.[136] Most LDCs would probably not welcome massive, tax-induced renunciations of citizenship by their emigrants. An LDC that successfully collected its tax from emigrants, however, could face this situation.

The likelihood of tax-induced renunciations is partially related to the financial burden imposed by the LDC tax. Although some emigrants might find any LDC tax offensive, a tax that imposed only a modest burden, such as a 5 percent surtax, would probably not provide a strong financial inducement to renunciation.

The experience of the Philippines is of little value in evaluating the probability of tax-motivated renunciations. Nonresident Filipinos presumably had no need to renounce their citizenship to avoid taxation—they could simply ignore the 1-2-3 tax with impunity. A Filipino's decision to obtain DC citizenship would be made for reasons independent of tax consideration.

LDCs can respond to this potential problem of renunciation by limiting a nonresident's tax exposure to that period of time an emigrant normally must wait before becoming a DC citizen.[137] This solution would eliminate the tax incentive for nonresidents to renounce their citizenship. For emigrants living in the United States, this approach would limit their exposure to an LDC tax to five years, the normal waiting period to become a U.S. citizen.

Summary and Conclusion

This case study questions whether Bhagwati's proposal to tax nonresident citizens can be unilaterally implemented by an LDC. To be sure, generalizations based upon the experience of only one LDC are subject to obvious limitations. The available pool of evidence upon which to base a judgment, however, will never be large because the Philippines and Mexico are the only LDCs to assert citizenship jurisdiction. Although a case study of the Mexican experience would be valuable, its results probably would not contradict those of the Philippine study.[138] Unless the behavior of Filipino nonresidents is idiosyncratic, noncompliance among emigrants—the group most likely to constitute an LDC's brain drain—can be expected.

Enforcement by the LDC will require the assistance of the host DC.[139] A host DC can provide assistance at each stage of the administration of the LDC tax by compiling a tax roll, assessing a nonresident's tax liability, and collecting the amount of tax owed. The most efficient way of combating widespread noncompliance would be for the host DC to collect the tax on behalf of the LDC.[140] DC collection of an LDC tax, however, as well as less interventionist roles, would far exceed the current limited amount of intergovernmental cooperation.[141]

For an LDC tax on nonresidents to be workable, a host DC would have to make costly and time-consuming changes in its existing procedures. For example, although a surtax would perhaps require fewer changes in DC practices than would other alternatives, the changes nevertheless would still be considerable. Initially it might appear that a surtax would only require a DC to add a line to its tax form. This simplicity is superficial because collecting a surtax from select groups of DC taxpayers—nonresident citizens of an LDC—would be equivalent in its administrative aspects to the adoption of a new DC tax. A DC tax administration would have to revise its tax forms and instructions, compile special tax rolls of persons subject to the tax, design special withholding tables and instructions, modify current payment programs for persons not subject to withholding, expand taxpayer education programs, respond to questions, and handle disputes.

This brief outline indicates that DC collection of an LDC tax, even one levied in its simplest form as a surtax, would demand numerous changes in DC practices. These changes would require a serious commitment on the part of a DC.[142] Because of the controversy surrounding the Bhagwati proposal, a DC would not be likely to make this commitment. Even if a DC were inclined to cooperate with an LDC, it still might not be willing to do so unless convinced that other DCs were similarly disposed. Otherwise a DC competing with other countries for specific types of emigrants, such as doctors, nurses, or engineers,[143] might fear that its efforts at policing an LDC tax would only divert immigration to those DCs not willing to cooperate.

In addition, a DC would be unlikely to participate in the enforcement of a tax on individuals who emigrated to escape religious, political, or social oppression. A DC might demand some guarantee that this group is exempt from the tax.[144] Such an exemption, however, may be impossible to administer fairly.[145]

A DC would probably require that an LDC tax impose equitable burdens on taxpayers. An LDC tax that was levied as a modest surtax would satisfy this condition; other versions of an LDC tax might not. At the very least a DC may insist that an LDC tax on the LDC's nonresidents will not deter individuals from emigrating.

Although a DC may view its assistance to the LDC as a form of foreign aid or as a gesture of goodwill, the DC itself is unlikely to derive any immediate benefit from such assistance. Accordingly a DC may have difficulty justifying costly or time-consuming changes in its existing procedures or law.

If host DCs refuse to play an active role in enforcing an LDC tax on nonresidents, supporters of the Bhagwati proposal will face a serious dilemma. They can of course continue to encourage the LDCs to levy taxes on nonresident citizens. At a minimum some revenue and foreign exchange will be generated. The tax will also serve as a moral statement about the responsibility of nonresidents to their country of citizenship. Indeed, over time, if enough LDCs levy a tax based on citizenship jurisdiction, perhaps the DCs will be convinced to provide the necessary administrative assistance. After a longer gestation period, the DCs might accept Bhagwati's argument that the benefits accruing from the brain drain impose an obligation upon them to cooperate with the LDCs in policing the tax.[146]

If the assistance of the DCs is not provided quickly, however, a tax on nonresident citizens may fall disproportionately on transient nonresidents such as contract workers and seamen, who tend to be unskilled or semi-skilled workers. If the Philippine experience is probative, the tax may be reduced to nothing more than a voluntary contribution by emigrants to their country of citizenship. Unless DCs actively assist in the collection of LDC taxes, Bhagwati's proposal would become a tax on the muscle drain rather than a tax on the brain drain, accomplishing few of its objectives.

Notes

I greatly appreciate the insights offered by Professors Michael J. McIntyre and Oliver Oldman upon their reading of a previous draft of this chapter. This chapter revises a study prepared for the World Bank. The opinions expressed herein do not necessarily reflect the official views of the World Bank or of its affiliates.

1. These conferences include Brain Drain and Income Taxation, Bellagio, Italy (Feb. 15–19, 1975); United Nations Conference on Trade and Development (UNCTAD) Group of Governmental Experts on Reverse Transfer of Technology, Geneva, Switzerland (Feb. 27–Mar. 7, 1978); Fifth Session of UNCTAD, Manila, Philippines (May 7–June 2, 1979); Extending Income Tax Jurisdiction over Citizens Working Abroad, New Delhi, India (Jan. 12–15, 1981).

2. Skilled workers also migrate among DCs. Indeed the term "brain drain" apparently made its contemporary debut in a 1962 report by the British Royal Society concerning the emigration of scientists and engineers from Britain to North America. (Congressional Research Service for Subcomm. on International Security and Scientific Affairs of the House Comm. on Foreign Affairs, 93d cong., 2d sess. 1974. *Brain Drain: A Study of the Persistent Issue of International Scientific Mobility.* p. 1057 comm. Print.) Migration also occurs among LDCs; for example, many Filipinos work in the Middle East. (UNCTAD. 1977. Case studies in reverse transfer of technology (brain drain); A survey of problems and policies in the Philippines. U.N. doc. TD/B/C.6/AC.4/5, p. iv [hereinafter cited as Case studies in reverse transfer].) Many countries also experience an internal brain drain when persons migrate from a country's less developed rural areas to its relatively more developed urban areas (see idem). As the title of the UNCTAD document suggests, the United Nations prefers the term "reverse transfer of technology" to the term "brain drain." The former is thought to be more neutral in connotation because it does not prejudge the issue of whether the emigration of skilled labor is, in fact, harmful to the LDCs. For stylistic convenience only, the term "brain drain" is used in this chapter.

The terms "developed countries" and "less developed countries" have no precise definitions and for this chapter it is unnecessary that any be formulated. (See generally Pomp and Oldman. 1979. Tax measures in response to the brain drain. *Harv. Intl. L. J.* 20, no. 1: 3 n7.)

3. See Bhagwati. 1972. The United States in the Nixon era: The end of innocence. *Daedalus* 101, no. 25: 41–44. Bhagwati's proposal was first discussed at a conference entitled Brain Drain and Income Taxation held in 1975 (see note 1). Some of the papers presented at that conference were published in volume three of *World Development* and volume two of the *Journal of Developmental Economics.* Additionally papers were reprinted in eds. J. Bhagwati and M. Partington. 1976. *Taxing the Brain Drain I: A Proposal* and ed. J. Bhagwati. 1976. *The Brain Drain and Taxation II: Theory and Empirical Analysis,* The Bhagwati proposal was also debated at UNCTAD's 1978 and 1979 meetings. (See UNCTAD. 1979. Reverse transfer of technology: A survey of its main features, causes and policy implications. U.N. doc. TD/B/C.6/47); UNCTAD. 1979. Technology: Development aspects of the

reverse transfer of technology. U.N. doc. TD/239.) In 1981 Bhagwati's proposal was the centerpiece of a conference in New Delhi, India (see note 1). Papers from this conference are published in this book.

4. See Pomp and Oldman (note 2), pp. 13–15.

5. See idem, pp. 15–16.

6. This version of the tax was first proposed in Pomp and Oldman. 1975. The brain drain: A tax analysis of the Bhagwati proposed. *World Dev.* 3, 751: 754–60.

7. See Pomp and Oldman (note 2), pp. 25–44.

8. See Internal Revenue Code of 1954, pub. l. no. 83-591, § 1, 68A stat. 5–7 (codified as amended at 26 U.S.C. (I.R.C.) § 1 (1982)); Treas. Reg. § 1.1-1(b) (1956).

9. See the next section.

10. Effective January 1, 1981, Mexico ceased taxing the worldwide income of its nonresident citizens. (See Massone. 1981. The Mexican income tax. *Bull. for Intl. Fiscal Doc.* 35: 389.)

11. Countries that assert citizenship jurisdiction rely on residency for taxing noncitizens. In other words either citizenship or residence status is sufficient for taxation. Resident noncitizens are taxable on their worldwide income in the same manner as resident citizens. Once the jurisdictional nexus of residency has been severed, however, nonresident noncitizens will no longer be taxed on their income from abroad, whereas nonresident citizens will continue to be taxed on their worldwide income (Pomp and Oldman (note 2), pp. 28–33).

12. Nonresidents will remain taxable on income received from within the taxing country (idem, pp. 28–33). In a minority of countries the source of income is the only jurisdictional nexus relied upon. These countries tax income from domestic sources regardless of the taxpayer's status; income from foreign sources is exempt (idem, pp. 28–29).

13. Idem, p. 30.

14. Alternatively an LDC could adopt an idiosyncratic definition of residence, one that relies heavily on a person's prior contacts with the country. Because this approach would deviate from international practice and custom, it could undermine the acceptability of the tax (idem, p. 31).

15. Idem, pp. 39–43.

16. At the New Delhi conference (see note 1), Gary Hufbauer, a former U.S. Treasury Department Deputy Assistant Secretary for Trade and Investment Policy, reported that the United States was generally successful in administering citizenship jurisdiction. He emphasized, however, that the United States has typically provided generous exemptions for income earned abroad, which have mitigated its administrative problems by reducing the number of nonresidents subject to the income tax. For example, from 1926 to 1953, U.S. citizens abroad generally could

exclude from U.S. taxable income all of their foreign-earned income. From 1952 to 1976, a ceiling was placed on the exemption. From 1978 to 1981 the exemption was eliminated for many persons and was replaced with a system of special deductions to adjust for certain living expenses abroad. Starting in 1982, the United States reinstituted the exemption. (Field and Greeg. 1976. U.S. taxation of foreign earned income of private employees. in *Essays in International Taxation* 99. See also I.R.C. § 911, 913 (1976), amended by I.R.C. § 911 (1982).)

More recently the General Accounting Office (GAO) conducted a study of nonresident U.S. taxpayers. The GAO estimated that 61 percent of its sample of nonresident citizens did not file a U.S. tax return. Because of the limited data available to the GAO, however, this figure may be seriously overstated. The Internal Revenue Service (IRS) believes that many U.S. citizens abroad are not filing income tax returns. (J. Finch. 8 May 1985. Statement before the Subcommittee on Commerce, Consumer and Monetary Affairs on United States citizens living in foreign countries and not filing federal income tax returns. pp. 2–4 (unpublished statement available in files of *NYU J. Int'l L. & Pol.*) (hereinafter cited as Finch Statement).) The Subcommittee on Commerce, Consumer and Monetary Affairs of the House Committee on Government Operations will publish hearings including the Finch Statement in Fall 1985.

17. Most LDCs are less sophisticated than the United States in enforcing their tax systems (see generally, eds. P. Kelley and O. Oldman. 1973. *Readings on Income Tax Administration*). The inefficiency of LDCs in administering their taxes domestically suggests that attempts at asserting jurisdiction over nonresidents may pose difficult administrative problems. Moreover LDCs may face the additional problem that many of their nonresident citizens may be emigrants who intend to become citizens of their host DCs. Emigrants may feel little pressure to comply with an LDC tax, especially if they do not anticipate returning to their LDCs. The United States is not faced with this problem on a large scale; commonly its citizens working outside the country alternate periods abroad with periods within the United States. The awareness of taxpayers abroad that they will eventually return home is likely to offset any inclination to ignore their tax obligations.

18. See Pomp and Oldman (note 2), pp. 3–4 nn8–9.

19. See Philippines Bureau of Internal Revenue. Revenue memorandum circular no. 40-71, § 1 (hereinafter cited as Bureau of Internal Revenue, mem. cir. no. 40-71).

20. Revenue Act of 1913, pub. l. no. 63-16, § II(A)(1), 38 Stat. 166 (1913). Internal revenue officers of the Philippine government administered the Revenue Act of 1913 within the Philippines. The revenue collected accrued to the Philippines and not to the United States. *Idem* § II(M).

21. U.S. Const. amend. XVI ("The Congress shall have power to lay and collect taxes on incomes, from whatever source derived, without apportionment among the several States, and without regard to any census or enumeration.").

22. Citizenship jurisdiction was adopted by the United States without any debate or discussion of alternatives and the Philippines hardly can be faulted for doing

likewise. According to Surrey, the U.S. decision was "apparently automatically made, without discussion, and apparently as an intuitive matter." (Surrey. 1956. Current issues in the taxation of corporate foreign investment. *Colum. L. Rev.* 56: 815, 817.)

23. Revenue Act of 1918, pub. l. no. 65-254, § 261, 40 stat. 1087-88 (1919).

24. See I. Evangelista. 1961. *Philippine Income Tax Law* 1.

25. See Philippines National Internal Revenue Code of 1939, §§ 21, 22, comm. act no. 466.

26. *Idem* § 30(c)(1)(B). Presumably, this provision was modeled after a similar one in the Internal Revenue Code. See I.R.C. § 904 (1954 and supp. 1985); see also Revenue Act of 1916, pub. l. no. 64-271, § 5(a)(3), 39 stat. 759 (1916).

27. If the United States government were to consider these Filipinos as residents for tax purposes, it would tax their worldwide income (See Treas. Reg. § 1.1-1(b) (1984).) Otherwise it would tax them only on income from U.S. sources (see I.R.C. § 871 (1982)).

Multiple taxation often arises because one country taxes individuals on the basis of residency or citizenship, and the other taxes them on the basis of the source of their income. International law has never required a country to provide relief from multiple taxation, although most countries that tax foreign income normally grant some relief by providing either a deduction or a credit for foreign taxes. (*See* Pomp and Oldman (note 2), pp. 36–37.)

28. Discussions with officials of the Central Bank in Manila (July, 1980). In conducting research for this chapter I interviewed numerous officials at all levels, with the understanding that comments and statements would not be attributed to specific individuals. Officials were extremely cooperative and provided complete access to the existing data. Unfortunately numerous weaknesses and gaps in the data make rigorous analysis and inquiry difficult. Consequently some of the observations in this chapter are based on the impressions of experienced and candid Philippine officials. The views of these officials, which were neither self-serving, uncritical, nor defensive, are consistent with the limited empirical data. (See notes 98–120 and accompanying text.)

29. For another example, consider a Filipino couple residing in the United States with $8,000 of taxable income. Assuming that a joint return was filed, the couple paid $1,380 in U.S. taxes for 1970. For a table of 1970 tax liabilities, see W. Andrews. 1979. *Basic Federal Income Taxation*. 2d ed. p. 793. Assume for simplicity that the couple's taxable income under Philippine law was also $8,000. At a conversion rate of 2 pesos to 1 U.S. dollar, the couple had a taxable income of 16,000 pesos. Their Philippine tax liability, before a credit for their U.S. tax, would be 1,960 pesos ($980). For the 1970 Philippine tax rates, see Joint Legislative-Executive Tax Commission. 1970. *A Short Guide to Philippine Taxes Revised*. The credit for their U.S. tax of $1,380 completely eliminated their Philippine tax of $980. Consequently at a conversion rate of 2 : 1 this couple did not owe a Philip-

pine tax. The overall effective tax rate on this couple was 17.3 percent ($1,380 divided by $8,000) and was determined solely by the U.S. tax rate.

After devaluation of the peso this couple had taxable income of 60,000 pesos ($8,000 times 7.5) (see text accompanying note 28), and a Philippine tax liability of 18,360 pesos ($2,448). The credit for their U.S. tax of $1,380 reduced their Philippine tax to $1,068 ($2,448 minus $1,380). The overall effective tax rate on this couple was 30.6 percent ($2,448 divided by $8,000) and their total taxes, U.S. and Philippine, increased from $1,380 to $2,448, an increase of 77 percent.

The devaluation more dramatically affected a couple having an income of $20,000. Their U.S. tax in 1970 was $4,380. Before devaluation their Philippine taxable income was 40,000 pesos, generating a precredit Philippine tax liability of 9,480 pesos ($4,740). After credit for their U.S. tax, the couple paid tax at an overall effective tax rate of 23.7 percent ($4,740 divided by $20,000). After devaluation the couple had a taxable income of 150,000 pesos (20,000 times 7.5) and a precredit Philippine tax liability of 69,640 pesos ($9,285). The credit for their U.S. tax of $4,380 reduced their Philippine tax to $4,905 ($9,285 minus $4,380). Their overall effective tax rate after the devaluation was 46.4 percent ($9,285 divided by $20,000). Their total taxes, U.S. and Philippine, increased about 96 percent from $4,740 to $9,285.

As these examples demonstrate, the effective tax rate for nonresident taxpayers was determined by the higher of the U.S. (or other DC) effective tax rate or the Philippine effective tax rate. Even though salaries in the United States were generally higher than those in the Philippines, the interaction of the fixed exchange rate of 2:1 and the respective rate structures of the United States and the Philippines did not necessarily generate a Philippine effective tax rate that exceeded the U.S. effective tax rate. At an exchange rate of 7.5:1, however, the Philippine effective tax rate for most taxpayers would exceed that of the United States.

30. Filipinos living in the United States were well organized, which enabled them to voice their complaints effectively (discussions with officials of the BIR in Manila, July, 1980).

31. Idem. This argument evidently had two facets. The first was that the Philippine tax code allowed certain deductions only if the expenditure was paid or incurred in the Philippines. For example, medical expenses and high school tuition payments for a taxpayer's dependents were deductible, subject to certain ceilings, only if incurred and paid in the Philippines. (See Philippines National Internal Revenue Code § 30(a)(2)(A) and (B).)

The second facet was directed at the BIR's interpretation of the statutory requirement that deductible expenses be "ordinary and necessary" (idem § 30(a)(1)). Some nonresidents complained that the BIR was too inflexible in its interpretation of the statute. They stated that the BIR denied deductions for expenditures that were commonplace abroad because they were uncommon within the Philippines. In some cases the BIR placed a ceiling on the amount of the deduction. This ceiling was based on what would have been reasonable had the expenditure been incurred in the Philippines, notwithstanding that the amount of the expenditure was reasonable under the standards of the DC where it actually was incurred.

32. For a discussion of these measures, see generally Oldman (note 17). Controlling income tax evasion. In *Readings on Income Tax Administration*. pp. 485–510.

33. See generally Surr. 1966. Intertax: Intergovernmental cooperation in taxation. *Harv. Intl. L. J.* 7. Although the Surr article was written in 1966, it generally still reflects current practices.

34. Discussions with officials of the BIR in Manila, July, 1980.

35. The United States also lacks a taxpayer roll of nonresident citizens (see Finch Statement (note 16), pp. 5–6). The creation of a master taxpayer roll is essential for an efficient tax administration (see Lemus (note 17). Establishment and maintenance of a register of taxpayers. In *Readings on Income Tax Administration*. p. 16). "The identification and register of taxpayers is absolutely essential for an efficient tax administration, and it might well be said that it constitutes one of the basic programs of highest priority, without which the other programs will lack assurance and effectiveness" (idem).

36. Discussion with officials of the Ministry of Labor in Manila, July, 1980.

37. Idem.

38. Discussions with officials of the BIR in Manila, July, 1980.

39. Idem.

40. Rarely do tax administrators from one country conduct their own investigation in another country (see Surr (note 33), p. 182). Occasionally, in cases involving potentially large sums of money, the BIR attempted to conduct audits at a consulate in the host DC. Taxpayers could, however, ignore requests to bring their books and accounts to the consulate and the BIR was powerless to deal with this recalcitrance. Furthermore, consulates were not always located near the taxpayer. Thus the problem of enforcement from a distance still remained. The BIR did have leverage over nonresident citizens, however, because it had the power to deny recalcitrant taxpayers the benefit of assistance from the consulate should they need help in the future. (Discussions with officials of the BIR in Manila July, 1980.)

41. Idem.

42. Idem.

43. Until I mentioned it, some BIR officials were unaware of a procedure in the United States whereby taxpayers may obtain certified copies of their tax returns from the Internal Revenue Service (see I.R.C. § 6103(p)(2)(A) (1982); Rev. Proc. 66-3, 1966-1 C.B. 601-06). Requiring taxpayers to submit a certified copy would reduce the BIR's problem of receiving copies of bogus U.S. returns. Appropriate safeguards would be necessary, however, to ensure that taxpayers would submit new certified copies every time they were to amend their U.S. returns. Otherwise nonresidents could file U.S. tax returns that were specially prepared to mislead the BIR, obtain certified copies, and then file amended U.S. returns that corrected their earlier returns.

If a host DC were willing, a nonresident's DC tax return could be made available to the Philippines. Such an arrangement could be made as part of a tax treaty, although it would exceed the current practice of the United States and other DCs. (See Pomp and Oldman (note 2), pp. 41–43.)

44. Discussions with officials of the BIR in Manila, July, 1980.

45. Idem. See generally Surr (note 33), p. 219 (discussion of the problem of collecting taxes from persons outside the country).

46. See Phil. Ann. Laws 72 § 346 (1956).

47. Bureau of Internal Revenue, rev. reg. no. V-32, 49 off. gaz. 443 (Feb., 1953), amended by Phil. Ann. Laws 72 § 346 (1956).

48. This power apparently is discretionary. Discussions with officials of the BIR in Manila, July, 1980. (See also Passport regulations. 1956. Reprinted in Phil. Ann. Laws 3 § 22.)

At one time the IRS also attempted to identify nonresident citizens who did not file returns when they sought to renew their passports. In the mid-1960s the IRS, in cooperation with the State Department, requested U.S. citizens living abroad to complete IRS Form 3966 (Internal Revenue Service Identification of U.S. Citizen Residing Abroad) when they renewed their passports. The form set forth the tax obligations of nonresident U.S. citizens and provided information on the availability of IRS taxpayer assistance abroad. The form requested information concerning the taxpayer's occupation and when and where he or she last filed a federal income tax return. In general the IRS's only source of information on nonresident citizens was Form 3966.

The IRS hoped that Form 3966 and the publicity surrounding it would encourage voluntary compliance abroad. The IRS experience was disappointing, however, primarily because there was no legal duty to file the form. A nonresident citizen was not precluded from renewing his or her passport if the form was not filed. Taxpayers also complained that the form violated their privacy rights. As a result, in 1979, the IRS discontinued the use of Form 3966. (See Finch Statement (note 16), pp. 9–10.)

49. See Phil. Ann. Laws 72 § 346 (1956).

50. Discussions with officials of the BIR in Manila, July, 1980.

51. Idem.

52. Idem.

53. If a nonresident claimed he or she was being supported by others and thus had no taxable income, the BIR occasionally required an affidavit to that effect from the person providing the support (idem).

54. Idem.

55. Between September 1, 1973, and July 1, 1974, 59,534 overseas Filipinos visited the Philippines spending an average of $500 each (Letter of Instruction no. 210

(1974)). Assuming an average exchange rate of 7.4 pesos to $1, each person spent an average of 3,700 pesos. By comparison for 1972 the tax collected per return under the 1-2-3 system (see text accompanying notes 79–98) averaged 329 pesos. The 1974 average was 171 pesos. (See text and table 2.1 accompanying notes 98–108.)

56. If the BIR had provided the names of Filipinos living in the host DC, the DC tax administration would have been able to check its files to see if a DC tax return had been filed. Information from this tax return could have been given to the BIR. But DC tax administrations would not have been in a position to help the BIR identify Filipinos who did not file Philippine tax returns. (See Pomp and Oldman (note 2), p. 56.)

57. Most DCs will not furnish tax information or collect foreign taxes except under limited and specific conditions delineated in a tax treaty. A typical tax treaty, however, is unlikely to provide a mechanism for dealing with the problems encountered by the BIR. The amount of information exchanged under a tax treaty is limited, and commonly does not involve areas relevant to the enforcement of a tax on nonresidents. Assistance in collection of foreign taxes is even more limited. (Idem, pp. 41–43.)

The current tax treaty between the Philippines and the United States does not commit the United States to cooperate in the collection of Philippine taxes on nonresidents. U.S. cooperation is limited to situations in which Filipinos wrongfully seek to obtain treaty benefits and would not cover nonresidents who refused to pay Philippine taxes. (See Assistance in collection. 1970. *Tax Treaties* 2 (CCH) ¶ 6630.)

The United States receives tax informaton from 17 of the 34 countries with which it has a tax treaty. In general the information pertains to investment income, such as data on interest and dividends, and not to data on wages and income earned through the performance of personal services. About one-third of the information returns that the United States receives as a result of these treaties are incomplete or are received too late to be of use. (See Finch Statement (note 16), pp. 10–12.)

58. Courts in the United States, Canada, and England generally do not recognize foreign tax judgments (see Pomp and Oldman (note 2), p. 41 n140).

59. Discussions with officials of the BIR in Manila, July, 1980.

60. See Ecevit and Zachariah. 1978. International labor migration. *Fin. & Dev.* 15: 32; H. Singer and J. Ansari. 1977. *Rich and Poor Countries.* pp. 222–224.

61. Discussions with officials of the BIR in Manila, July, 1980.

62. Idem.

63. The number of transient nonresidents was small until 1975 or 1976 (see text accompanying notes 111-114).

64. See Bureau of Internal Revenue, mem. cir. no. 40-71.

65. Idem § 3.

66. Idem.

67. Discussions with officials of the BIR in Manila, July, 1980.

68. Bureau of Internal Revenue, mem. cir. no. 40-71, § 1.

69. Idem § 2. The deduction also applied to transportation expenses incurred in moving from one country to another (idem).

70. Idem § 3.

71. Idem. The deduction for foreign taxes also was expanded to include city, county, and state income taxes, but most taxpayers presumably would have still chosen the credit rather than the deduction (see text accompanying note 27).

72. Discussions with officials of the BIR in Manila, July, 1980.

73. For an illustration of the problem caused by the floating of the peso, see note 29 and accompanying text.

74. See Bureau of Internal Revenue, rev. reg. no. 9-73, § 3(D).

75. Discussions with officials of the BIR in Manila, July, 1980.

76. The law stated:

All allowable deductions contained in the income tax returns filed in the country where [the taxpayers] earn their income [shall be allowed as deductions on the Philippine income tax returns]. Such deductions will be allowed ... in addition to the deductions allowed under the Income Tax Law of the Republic of the Philippines.

(See Bureau of Internal Revenue, mem. cir. no. 40-71, § 1.)
    The BIR interpreted the language "in addition to the deductions allowed under the Income Tax Law of the Republic of the Philippines" as intending to clarify that foreign tax law did not displace Philippine law. Hence a nonresident did not lose any deductions available under Philippine tax law that were not allowed under foreign tax law. According to the BIR, the language was not intended to allow taxpayers to deduct the same item twice. (Discussion with officials of the BIR in Manila, July, 1980.)

77. For example, expenses identified or labeled in one manner on the Philippine tax return might be categorized differently on the DC tax return (idem).

78. Discussions with officials of the BIR in Manila, July, 1980.

79. Idem.

80. Adjusted gross income is equal to gross income less the personal exemption and deduction for income taxes paid to the foreign country where the income was earned.

81. Presidential Decree No. 69 (1972). The 1972 changes apply only to foreign

income received by nonresident citizens. Income received from domestic sources is taxable under the same rules that apply to resident taxpayers.

82. Presidental Decree No. 323 (1973).

83. See Presidential Decrees Nos. 69 (1972), 323 (1973).

84. Bureau of Internal Revenue, rev. reg. no. 9-73.

85. Idem.

86. See note 117.

87. Discussion with officials of the BIR in Manila, July, 1980.

88. To illustrate the modest burden imposed by the Philippine tax, consider an unmarried taxpayer with $29,800 of salary income who lives and works in the United States. In 1983, assuming the taxpayer did not claim any itemized deductions, his or her U.S. income tax is $6,045. For purposes of the 1-2-3 tax, the adjusted gross income is $21,755 ($29,800 less a $2,000 personal exemption and less the U.S. tax of $6,045), generating a Philippine tax of $375 (1 percent of $6,000 plus 2 percent of $15,755). Compared with the U.S. tax, this taxpayer experiences a 6 percent increase in income tax burden ($375 divided by $6,045).

89. Because the rates of tax (1 percent, 2 percent, 3 percent) are so low, a non-resident's foreign income taxes typically will exceed the Philippine tax. If the Philippines had continued its prior practice of allowing a credit for foreign taxes (see text accompanying notes 26 and 27), the Philippine tax would have been eliminated for most nonresidents.

90. See text accompanying notes 28–30. Nonresident citizens receiving income in a currency other than the U.S. dollar must convert such income into dollars. The conversion is made at the average annual rate of exchange of the foreign currency and the U.S. dollar. (Bureau of Internal Revenue, rev. reg. no. 9-73, § 4(A)(1).) Theoretically the pre-1972 problem can still affect nonresidents receiving income in currencies stronger than the U.S. dollar. The low rates of Philippine tax, however, greatly reduce the severity of this problem.

91. Discussions with officials of the BIR in Manila, July, 1980.

92. For example, assume that deductions constitute 20 percent of gross income for all taxpayers. Any rate of tax [r] levied on net income can be translated into an equivalent rate of tax [.80r] levied on gross income.

93. Discussions with officials of the BIR in Manila (July, 1980).

94. Idem.

95. Bureau of Internal Revenue, rev. reg. no. 9-73, § 3(D).

96. Discussions with officials of the BIR in Manila, July, 1980. See text accompanying notes 43 and 44.

97. Discussions with officials of the BIR in Manila, July, 1980. The BIR has never charged a nonresident with evasion of the 1-2-3 tax. The small amounts of tax involved in most cases and the difficulty of enforcing a conviction make it futile to pursue such cases.

98. The BIR's Office of International Operations, which administers the 1-2-3 system, was created in 1973. The collection of data before the creation of this office was somewhat erratic. Events leading up to the declaration of martial law in 1972 interfered with the orderly processes of the government and made data collection difficult.

99. See *Readings on Income Tax Administration* (note 17), p. 432; Groves. 1958. Empirical studies of income-tax compliance. *Natl. Tax J.* 11: 291.

100. Discussions with officials of the BIR and the Central Bank in Manila, July, 1980.

101. See Harris. 1980. Underground economy: What can and should be done: The federal role. *Natl. Tax A.-Tax Inst. of Am.* 73: 262, 262–263.

102. Discussions with officials of the BIR in Manila, July, 1980. This estimate is based on information provided by Philippine embassies and consulates. Another estimate, not made by the BIR, places the number of Filipino workers and seamen abroad at 705,000. Although it is unclear, this estimate is evidently for 1974. (See Case studies in reverse transfer (note 2), p. 20 n28, citing M. Abella, Export of Filipino Labor in Relation to Development (updated paper).) On the basis of this estimate, the BIR received returns in 1974 from approximately 4 percent of the taxpaying population. The estimate of 705,000 may be too high, however, because not all of these workers necessarily would qualify as nonresidents for purposes of the 1-2-3 tax. (See text accompanying notes 84–86, and see note 117).

The Office of Emigrant Affairs estimates that as of December, 1979, the total number of overseas Filipinos was 1,674,722 (Office of Emigrant Affairs, Philippines Ministry of Labor and Employment. 1980. A Special Report on Profile of Filipinos Overseas. p. 2 (hereinafter cited as Office of Emigrant Affairs)). This figure, however, cannot be used for estimating the number of potential taxpayers under the 1-2-3 system because it is based solely on outflows and is not adjusted for deaths, changes of citizenship, or persons who return to the Philippines. This last factor is especially important because of the large number of contract workers only temporarily abroad. (See note 113 and accompanying text.)

103. See Presidential Decrees Nos. 23 (1972), 67 (1972), 68 (1972), 156 (1973), 157 (1973), 161 (1973), 370 (1974), 563 (1974), 631 (1975).

104. For example, the large increase in filers and tax revenue from 1971 (the last year under the prior tax regime) to 1973 (the first year for which data are available under the 1-2-3 system) supports a conclusion that the 1-2-3 system successfully increased taxpayer compliance. This conclusion would be erroneous, however, if the increase in filers and in revenue were attributable to nonresident citizens availing themselves of the tax amnesty. An additional complication arises from the increase in emigration that evidently occurred during this period, which would also

explain the increase in filers and revenue collected. (See Case studies in reverse transfer (note 2), p. 3.) Measuring the increase in emigration is difficult because reliable data have been kept only since 1975 (Discussions with officials of the Ministry of Labor in Manila, July, 1980). Analysis of the data in table 2.1 is hindered further by the declaration of a new amnesty in early 1973 that applied to acts of tax evasion regarding income realized before 1973 (see Presidential Decrees Nos. 157 (1973), 370 (1974), 563 (1974), 631 (1975)).

105. See Letter of Instruction No. 105 (1973).

106. A possible third objective is to grant a certain degree of legitimacy to the government by persuading nonresidents to return home, if only for a visit.

107. See Letters of Instruction Nos. 105 (1973), 163 (1974), 210 (1974); Presidential Decrees Nos. 439 (1974), 592 (1974), 819 (1975).

108. If tax clearance certificates were previously effective in encouraging taxpayer compliance, their suspension would be expected to result in some loss of tax revenue and a reduction in the number of returns filed. The data for 1974 are consistent with this explanation.

Alternatively if tax clearance certificates were never very effective, the 1974 data also could be explained as a return to more normal levels of taxpayer compliance after the increase in 1973 attributable to a tax amnesty (see note 104). Without disaggregating the data, it is difficult to reach a conclusion.

The 1974 decline in filers and revenue also would be explained if a large number of nonresidents decided to return to the Philippines and thus were no longer subject to the 1-2-3 system. Because no data are compiled on inflows of nonresidents, this hypothesis cannot be tested. Any inflow of nonresidents, however, would be offset by the sharp increase in emigration that occurred in 1973 and 1974. (See Case studies in reverse transfer (note 2), p. 3.)

109. Discussions with officials of the BIR in Manila, July, 1980.

110. For example, assume that a self-employed nonresident has gross income of $100 and business expenses of $90. Ignoring the personal exemption and the deduction for foreign taxes, a 3 percent marginal tax rate on the nonresident's gross income of $100 produces a tax of $3. This equals a 30 percent marginal tax rate on his or her net income of $10.

To the extent that the business deductions denied to self-employed persons represent a larger percentage of their gross income than do the business deductions denied employees, self-employed persons are effectively taxed on their net incomes at rates greater than those imposed on employees. For example, assume that in the preceding hypothetical example, an employee had $100 of gross income and deductions of $10. A 3 percent marginal tax rate on the employee's gross income of $100 produces a tax of $3. This is equal to a 3.33 percent marginal tax rate on his or her net income of $90 (ignoring the personal exemption and deduction for foreign income taxes).

Under the 1-2-3 system, uniform rates of tax on net income are not likely to result in the case of all self-employed persons. The costs of doing business as a percentage of gross income probably vary on the nature of the business. To the extent that such costs vary, self-employed persons are taxed on their net incomes at different rates. For example, a self-employed businessperson with $100 of gross income and $90 of expenses is taxed on net income at a marginal rate of 30 percent. By comparison, another self-employed businessperson with $100 of gross income and $10 of costs is taxed on net income at a marginal rate of 3.33 percent.

111. See Case studies in reverse transfer (note 2), p. 21.

112. Office of Emigrant Affairs (note 102), pp. 11, 14.

113. Idem, pp. 8–9. The total number of contract workers hired by these private agencies has increased dramatically since 1976. The figures for the 1976–1979 period are

Year	Number	Increase Over Prior Year
1976	13,960	—
1977	26,191	88%
1978	37,340	43%
1979	75,693	103%
	153,184	

(Idem, p. 10.) The workers in highest demand during these years were fitters, welders, and construction workers (idem, p. 17).

114. Idem, p. 15. The number of seamen aboard foreign-bound ships has increased steadily since 1976. The figures for the 1976–1979 period are

Year	Number	Increase Over Prior Year
1976	28,614	—
1977	33,378	17%
1978	37,951	14%
1979	45,226	16%

Idem, p. 15.

115. The figures for the 1976–1979 period are

Year	Number	Increase (Decrease) Over Prior Year
1976	37,690	—
1977	39,451	5%
1978	38,345	(3%)
1979	49,450	5%

Idem, p. 5.

116. See notes 111–114 and accompanying text.

117. The increase in the number of filers from 1975 to 1979 may support the BIR's view that transient nonresidents have a higher rate of compliance with the 1-2-3 system than do emigrants. For example, in 1977, 1978, and 1979, the number of returns filed increased by more than the percentage increase in emigrants leaving the Philippines (compare table 2.1 with table in note 115). One way to test the BIR's views empirically would be to compare with the data in table 2.1 the number of transient nonresidents who left the Philippines each year. Although detailed statistics have been kept since 1975 on the number of contract workers and seamen going abroad annually, no data exist on the number returning to the Philippines each year at the expiration of their contracts. Without these data the net increase in transient nonresidents cannot be calculated and compared with the increase in filers and tax revenue shown in table 2.1.

Estimating the number of returning contract workers from the data on outflows is difficult because information on the length of contracts and on the number of Filipinos who renew their contracts while abroad is not available. A change in the definition of a nonresident further complicates the calculations. As of 1978 contract workers are considered to be nonresidents if they are abroad for at least 183 days during the taxable year (Bureau of Internal Revenue, rev. reg. no. 1-79, § 2(c)). This change liberalized the definition of a nonresident (see text accompanying notes 84–86) and resulted in more contract workers becoming taxable under the 1-2-3 system. The large increase in the number of filers in 1978 probably is explained, at least in part, by the broader definition of a nonresident rather than by an increase in migration.

118. Characterizing the revenue collected under the 1-2-3 system as a windfall assumes that the taxes otherwise would not have been collected. Such an assumption can be questioned in the case of contract workers, who, for the reasons already discussed in the text, may present few compliance problems.

119. In addition to assisting nonresident citizens in the filing of their returns, the revenue attaché or representative disseminates information on the tax aspects of foreign trade and investment in the Philippines and assists foreign corporations and nonresident aliens engaged in business in the Philippines (discussions with officials of the BIR in Manila, July, 1980).

120. Idem.

121. Pomp and Oldman (note 2), pp. 39–43.

122. At each income level the effective LDC tax rate generally will exceed the effective DC tax rate (see Hamada. 1977. Taxing the brain drain: A global point of view. In ed. J. Bhagwati. *The New International Economic Order: The North-South Debate*. pp. 125, 143).

The United States has resolved the problem of designing a suitable set of rates by providing an exemption for certain amounts of foreign earned income (see note 16). For a short time this exemption was replaced for most taxpayers with a series of special deductions to take into account the higher costs of living abroad (see

Tax Treatment Extension Act of 1977, pub. l. no. 95-615, §913, 92 stat. 3100-06 (1978), repealed by Economic Recovery Tax Act of 1981, pub. l. no. 74-34 tit. I §112(a), 95 stat. 194 (1981)). This change increased the tax burden on many persons abroad. Because of fears that this increased tax burden was resulting in less employment abroad for U.S. citizens, the exemption was reinstituted. (See I.R.C. §911 (1984). See also U.S. Comptroller General. 1981. Report to the Congress: American employment abroad discouraged by U.S. income tax laws; U.S. Comptroller General. 1978. Report to the Congress: Impact on trade of changes in taxation of U.S. citizens employed overseas (hereinafter cited as Impact on trade); Hirsch and Rodriguez. 1978. Taxation—United States Expatriates—Foreign Earned Income Act of 1978. *Harv. Intl. L.J.* 19: 633).

123. See Pomp and Oldman (note 2), pp. 52–57.

124. Taxpayers residing in the United States could be required to submit certified copies of their U.S. tax returns (see note 43).

125. The problem of defining a tax base for nonresidents is much less severe for the United States. U.S. law is complex and sophisticated and evidently can cope with business conditions elsewhere. U.S. rules on business deductions appear to work satisfactorily when applied to situations abroad. (See generally Pomp and Oldman (note 2).)

126. The tax system for nonresidents between 1970 and 1971 was based on gross income calculated under Philippine law, and allowed nonresidents to claim deductions under both DC and Philippine tax law. These tax laws proved difficult to interpret (see note 76), and the BIR had trouble verifying deductions allowed by Philippine law (see text accompanying notes 74–75). The surtax approach would eliminate these problems because the Philippine tax would be based on the DC tax and, other than the tax rate, would not be determined by Philippine law.

127. For example, a 5 percent surtax ensures that the additional burden arising from both the LDC and the DC taxing the same income is limited to 5 percent. An alternative characterization of the 5 percent surtax is to view the LDC as levying its tax at an effective rate equal to 105 percent of the DC effective tax rate, with a credit provided for the DC tax.

128. If an LDC wanted to deviate from the DC rate schedule, it could design its own rates. These rates could be a function of the DC tax. For example, an LDC might wish to levy a 5 percent surtax as long as the DC tax were less than a certain amount, but might wish to either increase or decrease the rate of the surtax if the DC tax were to exceed a certain amount. This approach would allow an LDC to obtain more or less progressivity than that reflected in the DC rate structure. Additional flexibility could be achieved by choosing a different rate of surtax for different DCs.

129. Employees of international organizations such as the World Bank or the United Nations usually are exempt from DC taxation on their earned income and therefore do not necessarily compute their DC taxable incomes. For the U.S. rules,

see I.R.C. § 893 (1982). These employees could, of course, be required to compute their income as if they were taxable under DC law, but the LDC tax administration then would be faced with having to ensure that the employees' computations were accurate.

Contract workers present a somewhat similar problem because they might not be subject to an income tax. For example, several of the Middle Eastern countries that employ contract workers (see text accompanying notes 111–113) do not have an income tax, or exempt salaries earned by foreigners (see International Bureau of Fiscal Documentation. 1977 and supp. 1983. Taxes and Investment in the Middle East § 8.1.) Seamen also may not be subject to a DC tax because of the limited amount of time they spend within the jurisdiction of any foreign country.

Tax policy theorists might argue that the surtax approach has another disadvantage: it deviates from a concept of horizontal equity. According to this concept, two taxpayers who have the same incomes and who are similar in all other respects should pay the same amount in income tax. The surtax arguably violates this concept because nonresidents and residents earning the same incomes would pay different amounts in tax (although horizontal equity would be improved by the surtax approach if compared to the Philippines's present approach, which taxes residents on their net income but taxes nonresidents on their gross income).

It is unclear, however, how the concept of horizontal equity should be formulated in the international context. For example, in the domestic context, nearly all theorists agree that a taxpayer's choice of where to live is irrelevant in determining his or her tax liability. In most countries two taxpayers who have the same incomes but live in different regions nevertheless pay the same amounts in income tax. It is tempting to extrapolate from this domestic situation and argue that a taxpayer's choice of residence abroad also should be ignored in levying an income tax, and that a country should tax nonresidents in the same manner as it taxes its residents. The application of horizontal equity is not self-evident, however, when taxpayers reside abroad. Nonresidents working abroad may experience an increase in their cost of living that is greater than any comparable increase that they would experience domestically if they were to move from one area of the country to another. For a short period of time the United States responded to these considerations by granting its nonresident citizens special deductions to offset the higher cost of living abroad, although no similar deduction was granted to taxpayers moving from low-cost areas within the country to high-cost areas. (See Tax Treatment Extension Act of 1977, pub. l. no. 95-615, § 913, 92 stat. 3100-06 (1978), repealed by Economic Recovery Tax Act of 1981, pub. l. no. 74-34, tit. I, § 112(a), 95 stat. 194 (1981).)

Formulating a concept of horizontal equity is further complicated by the problem of converting a nonresident's foreign income into LDC currency. Theoretically a nonresident's income could be translated into its "equivalent" LDC income, based on the nonresident's purchasing power and standard of living, and this "equivalent" income could be taxed. Implementing this approach obviously would be difficult. (See generally Impact on trade (note 122), pp. 74–78; Gravelle and Keifer 1979. U.S. taxation of citizens working in other countries: An economic analysis, in *Studies in Taxation, Public Finance and Related Subjects* 3: 72 (1979).)

130. See *Readings on Income Tax Administration* (note 17), pp. 483—485. See also Crockett. 1965. Common obstacles to effective tax administration in Latin America. In *Problems of Tax Administration in Latin America.* p. 10. Crockett states:

But is [widespread tax evasion in Latin America] true because the Latin American is different by nature or training or outlook from the more compliant publics of North American and Europe, as some cynical Latin Americans have seemed to think? I am convinced that no such conclusion is warranted. On the contrary, I venture to assert that if the limited enforcement powers, the operational obstacles, the administrative handicaps that are prevalent in Latin America were present in the countries of North America and Europe, a great decay would begin to permeate their presently more productive tax departments, and as their publics became increasingly aware that impunity and not penalty would follow evasion, the relatively high degree of voluntary compliance that vigorous enforcement has slowly built up in them over the years would gradually sink to very low levels.

131. Interview with Juan Teran, former official, Ministry of Finance, Mexico, Jan., 1982. The limited evidence on the noncompliance of U.S. citizens abroad is also consistent with the experience of the Philippines and of Mexico. (See generally Finch Statement (note 16).)

132. See Ekstrand. 1980. Factors affecting compliance: Focus group and survey results. In 73 *Natl. Tax A.-Tax Inst. of Am.* 253—262; Wolfe. Magnitude and nature of individual income tax noncompliance. Idem, pp. 271—277; Harris (note 101), pp. 262—265.

133. Conceivably former citizens could be identified at the time they entered the Philippines for a visit and a determination could be made as to whether they were nonfilers or had any outstanding tax liabilities accrued during the period that they were citizens. Such an approach, even assuming it could be implemented, could be easily thwarted. (See text accompanying notes 50 and 51.)

134. Some LDCs have adopted elaborate incentives to encourage nonresidents to return home permanently. For the incentives offered by India, see Council of Scientific and Industrial Research of India. 1977. Case Study in reverse transfer of technology (brain drain): A survey of problems and policies in India. U.N. doc. TD/B/C.6/AC.4/6, pp. 21—23. Sri Lanka is reported as having tried to implement a "return-of-talent" scheme (see Marga Institute. 1977. Case studies in reverse transfer of technology (brain drain): A survey of problems and policies in Sri Lanka. U.N. doc. TD/B/C.6/AC.4/4, pp. 15—22).

135. The LDC could require a tax certificate in conjunction with any affirmative act requested by the nonresident, including the renewal of a medical or engineering license. Venezuela uses such a system, requiring certificates of solvency—proof of tax payment—for licenses as well as for permission to leave the country. (See C. Shoup, J. Duc, L. Fitch, D. MacDougall, O. Oldman, and S. Surrey. 1959. *The Fiscal System of Venezuela: A Report.* pp. 195—196, 216—220.)

136. See Pomp and Oldman (note 2), pp. 31—33, 48—49.

137. Even if the renunciation of citizenship is not a serious threat, a time limitation would be desirable for other reasons. Once individuals have been abroad for

substantial periods of time, the justice of continuing to subject them to LDC taxation becomes questionable (idem, p. 49). An LDC tax limited in time, however, would obviously not produce as much revenue as one imposed over a nonresident's lifetime. Moreover, sophisticated nonresidents might intentionally work under a deferred compensation arrangement to reduce their incomes during the period in which they would be subject to the LDC tax.

138. See text accompanying note 131. The limited information on the U.S. experience is also not encouraging (see generally Finch Statement (note 16)).

139. Certain draconian measures might in theory permit an LDC to collect the tax without the host DC's assistance. Whether an LDC would be capable of implementing highly sophisticated or intricate procedures is highly problematic. (See Pomp and Oldman (note 2), pp. 39–41.)

140. Idem, p. 41.

141. Idem, pp. 41–43.

142. Idem, pp. 56–57.

143. The DCs actively compete with each other for skilled immigrants (idem, pp. 12–13).

144. Even if practicable, such an exemption might not satisfy those DCs that would refuse to cooperate with certain LDCs under any circumstances (idem, p. 46).

145. Perhaps the exemption could be granted, at a minimum, to refugees protected by the United Nations Convention and Protocol Relating to the Status of Refugees, July 28, 1951, 19 U.S.T. 6223, T.I.A.S. no. 6577, 189 U.N.T.S. 150.

146. For a discussion of this argument, see Pomp and Oldman (note 2), pp. 16–18.

3   The State, the Individual, and the Taxation of Economic Migration

Gary Clyde Hufbauer

Introduction

Economic migration between states can be divided into four types:

1. the exportation of capital services (including financial capital, physical capital, and intellectual capital);
2. the exportation of labor services (citizens working abroad);
3. the importation of capital services;
4. the importation of labor services.

Corresponding to these four types of migration are four types of tax regimes that each state can apply to foreign income and the income of foreigners. This chapter focuses on just one of those regimes, the taxation of citizens working outside the state. Limited consideration is also given to the taxation of aliens working inside the state.

Economists usually approach the taxation of citizens working outside the state and aliens working inside the state with a view to productive efficiency and redistributive welfare. Suppose that tax regime T_1 is applied to citizens working inside the state, tax regime T_2 is applied to citizens working outside the state, and tax regime T_3 is applied to aliens working inside the state. Economists usually consider the following questions: First, what result will these respective tax regimes have on the productivity and mobility of the three classes of individuals? Second, how can these regimes be adjusted to improve the welfare of resident citizens, perhaps, but not necessarily, giving less weight to the welfare of the other two classes of individuals?

Lawyers customarily approach these same tax issues from the perspectives of power and equity. That is to say, lawyers usually consider the following questions: First, what is the state's own constitutional power and administrative ability to apply different tax regimes to the three classes of individuals? Second, what are the accepted international limits to the state's exercise of its municipal taxing powers? In other words, at what point does a state's tax regime conflict with the sovereign rights of other states? Third, what considerations of equity ought to cause a state either to exercise less than its full jurisdictional ability to discriminate between classes of individuals or to moderate the extraterritorial reach of its tax system?

These customary inquiries are intriguing. But the taxation of migratory individuals cannot be examined solely in terms of efficiency, redistribution, power, and equity. The very act of migration calls into question the fundamental nature of the state and the fundamental relationship between the state and the individual.

I propose, therefore, to devote this essay to a discussion of fundamental issues.

The Nature of the State

The creation and extinction of states is a fascinating process. It works by mirrors. A state exists through the acknowledgment of other states and it ceases to exist when that acknowledgment is withdrawn. One is reminded of a tree falling in the forest: Is there a sound if no creature is there to hear it? In the case of states, no state exists if no other state recognizes it.

Usually the existing community of states acknowledges a new state or withdraws its acknowledgment from an old state en masse. Acknowledgments usually, but not always, follow the actual and exclusive dominion by the state over a defined territory and population. Some states still recognize Lithuania and Estonia even though they have long ceased to exist as factual entities. For many years the United States refused to recognize the People's Republic of China, despite Beijing's clear dominion over a large mass of territory and population. And many states have withdrawn recognition from the Republic of China, even though it indisputably controls the people and territory of Taiwan. Increasingly the Palestinian Liberation Organization, which controls population but not territory, is gaining recognition as a state.

In short a state can exist with or without territory and population. A fortiori, neither the creation nor extinction of a state depends on the means by which the state exercises dominion, if it exercises dominion at all. A state can rule by force, by benevolence, or by consensus; the ruling apparatus can range from a class that is distinct from and unresponsive to the governed population, to a class that is a microcosm of and instantly responsive to the governed population.

Western scholars, in analyzing alternative tax regimes, all too readily assume that the state exercises actual and exclusive dominion over a defined territory and population and that the ruling apparatus reflects and represents the governed population. As a factual matter these assumptions are often incorrect. Most states are governed either by force (even terror) or by benevolence and not by consensus, and in most states the ruling apparatus is quite distinct from and unresponsive to the populace. Malign states are far more commonplace than benign states.

The distinction between the state and populace is readily illustrated by regimes remote in time and place. The ancient and magnificent Golaconde Fort in Hyderabad, with its ruined pleasure baths for royal maidens and its military command of the Deccan plain, stands as visual testimony to the separation between rulers and ruled. The more recent regimes of Idi Amin, Kim Il Sung, Pol Pot, and the Shah of Iran illustrate the same distinction.

The distinction between state and population is not, however, confined to ancient and modern despots. A great many Americans passionately believed in the 1960s that the Vietnam War was wrong. In the expression of the day they were "alienated" from the state. Similar events have occurred from time to time in Canada, France, India, and other parliamentary democracies.

The point of this discussion is simple: It is more accurate to characterize the state as an entity distinct from the populace, with its own peculiar goals, than as the responsive servant of the populace so frequently assumed in Western economic and legal analysis of tax issues.

What peculiar goals of state are generally not shared with the same enthusiasm by the populace? One goal, common to ancient and modern despots, is a luxurious style of life for the governing class. Another goal, of greater importance for our inquiry, is the aggrandizement of economic and political power. A ravenous appetite for power characterizes nearly all states.

Whatever their pronouncements about the common good, political leaders savor the exercise of power as an end in itself. This was true not only of Adolf Hitler, Josef Stalin, and Mao Tse-tung; it was also true of Franklin Roosevelt, Jawaharlal Nehru, and Charles de Gaulle. And what was true of great leaders is also true of small bureaucrats: a bigger bureau becomes life's goal.

But joy of power is not the only explanation for persistent aggrandizement of the state. In many states, especially welfare states, numerous groups clamor at the public trough.[1] Each group fully knows that its own success will impose costs; but it also knows that those costs will be borne by society at large. Indeed a decision *not* to clamor is a decision to accept disproportionate burdens. Thus aggrandizement of power epitomizes the modern welfare state: Sweden, Denmark, and (until now) New Zealand. In such states "welfare" goes far beyond assuring a decent life to the poor. Instead it has developed into a massive system of transfers *within* the middle class, and indeed from the left pocket to the right pocket of individual members of the middle class. In the process of making these transfers, the state enormously increases its own power over economic life.

Fortunately many states contain systemic limitations on the aggrandizement of state power over individual life. Indeed a critical distinction between benign states and malign states is the vitality of these limitations. The most important systemic limitations are supplied by internal institutions. The paradigm is the written constitution, interpreted by an independent judiciary. Other institutions serve the same purpose: unwritten constitutions, universities, the press, the church, powerful private corporations.

In the realm of economic life, however, these limitations on state power are losing force. For example, in the United States, the Supreme Court rarely strikes down a federal economic statute for exceeding the powers granted to congress under the interstate and foreign commerce clause of the Constitution or for violating either the due process clause of the Fifth Amendment or the equal protection clause of the Fourteenth Amendment. The universities, the press, and the church are more concerned with propagating ideas than enhancing economic liberty, and powerful private corporations are increasingly drawn by an elaborate system of regulation and rewards into collaboration with the state apparatus.

Systemic limitations on state power over individual life are also provided by competition between states. This competition takes four main forms. At one extreme there is the acquisition of the territory of one state by another state, usually through conquest or civil war. Competition of this type may or may not result in a loosening of state control over the life of individuals, depending on the institutions of the victorious and the vanquished state and on whether the motive for combat was to liberate the oppressed or to oppress the liberated. A milder form of competition occurs when one state espouses individual liberties in another state, using diplomatic and even economic leverage to attain its goals.[2] Cases in point include French concern for the Quebecois, American concern for Soviet Jews, and the concern of many states for South African blacks. Third, and

still milder, there is the normal range of cultural and commercial competition that takes place between any two states that exchange goods and
ideas with one another. The fourth and final form of competition that limits
state power is migration. In 1956 Charles Tiebout elevated the concept of
"voting with one's feet" to landmark proportions in the theory of local
finance.³ Tiebout's analysis has far wider implications than competition
between the Massachusetts towns of Brookline and Newton in their respective mixes of taxes and services. The ability of an individual to emigrate affords both an escape hatch and a defense against political and
economic oppression at the national level.

Restraints on Emigration

Emigration in response to political adversity is generally applauded, but
emigration in response to economic adversity is often scorned. It is
considered noble to escape political harassment or imprisonment; it is
considered less noble to escape unemployment, low pay, or high taxes.

But consider this: Whereas the political emigrant may simply remove
an irritant to the state apparatus, the economic emigrant may actually
contribute to a better life for those left behind. When skilled but unemployed graduates leave India, their emigration mercifully reduces the
number of idle job seekers. And their departure forcefully notifies the state
of a mismatch between training and opportunities. When fully employed
professionals leave Britain or Sweden because of inadequate pay or
extravagant taxation, their emigration dramatically alerts society at large
that the state's incentive structure needs review. The classic case involves
the tax emigration of just three Swedes: Ingmar Bergman, Bjorn Borg, and
Ingemar Stenmark. Their departure, widely publicized in the newspapers,
has done more to focus Swedish attention on the enormous erosion of
incentives than the writings of all the economists between Stockholm and
Stanford.⁴

Individual freedom would be greatest if each individual could choose
between citizenship in his or her patriate state and citizenship elsewhere.
To be sure, some limits must be placed on "free-choice citizenship."
Otherwise individuals might abandon their patriate states in national
emergencies, only to return as free riders on better times. The present
danger, however, is not that the nations of the world allow too much
choice of citizenship but that they allow far too little.

Emigration controls are generally "justified" by notions that the state
enjoys a quasi-property interest in the individual, more particularly in his

or her talents and training. In the nineteenth century and before, property interests in human beings were institutionalized as slavery. In more recent times "brain drain," "loss of human capital," and "emigration rents" have gained currency as expressions for much weaker, but still recognizable, quasi-property interests.

In extreme cases states have sought to protect their quasi-property claims by creating a no-man's-land at the border. The Soviet Union and its Eastern European colonies come to mind. In less extreme cases states have imposed exit taxes both to retard emigration and to capture the economic rents generated by it. Shadowy understandings of this sort are said to characterize immigration relations between East and West Germany and between Romania and Israel.

As a much milder technique a few states, namely, the United States, the Philippines, Mexico, and the Soviet Union, have asserted their constitutional prerogative to tax the income of expatriate citizens solely on the basis of citizenship. As a still milder technique, a great many states utter the rhetoric of "lost human capital," but firmly believe that the yield on their quasi-property claims will be greatest if allowed to take the form of voluntary remittances, greater export sales, and the possible future homecoming of entrepreneurs and retirees.

Decisive humanitarian differences clearly separate these various state techniques for asserting quasi-property claims. But in a sense techniques are a matter of administrative detail. The basic issue is the validity of *any* quasi-property interest in a departing citizen. In short can the state rightfully expect *any* economic return on its citizens who leave to take up residence or citizenship in another country?

Respectable intellectual clothing has been given to the notion that the state enjoys a quasi-property claim on its citizens. One piece of intellectual clothing, offered under the label of "brain drain" or "loss of human capital," is based on the idea that departing citizens should account to the state for benefits received. The accounting in question refers not merely to benefits acquired on a contractual basis, but also to accumulated training in the widest sense of the term. On this argument the Lebanese merchant who leaves Beirut to begin anew in New York should pay a Lebanese income tax on his or her American income, no matter what the source of his or her training or talent.

The other piece of intellectual clothing is derived from the observation that strict immigration controls give rise to "emigration rents." Thus the lucky Turk who emigrates to Switzerland should—according to the theology of "find a rent, tax it"—share his or her good fortune with those left at home. Supposedly this sharing is best accomplished if the emigrant pays Turkish exit taxes upon departure, or Turkish income taxes on Swiss wages.

But these intellectual garments have no greater substance than the emperor's new clothes unless some entity other than the individual has a proper claim to the emigrant's talents, training, and good fortune. Without such a claim there can been no "drain," "loss," "accounting," or "rent" that the state can rightfully assert.

To determine whether the state has a rightful claim, we must briefly digress on the contract of citizenship. The terms of the most important contracts that individuals enter into during their lifespan are written by the state. I refer to the contracts of marriage, parenthood, and citizenship. All three are status contracts, that is to say, contracts of adhesion not of negotiation. Each of these contracts contains four groups of terms: those governing the creation of the status, those relating to individuals' rights, those relating to their duties, and those relating to the termination of the status.

Within extremely broad limits each state has historically acknowledged the prerogative of every other state to specify and change the terms of its own status contracts. It follows that each state is acting within its traditional sovereign rights if it chooses to prohibit emigration, to tax emigrants on departure, or to tax expatriate citizens. Nevertheless, because the gestation of states contains no mechanism to abort the birth of monsters and trolls, we are entitled to ask what limits *should* be placed on the exercise of the state's prerogatives.

Direct restraints on emigration are condemned by Article 13(2) of the Universal Declaration of Human Rights, adopted by the General Assembly of the United Nations, which states that "... everyone has the right to leave any country, including his own, and return to his country...."[5]

Echoing the U.N. declaration, Section 402(a) of the U.S. Trade Act of 1974 declared[6]

To assure the continued dedication of the United States to fundamental human rights, and notwithstanding any other provision of law, on or after the date of enactment of this Act products from any nonmarket economy country shall not be eligible to receive nondiscriminatory treatment (most-favored-nation treatment), such country shall not participate in any program of the Government of the United States which extends credits or credit guarantees or investment guarantees, directly or indirectly, and the President of the United States shall not conclude a commercial agreement with any such country, during the period beginning with the date on which the President determines that such country—

1. denies its citizens the right or opportunity to emigrate;

2. imposes more than a nominal tax on emigration or on the visas or other documents required for emigration, for any purpose or cause whatsoever; or

3. imposes more than a nominal tax, levy, fine, fee, or other charge on any citizen as a consequence of the desire of such citizen to emigrate to the country of his choice, . . .

Neither the U.N. Declaration of Human Rights nor the U.S. Trade Act of 1974 has achieved the standing of customary international law. But both signal an international aversion to direct restraints on emigration. Surely a line must be drawn between the claims of the state and the claims of the individual. And surely that line must allow the citizen an unfettered right to remove himself from the physical terrain of the state. Thus closed borders and exit taxes are inherently outrageous: they impose a direct restraint on emigration of the sort condemned by the U.N. Declaration of Human Rights, by the U.S. Trade Act of 1974, and by civilized opinion.

The more difficult question is whether the taxation of the earned income of expatriate citizens should be likewise condemned. Taxation based on citizenship does not directly restrain emigration, although it may discourage some citizens from accepting employment or continuing employment abroad. Clearly the U.N. declaration is aimed at direct restraints, not minor economic disincentives. Thus a case against the taxation of expatriate citizens on their foreign earnings must rest on an argument that such taxation involves an improper state claim on "human capital" or "emigration rents." But why should the taxation of expatriate citizens involve an improper claim when the same taxation of resident citizens involves a perfectly proper obligation?

The basic reason is that individuals have no power to bargain over the elements in their contract of citizenship. Their only choice, when they enjoy even this choice, is to accept or reject the entire citizenship "package."

Accordingly citizens who choose to remain in their patriate state have either decided that the family, cultural, and other associations, and the public goods and other benefits of resident citizenship provided by that state at least equal whatever taxes and obligations the state exacts from them or they have decided that they are willing, even glad, to contribute any deficiency between benefits and burdens to the commonwealth. Under these circumstances the state is hardly making an improper claim on the individual. The contract of citizenship, taken as a whole, is accepted as a matter of free choice by the individual.

By contrast citizens who choose to earn a living abroad have clearly decided that the burdens of continued residence in the state outweigh its benefits. Taxation is essentially an economic obligation, and the expatriate citizens have clearly cast their economic lot with an alien state. They earn income in that state; they buy their sustenance, shelter, and luxuries in that state; they pay taxes to that state. Once the citizens have established residence abroad, they retain only one indisputable benefit of citizenship: the right to return to their patriate state. Otherwise they have surrendered daily access to the associations and public goods of their native land. The question becomes: Does the right to return, standing alone, provide justification for taxing expatriate citizens' foreign-earned income?

The right to return is enshrined in the U.N. Universal Declaration of Human Rights. How can so basic a right become the occasion for taxation? Indeed what is the meaning of a basic human right when its mere *potential* exercise becomes the rationale for imposing taxation? The United States Supreme Court has held that the basic right to vote in state elections cannot be qualified by a poll tax[7] or by a residency requirement longer than 50 days.[8] Surely the logic of these decisions argues against grounding the taxation of expatriate citizens on their right to return.

Additional considerations buttress this argument. Suppose, *arguendo*, that India decided to impose a citizenship tax. Gupta, an Indian expatriate, acquires the citizenship of France and renounces his Indian citizenship. But suppose that Indian law does not allow renunciation. Instead it follows the maxim "Born an Indian, die an Indian." No one would contend that Gupta's involuntary dual citizenship, complete with right of return, should entail a tax obligation to India. But how different is this situation from the imposition of a citizenship tax on Sen, an ordinary Indian expatriate working abroad as a resident alien?

Two features distinguish the Gupta hypothetical example from the Sen hypothetical example: first, Gupta's act of acquiring a new citizenship; second, Gupta's act of renouncing his old citizenship. Let us examine these two features closely. Instant citizenship is rarely granted. Instead most countries impose a waiting period before permitting resident aliens to become citizens. In the United States the customary waiting period is five years; in Switzerland the waiting period is as least twelve years; in Kuwait and Saudi Arabia the waiting period is forever. Thus if we were to specify that the act of acquiring a new citizenship is the decisive step that frees an individual from the quasi-property claims of his or her birth state, we would reach a curious and untenable conclusion: if emigrant Sen devoutly desires to sever all bonds with India at the moment his plane leaves

Bombay, he would be forced by the laws of his new resident state to wait five years, twelve years, or a lifetime to achieve that result.

Perhaps, instead, the critical step should be Sen's decision to voluntarily renounce his Indian citizenship. Suppose that India recognizes renunciation. But suppose that Sen does not yet qualify for citizenship in his country of residence. Then we would reach another curious and untenable conclusion: the price of breaking India's quasi-property claim is for Sen to become a stateless person. That price is excessive.

In short the citizenship tax on expatriate Sen is an improper quasi-property claim, *unless* Sen values his Indian citizenship, does not seek the citizenship of another country, and is willing to proclaim these matters when presented with his Indian tax bill. But now I am describing not the ordinary emigrant, emigrant Sen, but a quite different individual, emigrant Lall. Emigrant Lalls are probably not very numerous, and it is hard to perceive the equity in an expatriate citizenship tax that reaches only the Lalls.

A further practical consideration deserves mention. It is very difficult for a state to tax its expatriate citizens on their foreign-earned income unless the majority of them, like emigrant Lall, voluntarily pay the tax. The state has little means of keeping track of the identity of expatriates, their addresses, or their income. And the state has no means of enforcing collection of the tax as long as the citizen remains abroad.

As a result of this practical consideration, some scholars have suggested that immigrant states should assist emigrant states in collecting their citizenship taxes. This suggestion encounters three objections. In the first place tax treaties between states have historically *relieved* taxpayers of double taxation or in other ways reduced their tax burden. It would be novel to negotiate a tax treaty that had, as its main purpose, the collection of additional taxes. In the second place most countries have ample administrative problems enforcing their own taxes without undertaking the burden of collecting other nations' taxes. In the third place ideological compatibility differs greatly between different country pairs. Although the United States and Canada might find common ideological ground for tax cooperation, the United Sates and Cuba cannot. In other words before a country departs from long-standing tradition and becomes involved in enforcing another country's personal income taxes, it would want to evaluate that other country's entire political system in terms of its own doctrines. A thorough evaluation would certainly be demanded by the United States, most Western European countries, Canada, Australia, and Japan. In practice this means that most industrial countries would not be willing to assist in enforcing the expatriate citizenship taxes of most developing countries. The industrial countries would find the gulf in political systems simply too great.

Conclusion

States come in many colors, shapes, and sizes, but the malign and unresponsive state is more commonplace than the benign and responsive state. The goals of the state, whether malign or benign, are often quite distinct from the goals of its citizens. In particular states relentlessly seek to increase their power over individual economic and political life. Domestic institutions and competition between states often serve to limit the abuses of state power.

One important form of interstate competition is economic migration. Closed borders and exit taxes directly curtail this form of competition. Such restrictions stand condemned by the U.N. Declaration of Human Rights.

Income taxes on the earned income of expatriate citizens are a much milder form of emigration restraint. But the assertion of these taxes amounts to the assertion of a quasi-property claim by the state, a claim not balanced by public goods or cultural associations offered by the state to the citizen living abroad.

The strongest argument for asserting a tax claim on expatriate citizens is that they have a right to return; but in a world where citizenship in other countries is not readily available, this basic right is not a proper foundation for taxation.

As a practical matter expatriate income taxes are difficult to enforce without cooperation from the immigrant state. For deep-seated reasons it is unlikely that this sort of tax cooperation will flourish in the near future.

Notes

I am indebted to David Bradford and Assar Lindbeck for valuable criticisms of the original draft.

1. Assar Lindbeck has often emphasized this point.

2. On the use of economic sanctions, see Gary Clyde Hufbauer and Jeffrey J. Schott. Oct. 1983. *Economic Sanctions in Support of Foreign Policy Goals.* Washington, D.C.: Institute for International Economics.

3. Charles Mills Tiebout. 1956. A pure theory of local expenditures. *Journal of Political Economy* Oct.

4. Assar Lindbeck. Dec. 1980. Work disincentives in the welfare state. Seminar paper 164, Institute for International Economic Studies, University of Stockholm. Lindbeck supplemented his paper by comments at the conference.

5. Adopted by the General Assembly of the United Nations on December 10, 1948, G.A. Resolution 217 (III) A. Similar language, but with qualifications preserving greater flexibility for state restrictions, appears in Article 12(2) of the International Covenant on Civil and Political Rights adopted by the General Assembly on December 16, 1966.

6. P.L. 93-618, 93d congress, January 3, 1975.

7. *Harper v. Virginia Board of Elections*, 383 U.S. 663 (1966).

8. *Dun v. Blumstein*, 405 U.S. 330 (1972); *Marsh v. Lewis*, 410 U.S. 679 (1973).

III

Theoretical Analyses

4   The Effect of Potential Emigration on the Optimal Linear Income Tax

John Douglas Wilson

Introduction

The study of optimal income taxation has made much use of a simple model originally developed by Mirrlees.[1] In this model there is one consumption good, which is produced from one type of labor, and the technology is characterized by constant returns to scale. Individual differences are completely described by a single parameter, which may be called ability; individuals differ only by the amount of income that they receive per unit of labor. Thus all utility functions are identical and depend only on consumption and labor.

Of concern to us here is the further assumption that migration is impossible. For countries in which emigration is an important phenomenon, this assumption is unsatisfactory. Individuals often have the opportunity to emigrate when they are taxed too heavily or, upon emigrating, to return when the taxes they face in their home country are lowered sufficiently. Emigration opportunities are likely to have a large effect on the optimal income tax and, consequently, on the utilities of those individuals who remain residents. In fact under the assumptions of Mirrlees's model, the only way in which emigration affects the utilities of residents is through its effect on the optimal income tax.

The purpose of this chapter is to present a study of how emigration opportunities affect the optimal income tax. To do so, I extend Mirrlees's model to include emigration opportunities. Social welfare is a function of individual utilities. Although few restrictions are placed on the form of this function, I do assume that the contribution of an individual's utility to social welfare is independent of whether he or she is a resident or an emigrant. I do not alter Mirrlees's assumption that there is a fixed number of individuals at each ability level who are included in the measurement of social welfare, instead concentrating on the effect of the income tax on the division of this fixed number between residents and emigrants. Thus the essential feature of the extension of Mirrlees's model is that the number of individuals subject to the income tax at each ability level is allowed to vary as the income tax schedule is changed.

Rather than follow Mirrlees by not restricting the functional form of the income tax schedule, I consider only linear income taxation. A linear income tax consists of a poll subsidy and a constant marginal tax on income. Thus I am able to analyze how actual tax parameters are affected by the presence of emigration opportunities.

The specific question is how the optimal tax parameters for an open economy differ from those for an economy that I call partially closed. In the open economy every individual is free to migrate at will. A partially closed economy is formed by taking an open economy with its tax set optimally and imposing the constraint that certain individuals may not enter or leave the home country; these individuals are no longer allowed to change their status as residents or emigrants. The economy is said to be partially closed because it is closed at some ability levels but remains open at other ability levels. Both the open economy and a partially closed economy have the same number of residents at each ability level when the tax for the open economy is set optimally. Also both economies are characterized by the same tastes and technology. Thus the comparison of optimal taxes for the two economies can be said to isolate the effect on the optimal tax of emigration opportunities at the ability levels where the economy is partially closed.

The results from this comparison can be simply stated. Emigration opportunities manifest themselves in what I call potential emigration. Potential emigrants exist at a given ability level if a small tax change from the open economy optimal tax alters the number of residents with this ability level. I find that the elimination of potential emigration at relatively low and high ability levels raises the optimal marginal tax and poll subsidy, whereas its elimination at ability levels in some intermediate interval lowers the optimal marginal tax. The exact statement of this result is contained in propositions 1 and 2.

My analysis is applicable to the migration of highly skilled individuals from developing countries (LDCs) to developed countries (DCs). It has been noted that the magnitude of this migration is likely to be most dependent on the restrictiveness of DC migration policies.[2] In the United States a system of national quotas was replaced in 1965 by legislation promoting quality immigration. Over the subsequent five years the U.S. experienced a great increase in both the share of LDCs in PTK (professional, technical, and kindred) immigration and the share of LDC immigration in total immigration. The model gives an indication of how a return to restrictive national quotas would affect the desirable income tax structures for LDCs.[3]

The plan of this chapter is as follows. Before getting into the details of the model, I first outline the basic argument behind the results. Then I present the model of an open economy and describe partially closed economies. In the fifth section I prove a proposition that shows how the distribution of the ability levels where the economy is partially closed determines the direction in which the tax may feasibly be changed from its optimal value for the open economy to increase social welfare. In the following section I extend the results to make a statement about the difference between the optimal taxes for open and partially closed economies. Before the concluding section, I apply the analysis to the case in which the utility function is Cobb-Douglas and the social welfare function is utilitarian.

The Basic Argument

Consider a small tax change from the open economy optimal tax that involves increases in the poll subsidy and marginal tax and leaves the government budget balanced in the open economy. Under reasonable assumptions, all individuals with ability levels less than some ability level n_2 are helped by this tax change, whereas those with ability levels greater than n_2 are hurt. Also individuals with ability levels less than some ability level n_1 are tax recipients at the optimal tax, whereas those with ability levels greater than n_1 are taxpayers.[4] Tax recipients receive a poll subsidy that is greater than the tax they pay on their earned income, and taxpayers receive a poll subsidy that is less than this tax.

Suppose that individuals move where their utilities are highest. At ability levels possessed by potential emigrants that are either less than n_1 and n_2 or greater than n_1 and n_2, the tax change induces either tax recipients to enter the home country or taxpayers to leave. The resulting losses in tax revenue can be prevented by partially closing the economy at these ability levels. Once the economy is partially closed, the same small tax change from the open economy optimal tax creates a budget surplus. Another tax change involving the same increase in the marginal tax but a greater increase in the poll subsidy is feasible. This tax change raises social welfare in the partially closed economy.

This result is reversed if the economy is partially closed at ability levels between n_1 and n_2 where potential emigrants exist. Again consider a small tax change from the open economy optimal tax that keeps the government budget balanced in the open economy, but now suppose that it involves reductions in the poll subsidy and marginal tax. In the partially closed economy, either tax recipients are prevented from entering the home country or taxpayers are prevented from leaving (depending on whether n_1 is greater or less than n_2). Consequently social welfare can be increased by a feasible tax change from the open economy optimal tax that involves a reduction in the marginal tax.

These results indicate that the effect of potential emigration on the optimal tax depends on the ability levels possessed by potential emigrants. The results are local, focusing on small welfare improvements. A following section makes the extension to global results concerning the difference between open and partially closed economy optimal taxes.

The Open Economy

Consider an economy composed of a home country and the rest of the world. The government of the home country desires to maximize a social welfare function that includes the utilities of a continuum of individuals. These individuals are indexed by ability levels N_1 to N_2, where $N_1 > 0$ and $N_2 < \infty$.[5] They are called residents if they reside in the home country and emigrants if they live abroad. There may exist individuals who are not included in the measurement of social welfare. But they are assumed not to affect the value of the optimal income tax, either because they are not subject to taxation while in the home country or because they are not allowed to enter the home country. Thus they are ignored in the following analysis. All residents included in the social welfare function are taxed. But the government is unable to tax emigrants.

Each individual possesses a home utility function $u(c, y)$, where c is consumption and y is labor. $u(c, y)$ is defined for $c > 0$ and $0 \leqq y < E$, where E is a common endowment of leisure. It is assumed that $u(c, y)$ is continuously differentiable and strictly concave, with $\partial u(c, y)/\partial c > 0$ and $\partial u(c, y)/\partial y < 0$. Consumption and leisure are assumed to be normal goods.

A resident with ability level n chooses c and y to solve

$$\max u(c, y)$$

subject to

$c = a + (1 - t)ny,$

where a is the poll subsidy and t is the marginal tax, $y(n, a, t)$ denotes the supply of labor; $z(n, a, t) = ny(n, a, t)$ is earned income; and $-a + tz(n, a, t)$ is the net tax.

Home utility is specified indirectly by the function $v(n, a, t)$, which has the properties

$$\frac{\partial v(n, a, t)}{\partial a} > 0 \tag{1}$$

and

$$\frac{\partial v(n, a, t)}{\partial t} = -z(n, a, t)\frac{\partial v(n, a, t)}{\partial a} \leqq 0. \tag{2}$$

Functions $v(n, a, t)$ and $z(n, a, t)$ are defined for all (a, t) in the set $\{(a, t): c > 0, 0 \leqq y < E, a + (1 - t)ny < c\}$. For those (a, t) not in this set, there is no way that individuals can use their endowments of leisure to obtain a positive level of consumption while satisfying their budget constraints.

The utilities that individuals can receive abroad are exogenously given in this model. Individuals live abroad if and only if their home utilities are less than their foreign utilities. A tax change raises (lowers) the number of resident n-individuals by raising (lowering) their home utilities. For mathematical convenience I specify the model so that these residential population changes depend continuously on the magnitudes of the changes in home utility. Individuals with the same ability level are assumed to receive different foreign utilities. $F(n, v)$ denotes the number of n-individuals with foreign utility levels less than v.[6] Then $F(n, v(n, a, t))$ is the number of resident n-individuals when the tax is (a, t). An increase in a or a reduction in t has a nonnegative effect on this number because it increases $v(n, a, t)$:

$$-\frac{\partial F}{\partial v}\frac{\partial v(n, a, t)}{\partial t} = \frac{\partial F}{\partial v}\frac{\partial v(n, a, t)}{\partial a}z(n, a, t) \geqq 0. \tag{3}$$

If the foreign utilities of n-individuals are either all lower or all higher than their home utility, then a small change in home utility has no effect on the number of resident n-individuals: $\partial F/\partial v = 0$. Potential emigrants with ability level n are said to exist at (a, t) if the only if $\partial F/\partial v \neq 0$. Much use of this definition will be made in the following.

Turning to the government, we assume that there are no public expenditures. Thus the government budget is balanced by setting government revenue net of poll subsidy payments equal to zero:

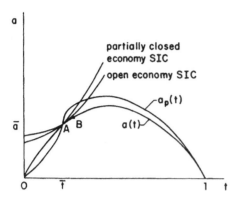

Figure 4.1

$$G(a, t) = \int_{N_1}^{N_2} (tz(n, a, t) - a)F(n, v(n, a, t))\, dn = 0. \tag{4}$$

Let $a(t)$ denote the maximum poll subsidy that satisfies this constraint at t. Borrowing the terminology of Romer (1975), we refer to the graph of $a(t)$ as the tax possibility frontier (TPF) for the open economy.

Tax parameters a and t are chosen subject to (4) to maximize social welfare, which is an increasing function of the utilities received by residents and emigrants.[7] An individual is assumed not to affect social welfare by migrating if his utility remains unchanged. In other words residents and emigrants are treated equally in the measurement of social welfare.

Because a and t uniquely determine individual utility levels (given foreign utility possibilities), social welfare can be written as a function of a and t: $W = W(a, t)$. This function is assumed to be continuously differentiable.[8] Clearly our assumptions imply that social welfare is raised by an increase in a or a reduction in t. Consequently social indifference curves, such as the one depicted in figure 4.1, slope up.

Partially Closed Economies

To partially close the economy at all ability levels in a set P, the tax is set optimally in the open economy.[9] Institutions are then formed to prevent the number of residents (and the number of emigrants) at each ability level in P from changing in response to any tax change. Letting $(\bar{a}, \bar{t})$ denote the optimal tax for the open economy,[10] the number of residents in the partially closed economy with an ability level belonging to P is fixed at $F(n, v(n, \bar{a}, \bar{t}))$.

Partially closing the economy does not alter the manner in which social welfare depends on individual utilities. But by restricting migration, it does alter the utilities some individuals receive at particular values of a and t. Consequently it changes the relation of social welfare to a and t. The new relation is denoted $W_P(a, t)$. We now study its properties.

Until the tax is changed from $(\bar{a}, \bar{t})$, partially closing the economy does not prevent migration. Thus the open and partially closed economies have the same level of social welfare at $(\bar{a}, \bar{t})$:

$$W_P(\bar{a}, \bar{t}) = W(\bar{a}, \bar{t}). \tag{5}$$

Partially closing the economy, however, may prevent individuals from migrating in response to various tax changes originating at $(\bar{a}, \bar{t})$. This prevention lowers social welfare because individuals wish to go where their utilities are highest. Thus

$$W_P(a, t) \leqq W(a, t), \qquad \text{for all } a, t. \tag{6}$$

Fig. 4.1 depicts the social indifference curves (SICs) for the open and partially closed economies that pass through $(\bar{a}, \bar{t})$. They are referred to as the open economy SIC and the partially closed economy SIC. By (5) they correspond to the same level of social welfare. By (5) and (6) the partially closed economy SIC cannot lie below the open economy SIC, but the two SICs are tangent at $(\bar{a}, \bar{t})$.[11]

For the partially closed economy let $G_P(a, t)$ denote government revenue net of poll subsidy payments at (a, t). Partially closing the economy has no effect on the residential population while the tax is at $(\bar{a}, \bar{t})$. Because the government budget is balanced at $(\bar{a}, \bar{t})$ in the open economy, it must also be balanced at $(\bar{a}, \bar{t})$ in the partially closed economy:

$$G_P(\bar{a}, \bar{t}) = G(\bar{a}, \bar{t}) = 0. \tag{7}$$

If the economy were completely closed, $G_P(a, t)$ would necessarily be a decreasing function of the poll subsidy. This follows from the normality of leisure, which implies that each resident's net tax (net of the poll subsidy) is a decreasing function of the poll subsidy. For simplicity, we assume that $G_P(a, t)$ is a decreasing function of a for all partial closings and taxes under consideration.[12] Then $\bar{a}$ is the maximum feasible poll subsidy at $\bar{t}$ in the partially closed economy. Thus the tax possibility frontier $a = a_P(t)$ passes through $(\bar{a}, \bar{t})$, as illustrated in figure 4.1. Furthermore the implicit function theorem implies that $a_P(t)$ and $a(t)$ are continuously differentiable.[13]

Welfare Improvements

If the economy is partially closed at ability levels possessed by potential emigrants, then potential emigration is said to be eliminated at these ability levels. In this section we relate the ability levels where potential emigration is eliminated to the direction in which the tax can be feasibly changed from $(\bar{a}, \bar{t})$ to increase social welfare.

Consider a small tax change that originates at $(\bar{a}, \bar{t})$ and takes place along the open economy TPF (A to B in fig. 4.1). By the definition of this TPF, the marginal change in tax revenue from this tax change is zero in the open economy:[14]

$$G'(a(\bar{t}), \bar{t}) = \frac{\partial G(\bar{a}, \bar{t})}{\partial a} a'(\bar{t}) + \frac{\partial G(\bar{a}, \bar{t})}{\partial t} = 0. \tag{8}$$

Consider the same tax change in an economy that is partially closed at all ability levels in a set P. $G'_P(a(\bar{t}), \bar{t})$ is the resulting total marginal change in tax revenue. This partial closing eliminates all residential population changes in P that would have been caused by the tax change. Subtracting $G'_P(a(\bar{t}), \bar{t})$ from $G'(a(\bar{t}), \bar{t})$ gives the marginal change in tax revenue from these residential population changes. Then (8) implies that $-G'_P(a(\bar{t}), \bar{t})$ is this marginal tax revenue change. In symbols,

$$-G'_P(a(\bar{t}), \bar{t}) = \int_P (tz - a) F_v v'(n, a(\bar{t}), \bar{t}) \, dn, \tag{9}$$

where, by our notational convention,

$$v'(n, a(\bar{t}), \bar{t}) = \frac{\partial v(n, \bar{a}, \bar{t})}{\partial a} a'(t) + \frac{\partial v(n, \bar{a}, \bar{t})}{\partial t}.$$

A tax change along the partially closed economy TPF leaves tax revenue unchanged in the partially closed economy: $G'_P(a_P(\bar{t}), \bar{t}) = 0$. Consequently if $G'_P(a(\bar{t}), \bar{t})$ is positive (negative), $a'_P(\bar{t})$ is greater (less) than $a'(\bar{t})$. A tax is called P-feasible if it is feasible in an economy that is partially closed at all ability levels in P. As shown in figure 4.1, if $a'_P(\bar{t}) > a'(\bar{t})$, there exists a P-feasible tax involving a greater poll subsidy and marginal tax than $(\bar{a}, \bar{t})$ and yielding a higher level of social welfare than $(\bar{a}, \bar{t})$. Similarly if $a'_P(\bar{t}) < a'(\bar{t})$, there exists a P-feasible tax giving a higher level of social welfare than $(\bar{a}, \bar{t})$, but involving a lower marginal tax.

To sign $G'_P(a(\bar{t}), \bar{t})$, we utilize the following two lemmas. Lemma 1 is valid only if $\bar{t}$ is greater than zero. Henceforth we assume that this condition holds.[15]

Lemma 1.   There exists an ability level $n_1 \in (N_1, N_2)$ such that

$$\bar{t}z(n, \bar{a}, \bar{t}) - \bar{a} \gtreqless 0 \quad \text{as} \quad n \gtreqless n_1. \tag{10}$$

Proof.   Under the assumption that consumption is a normal good, $z(n, a, t)$ can be shown to be increasing in n.[16] Also the definition of $\bar{a}(= a(\bar{t}))$ and the assumption that there are no public expenditures imply that some individuals are taxpayers and others are tax recipients when the tax is set at $(\bar{a}, \bar{t})$. Thus (10) must hold for some $n_1 \in (N_1, N_2)$.   Q.E.D.

Lemma 2.   There exists an ability level $n_2 \in (N_1, N_2)$ such that

$$v'(n, a(\bar{t}), \bar{t}) \lesseqgtr 0 \quad \text{as} \quad n \gtreqless n_2. \tag{11}$$

Proof.   By (2) (Roy's Identity),

$$v'(n, a(\bar{t}), \bar{t}) = \frac{\partial v(n, \bar{a}, \bar{t})}{\partial a}(a'(\bar{t}) - z(n, \bar{a}, \bar{t})). \tag{12}$$

This condition implies that (11) holds for some n_2 because $z(n, a, t)$ is increasing in n. Because the open economy TPF and SIC are tangent at $(\bar{a}, \bar{t})$, a small tax change along the open economy TPF from $(\bar{a}, \bar{t})$ can neither raise all home utilities nor lower all home utilities. Thus $n_2 \in (N_1, N_2)$.   Q.E.D.

Let

$$n^l = \min(n_1, n_2) \quad \text{and} \quad n^u = \max(n_1, n_2). \tag{13}$$

We now prove the results given in the second section.

Proposition 1. n^l and n^u have the following properties:

(a) $N_1 < n^l \leq n^u < N_2$.

(b) If $P \subset P_1 = \{n: n < n^l \text{ or } n > n^u\}$ and potential emigrants exist at $(\bar{a}, \bar{t})$ with ability levels in P,[17] then there exists a tax (a, t) such that

1. (a, t) is P-feasible;
2. $W_P(a, t) > W(\bar{a}, \bar{t})$;
3. $t > \bar{t}$;
4. $a > \bar{a}$.

(c) If $P \subset P_2 = \{n: n^l < n < n^u\}$ and potential emigrants exist at $(\bar{a}, \bar{t})$ with ability levels in P, then there exists a tax (a, t) such that

1. (a, t) is P-feasible;

2. $W_P(a, t) > W(\overline{a}, \overline{t})$;

3. $t < \overline{t}$.

Proof of (a).   By lemmas 1 and 2, n_1 and n_2 belong to (N_1, N_2). Then (a) follows from the definitions of n^l and n^u.

Proof of (b).   From lemmas 1 and 2 we see that P_1 has been defined so that $\overline{t}z(n, \overline{a}, \overline{t}) - \overline{a}$ and $v'(n, a(\overline{t}), \overline{t})$ have opposite signs for all n in P_1. Then (9) implies that $G_P'(a(\overline{t}), \overline{t}) > 0$ for all P in P_1 with ability levels possessed by potential emigrants at $(\overline{a}, \overline{t})$ (ability levels where $F_v \neq 0$). By the previous remarks this proves the existence of a tax $(\overline{a}, \overline{t})$ with the four properties in (b).

Proof of (c).   By lemmas 1 and 2, $\overline{t}z(n, \overline{a}, \overline{t}) - \overline{a}$ and $v'(n, a(\overline{t}), \overline{t})$ have the same sign for all n in P_2. Using (9), this implies that $G_P'(a(\overline{t}), \overline{t}) < 0$ for all P in P_2 with ability levels possessed by potential emigrants at $(\overline{a}, \overline{t})$. By the previous remarks this proves (c).

Proposition 1 indicates that potential emigration among low- and high-ability members of the economy prevents social welfare from being increased by making the tax structure more egalitarian. Intuitively, more redistribution is good when this potential emigration is eliminated because residential population changes that cause a tax revenue loss are eliminated.

Proposition 1 also indicates that, if $n^l \neq n^u$, then there exists an intermediate interval of ability levels in which the elimination of potential emigration makes feasible a tax change from $(\overline{a}, \overline{t})$ that increases social welfare and involves a reduction in the marginal tax. The change in the poll subsidy appears to be ambiguous. It may be possible to both reduce the marginal tax and increase the poll subsidy, in which case every resident benefits from the partial closing of the economy. Such a tax change would not be feasible in the open economy because it would induce an influx of tax recipients

Ability levels n^l and n^u equal, respectively, the minimum and maximum of n_1 and n_2. Lemmas 1 and 2 and their proofs show that n_1 is the ability level at which $z = \overline{a}/\overline{t}$, whereas n_2 is the ability level at which $z = a'(\overline{t})$. I venture to speculate that they almost always have different values. Which value is largest is inconsequential to the analysis.

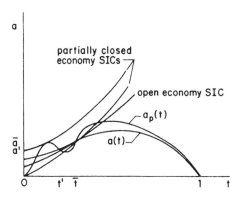

Figure 4.2

The Global Optima

If $W_p(a_p(t), t)$ is concave in t, then the direction from $\bar{t}$ in which a small feasible tax change increases social welfare once the economy is partially closed is the same direction in which the partially closed economy optimal tax lies. We can then use proposition 1 to compare open and partially closed economy optimal taxes. However, there is no reason for this concavity to hold. Figure 4.2 illustrates a partial closing that lowers the optimal marginal tax but makes feasible increases in the poll subsidy and marginal tax from $(\bar{a}, \bar{t})$ that raise social welfare. As shown, although the partially closed economy TPF dips below the open economy TPF immediately to the left of $\bar{t}$, it then rises sufficiently far above the open economy TPF for the optimal marginal tax to lie to the left of $\bar{t}$.

Intuition suggests that this possibility is ruled out if the set of ability levels in which the economy is partially closed in sufficiently small. The argument is that once the partially closed economy TPF dips below the open economy TPF on one side of $\bar{t}$, small partial closings cannot raise it high enough on this side to create feasible taxes with a higher level of social welfare than $W(\bar{a}, \bar{t})$. The situation illustrated in figure 4.2 does not occur.

Two qualifications must be added to this intuitive argument for it to be correct. First, the optimal tax for the open economy must be unique; this means that $\bar{t}$ is the only marginal tax where the open economy SIC and TPF are tangent. Second, attention must be limited to a set of partial closings for which there exists a neighborhood of $\bar{t}$ where the open and partially closed economy TPFs cross only at $\bar{t}$. This latter condition is satisfied by considering only partial closings at ability levels outside of some fixed neighborhoods of n^l and n^u.

With these two qualifications the partially closed economy optimal tax and small feasible tax changes that increase social welfare lie in the same direction from $\bar{t}$ if the partial closing is sufficiently small. The exact statement of this result is now given without proof.[18] To restrict the size of the partial closings, let us use the concept of a Lebesgue measure. The Lebesgue measure of a measurable set P is denoted mP.[19] $(\bar{a}_P, \bar{t}_P)$ is the optimal tax for an economy that is partially closed at all ability levels in P.[20]

Proposition 2. Suppose that $(\bar{a}, \bar{t})$ is the unique open economy optimal tax. Then for any $\varepsilon > 0$, there exists a $\delta > 0$ such that the following is true for any set P of ability levels that contains potential emigrants and satisfies $mP < \delta$.

(a) If $P \subset \{n: n < n^l - \varepsilon$ or $n > n^u + \varepsilon\}$, then $\bar{t}_P > \bar{t}$ and $\bar{a}_P > \bar{a}$.

(b) If $P \subset \{n: n^l + \varepsilon < n < n^u - \varepsilon\}$, then $\bar{t}_P < \bar{t}$.

An Example

One implication of proposition 2 is that eliminating potential emigration at ability levels that are sufficiently high raises the optimal poll subsidy and marginal tax. More precisely there exists an $\bar{n} < N_2$ such that if a set P contains potential emigrants and belongs to $(\bar{n}, N_2]$, then partially closing the economy at all ability levels in P raises the optimal poll subsidy and marginal tax. To obtain some feeling about what constitutes "sufficiently high," let us make the following assumptions: 1. The utility function is Cobb-Douglas: $u(c, y) = c^{1-\alpha}(1 - y)^\alpha$, $0 < \alpha < 1$. 2. The social welfare function is utilitarian (the sum of the utilities of residents and emigrants). 3. Everyone works at $(\bar{a}, \bar{t})$ $(z(n, \bar{a}, \bar{t}) > 0$ for all n). 4. Each partially closed economy optimal tax is greater than zero. Given these assumptions, we now develop an interesting expression for $\bar{n}$ and outline the proof that it has the above property.[21]

For an economy that is partially closed at all ability levels in a set P, let $\bar{n}_P(t)$ denote the mean ability level of residents when the tax is on the open economy SIC at t. Let

$$\bar{n} = \max\{\bar{n}_P(t): P \subset [N_1, N_2], t \in [0, \bar{t}]\}. \tag{14}$$

In words, $\bar{n}$ is the maximum mean ability level of residents for open and partially closed economies in which the tax is set at a point on the open economy SIC between 0 and $\bar{t}$.[22] Under our assumptions $\bar{n}$ can be shown greater than $n^u = \max(n_1, n_2)$ by proving that n_2 is less than n_1 and n_1 equals $\bar{n}_P(\bar{t})$.[23] Then part (a) of proposition 1 implies that partially closing the economy at ability levels above $\bar{n}$ at which potential emigrants exist alters the optimal tax. We want to show that $\bar{t}_P > \bar{t}$. Suppose, to the contrary, that $\bar{t}_P < \bar{t}$. Then, as shown in figure 4.2, there exists a tax (a', t'), $t' < \bar{t}$, where the open economy SIC and partially closed economy TPF cross. It is possible to show that the tax change from $(\bar{a}, \bar{t})$ to (a', t') increases the utilities of residents with ability levels greater than $\bar{n}_P(t')$. Thus it can only increase the residential population at these ability levels. Furthermore all individuals with these ability levels can be shown to be taxpayers at (a', t'). Consequently preventing these residential population changes causes a decline in tax revenue at (a', t'). It follows that (a', t') is not feasible in an economy that is partially closed only at ability levels greater than $\bar{n}(> \bar{n}_P(t'))$, because it is not feasible in the open economy. The assumption that (a', t') lies on the partially closed economy TPF is contradicted. We may conclude that $\bar{t}_P$ cannot be less than $\bar{t}$ if P is a subset of $(\bar{n}, N_2]$.

We have shown that eliminating potential emigration at ability levels above $\bar{n}$ raises the optimal marginal tax and poll subsidy. The significance of this result rests on our feelings about the location of $\bar{n}$ in $[N_1, N_2]$. Because $\bar{n}$ is the mean ability level of residents for some economy, we may reasonably expect $\bar{n}$ to be centrally located. Of course it is quite possible for $\bar{n}$ to be closer to N_2 than to N_1. But except for extreme cases $(\bar{n}, N_2]$ should be sizable.

Concluding Remarks

In this chapter I have attempted to characterize the effect of potential emigration on the optimal linear income tax. Simply stated, I have found that potential emigration among low- and high-ability individuals tends to lower the optimal marginal tax, whereas potential emigration among individuals with ability levels in some intermediate interval tends to raise it. The bulk of the work in this chapter has gone into giving an exact meaning to this statement.

The applicability of my analysis is subject to the usual limitations of Mirrlees's model of optimal income taxation. A limitation that is specific to the study of emigration opportunities is the assumption that the number of individuals included in the social welfare function at each ability level is fixed. The seriousness of this asumption is hidden by the absence of any consideration of time in the model. In a model involving time one would presumably want to have some rule to determine who is included in the social welfare function. For example, we might include only those individuals born in the home country. But then the current number of residents at each ability level is likely to influence future numbers of individuals in the social welfare function at each ability level. Because the current number of residents depends on the current value of the income tax, this value is likely to affect future numbers of individuals in the social welfare function. This dynamic consideration is not accounted for in the static model presented here.

In spite of the inherent limitations of my analysis, I believe that my characterizations of the effect of potential emigration on the optimal income tax provide a useful way of understanding the manner in which emigration opportunities enter into the determination of the optimal income tax.

Notes

I am grateful to J. N. Bhagwati, P. A. Diamond, K. W. S. Roberts, and two anonymous referees for helpful comments and suggestions.

1. Mirrlees 1971.

2. See Bhagwati 1977.

3. Of course restrictive quotas in the United States may simply divert migration to other DCs. Bhagwati (1976) speculates that the 1965 easing of restrictions may have lessened PTK migration to Canada.

4. We assume that there are no public expenditures.

5. All functions in this paper that have ability levels as arguments are defined only at ability levels in the interval $[N_1, N_2]$.

6. $F(n, v)$ is assumed to be continuously differentiable.

7. More accurately, because we are dealing with a continuum of individuals, social welfare is a function of the utility levels over this continuum. An increase in the utilities possessed by all individuals with ability levels in any set with a positive measure is assumed to raise social welfare. Note also that we are assuming the home government does not count the tax payments by emigrants to foreign governments in its measure of social welfare. This means that the home government is concerned only with the welfare of its own population (emigrants and residents), rather than with some measure of "world social welfare."

8. An example of social welfare function that satisfies our assumptions is the utilitarian social welfare function, which is the sum of the utilities of residents and emigrants.

9. Unless otherwise specified, the set P is taken to be any nonempty measurable subset of $[N_1, N_2]$.

10. $(\bar{a}, \bar{t})$ need not be the only optimal tax for the open economy. If there are other optimal taxes, then we must specify the one at which the economy is partially closed. Our results concerning local welfare improvements do not require the existence of a unique optimal tax for the open economy. This uniqueness assumption, however, must be made to obtain our global results.

11. This result relies on the two SICs being continuously differentiable at $(\bar{a}, \bar{t})$. This property follows from the implicit function theorem.

12. Our results concerning local welfare improvements can be proved without this assumption. The global results in the section on the global optima hold under the much weaker assumption that $\partial G(\bar{a}, \bar{t})/\partial a$ and $\partial G(\bar{a}, \bar{t})/\partial t$ do not both equal zero.

13. The assumption that $G_P(a, t)$ is decreasing in a for all measurable nonempty $P \subset [N_1, N_2]$ implies that $G(a, t)$ is also decreasing in a.

14. Throughout this paper a prime is used to denote a total derivative with respect to t.

15. Sheshinski (1972) has shown that the optimal marginal tax for a completely closed economy is greater than zero when labor is a nondecreasing function of the net wage rate.

16. I am indebted to Professor Peter Diamond for showing me a simple proof of this statement.

17. This statement is taken here and everywhere else to mean that the set of ability levels in P in which potential emigrants exist has a positive measure.

18. See Wilson (1979).

19. If P consists of a sequence of disjoint intervals, then mP is the sum of the lengths of these intervals. More generally mP is the outer measure of the measurable set P. (See Royden 1968, ch. 3.)

20. $(\bar{a}_P, \bar{t}_P)$ need not be the only optimal tax for an economy that is partially closed at all ability levels in P. If there are others, then the particular optimal tax under consideration may be assumed to be arbitrarily chosen.

21. See Wilson (1979) for the details of the proof.

22. Given our continuity assumptions, this maximum can be shown to exist.

23. The latter result follows from the analysis of Itsumi (1974) and Romer (1975).

References

Bhagwati, J. N. 1976. The international brain drain and taxation: A survey of the issues. In *The Brain Drain and Taxation*, ed. J. Bhagwati. Amsterdam: North-Holland, pp. 3–27.

Bhagwati, J. N. 1977. The brain drain: International resource flow accounting, compensation, taxation and related proposals. Mimeo, MIT, Cambridge, Mass.

Itsumi, Y. 1974. Distributional effects of linear income tax schedules. *Review of Economic Studies* 41: 371–381.

Mirrlees, J. A. 1971. An exploration in the theory of optimal income taxation. *Review of Economic Studies* 38: 175–208.

Romer, T. 1975. Individual welfare, majority voting, and the properties of a linear income tax. *Journal of Public Economics* 4: 163–186.

Royden, H. L. 1968. *Real Analysis*. New York: Macmillan.

Sheshinski, E. 1972. The optimal linear income tax. *Review of Economic Studies* 39: 297–302.

Wilson, J. D. 1979. The effect of potential emigration on the optimal linear income tax. Unpublished dissertation, MIT, Cambridge, Mass.

5   Tax Policy in the Presence of Emigration

Jagdish N. Bhagwati and
Koichi Hamada

Introduction

Recent policy and theoretical discussions of the effects of highly skilled migration from the underdeveloped countries, the so-called brain drain, have focused on a proposal (Bhagwati 1972) to levy a (supplementary) income tax on those who migrate, the proceeds of such a tax to be transmitted to the developing country of origin or to developing countries *en bloc* for developmental spending.[1]

The welfare implications of such a tax were analyzed in an earlier paper of ours (Bhagwati and Hamada 1974) in the context of a model of the country of emigration, characterized by sticky wages and Harris-Todaro (1971) type of unemployment. In subsequent papers the tax has been analyzed also in the context of modified models, still incorporating the unemployment phenomena, by Rodriguez (1975) and McCulloch and Yellen (1975).[2] Essentially these models analyze the impact of the income tax on emigrants' incomes as arising primarily through the reduced differential between foreign (net of tax) and domestic salaries for the emigrant class of labor. This reduction in differential, in turn, reduces the expected and possibly the actual salaries in the home countries and thus generates consequences for education, unemployment, income, and income distribution (among the educated, uneducated, employed, and unemployed).

In this chapter we take an altogether different, public-finance-theoretic approach to the analysis of the income tax on emigrants. We use rather the framework of income taxation originated by Mirrlees (1971), and particularly in the form developed by Atkinson (1973). There the choice for individuals is the length of education, which affects their productivities after graduation so that education increases the earnings of individuals while simultaneously postponing the realization of these earnings. Atkinson studies, in the context of this model, the conflict between efficiency and equity: the income tax would redistribute income but also distort the educational choice and hence reduce efficiency.[3]

In this chapter we use this basic model to analyze the welfare impact of the possibility of emigration to earn incomes abroad and to assess the role of taxing migrants' incomes under alternative assumptions within the model.

In the next section we lay out the model with the required modification to consider foreign earnings by migrants. It also outlines three policy instruments—the income tax (on domestically earned incomes), an educational subsidy, and the income tax on migrants' foreign earnings—that are appropriate to analyze in the model, for reasons spelled out herein. Then we consider the use of only one policy instrument, the tax on nonmigrants' incomes, which throughout we will refer to simply as the "income tax."[4] In the following section, on the other hand, we consider the case in which the home country can use both the income tax *and* an income tax on migrants' incomes, simply called hereafter an "income tax on migrants."[5] In the fifth section we consider the case in which *all three* instruments are available to the home country. To close, we offer concluding observations, including the possible extension of our results for tax policy in relation to migrants.

The Model and Policy Instruments

The Model

Following Atkinson's model of optimal income taxation, we assume that differences exist in the innate ability of the individuals of the home country. Let n be the index of innate ability and S be the length of education that an individual undertakes. The innate ability in the initial population, before immigration possibility opens, is assumed to be distributed by the density function $p(n)$, such that

$$\int_{n_1}^{\infty} p(n)\, dn = 1,$$

where n_1 indicates the lower bound of the index of innate ability. Let the domestic earning of an individual be a function of his or her ability and length of education such that $f(n, S)$ indicates the resulting earnings.[6] Let $f^*(n, S)$ be the earnings if the individual migrates and therefore has foreign earnings instead, even though we assume that he or she was educated at home. These earnings are defined *gross* of income tax levied by the foreign country. Moreover these earning functions are assumed to be increasing functions of n and S, whereas the marginal productivity of S is assumed to be nonincreasing. That is to say,

$$f_n, f_n^* > 0, \qquad f_S, f_S^* > 0, \qquad f_{SS}, f_{SS}^* \leqq 0,$$

with subscripts denoting the partial derivatives with respect to the subscripted variables. We further assume, for simplicity, that the length of working period after education is identical at home and abroad and we designate it as R.

The decision whether or not to migrate is then assumed to depend on the comparison between the discounted earnings stream at home and that in the country of immigration. We assume that if the former exceeds the latter, individuals will remain at home; if the former is less than the latter, they will decide to migrate and work abroad instead.[7] Further assumptions on the migration decision will be spelled out in the next section.

The Policy Instruments

With this basic framework set up, we now list the three policy instruments that we consider in this chapter.

1. *Linear income tax.* Following Atkinson (1973), a linear income tax implies that the after-tax (nonmigrants') income is written in the form $[\alpha + \beta f]$, where $\alpha > 0$, $1 > \beta \geqq 0$, $(1 - \beta)$ is the marginal rate of taxation and α constitutes the uniform lump-sum payment to each individual.

2. *Subsidy to education.* Following Hamada (1974), who demonstrated that the use of an appropriate educational subsidy could virtually resolve the Atkinson conflict between equity and efficiency, an educational subsidy is considered as implying that the subsidy (G) is given directly to individuals enrolled in the educational system.

3. *Linear income tax on migrants.* Following Bhagwati, we consider a linear income tax on migrants so that their income after home-country tax can be written in the form $[\alpha^* + \beta^* f^*]$, with the asterisk indicating migrants. If we assume that the country of immigration levies its own income tax on the migrants' income such that $y^* = \gamma + \delta f^*$, where y^* is then the net immigration-country tax income of the migrant, and that the home country's income tax on migrants is levied on y^* so as to leave the migrant finally with net income equal to $[t + \tau y^*]$, then we must have $\alpha^* + \beta f^* = t + \tau(\gamma + \delta f^*)$ so that we obtain the following relationship between the tax parameters:[8]

$$\alpha^* = t + \tau\gamma; \qquad \beta^* = \tau\delta.$$

4. *The welfare criteria.* Next we note that three alternative welfare criteria might be deployed to analyze the outcomes under these alternative policy combinations. We generally deploy the criterion of the welfare impact of the migration on those left behind (TLBs), examining in turn their average income or utility and alternatively the minimum income among them à la Rawls (1971). Alternatively we could have examined the welfare impact on TLBs plus the migrants,[9] as discussed briefly in the concluding section.[10] Finally we could have taken a global or "internationalist" criterion embracing the nonmigrant nationals of the country of immigration as well in a two-country framework.

Income Tax in the Presence of Migration

We now consider the case, applicable to countries that neither subsidize education nor exercise their income tax jurisdiction over citizens working abroad, in which the home country has only an income tax (on domestic incomes) at its command. Precisely we will analyze the welfare impact on TLBs when, in the presence of the possibility of migration to work abroad, the income tax is levied at an optimal rate.[11] Our reference point will be the standard Atkinson solution in which the possibility of migration is not allowed, so that we will then be able to deduce what the introduction of the possibility of migration implies for the welfare of the TLBs and the associated optimal parameters/rates of income taxation.

Two Fundamental Individual Decisions

We begin by first indicating how the possibility of migration to earn foreign income will influence the two fundamental choices facing an individual in this modified Atkinson economy: the choice of the length of education and the decision to migrate or work at home. Note immediately, however, that in the Atkinson model without migration, efficiency is sacrificed for equity, the loss of efficiency taking the form of a reduced length of education because individuals are taxed on their (education-augmented) earnings. In our modified version with migration, on the other hand, the sacrifice of efficiency will occur on two dimensions: a distorted length of education by migrants and nonmigrants, *and* overmigration because migrants escape (whereas nonmigrants must pay) the income tax because the home country fails to exercise its tax jurisdiction over citizens working abroad.

Choice of Length of Education

Assuming throughout that education is always undertaken at home, we can see that an individual will maximize his or her lifetime income from domestic earnings, I_d, with respect to S (the length of education). Now

$$I_d = \int_S^{S+R} (\alpha + \beta f(n, S))e^{-it} \, dt$$

$$= A(\alpha + \beta f)e^{-iS},$$

(1)

where i is the rate of discount, R is the length of working period, and $A \equiv (1 - e^{-iR})/i$. Because we assume that R is constant,[12] A can also be regarded as a constant. Maximizing I_d with respect to S, we then obtain the first-order condition for a privately optimal decision:

$$A\{-i(\alpha + \beta f) + \beta f_S\} = 0.$$

(2)

The second-order condition is satisfied because of the assumption that $f_{SS} \leq 0$.

Similarly if the individual concentrates on foreign earnings as a migrant, he or she will maximize

$$I_f = \int_S^{S+R} (\alpha^* + \beta^* f^*(n, S))e^{-it} \, dt - Ce^{-iS}$$

$$= A(\alpha^* + \beta^* f^*)e^{-iS} - Ce^{-iS},$$

(1a)

where C is the lump-sum cost of migration (for example, transportation and the like) that is incurred at the time of departure, $f^*(n, S)$ is the foreign income to be earned before tax by an individual with index n, and $(\alpha^* + \beta^* f^*)$ is the foreign income of the migrant net of all income taxation. Recall from our earlier discussion of policy instruments that when the home country does not tax citizens abroad, α^* and β^* will equal the parameters of the income tax schedule of the *foreign* country, that is, $\alpha^* = \gamma$ and $\beta^* = \delta$.

The corresponding first-order condition for the migrants' privately optimal decision then is yielded by maximizing I_f with respect to S, and is

$$A\{-i(\alpha^* + \beta^* f^*) + \beta^* f_S^*\} + iC = 0.$$

(2a)

Decision to Migrate and Work Abroad

Next consider the problem of the choice between staying at home and working abroad. Potential migrants are assumed to decide whether or not to migrate by comparing the discounted value of income streams to be obtained from home and abroad. They decide to migrate therefore if the following expression is positive and not to migrate if it is nonpositive:

$$\Gamma(n) = \{A(\alpha^* + \beta^* f^*(n, S^*))e^{-iS^*} - Ce^{-iS^*}\} - A(\alpha + \beta f(n, S))e^{-iS}. \quad (3)$$

Here S and S^* indicate, respectively, the length of education given the opportunity to work at home or abroad.

To facilitate our analysis, we additionally assume now that corresponding to the parameters of the income tax schedules of the home country and the foreign country there is a *unique* value n^* of ability above which everyone will migrate.[13] Hence

$$\Gamma(n) > 0, \quad \text{if } n > n^*, \qquad \Gamma(n) \leqq 0, \quad \text{if } n \leqq n^*. \quad (4)$$

Evidently the value of n^* depends on the tax parameters, α and β, through their effect on realized discounted incomes. Moreover because β's effect on this income equals α's effect multiplied by $f(n, S)$, we can show that[14]

$$\frac{\partial n^*}{\partial \alpha} > 0; \qquad \frac{\partial n^*}{\partial \beta} = f(n^*, S)\frac{\partial n^*}{\partial \alpha} > 0. \quad (5)$$

Next, reflecting the reality that migration is feasible often for the skilled alone (thanks to the nature of immigration restrictions that are biased in favor of professional, skilled immigrants), we will assume that this critical value n^* is larger than the mean value $\bar{n}$ of the ability index, that is,

$$n^* > \bar{n}. \quad (6)$$

Finally, the reader may find it illuminating to consider the critical value n^* in figure 5.1, where I_d and I_f are drawn as functions of the ability index n and the given tax parameters. Our assumption underlying (4) implies that

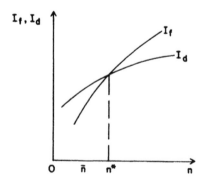

Figure 5.1

the I_f curve intersects the I_d curve from below only once, with the value of n at the intersection being n^*. I_d shifts upward with an increase in either α or β. However, the increase in the latter case is proportionally $f(n, S)$ times greater than in the former case. It follows that the value of n^* will increase with either α or β, as in (5).

Defining TLBs

Next, before we undertake our analysis of the nature of the optimal income tax schedule in the presence of migration, we must carefully consider the implication of the welfare criterion we plan to adopt, that is, the impact on TLBs. This is because one final complexity needs to be cleared up in discussing the TLBs in our modified Atkinson economy. The TLBs turn out in general to be a variable number of individuals because the critical value n^* that serves to divide the population in the home country into migrants and nonmigrants is a function of the tax parameters, α and β. Thus if we were to compare (say) the average welfare of TLBs under one set of (α, β) with the average welfare of TLBs under another set of (α, β), we would in fact be comparing different subsets of original population.[15] To avoid this difficulty, we resort to the following stratagem. We take a value N such that $N \leqq n^*$ for *all* n^*'s associated with the range of tax parameters,[16] α and β, that emerge in our analysis. We then redefine TLBs to include only those whose ability index lies in the interval $[n_1, N]$. This procedure clearly avoids the ambiguity concerning the size of the TLB population by making it invariant to changes in n^*.

The Formal Optimization Problem

We are now in a position to analyze the optimal choice of the tax parameters, α and β, in this modified, "open" Atkinson economy. Consider first the utilitarian criterion for judging welfare impact on TLBs. We then have the formal problem of maximizing[17]

$$\int_{n_1}^{N} U(I_d(n, \alpha, \beta))p(n)\, dn \tag{7}$$

subject to the budget constraint

$$\alpha \int_{n_1}^{n^*} p(n)\, dn = (1 - \beta) \int_{n_1}^{n^*} f(n, S)p(n)\, dn. \tag{8}$$

Because the general solution to this problem is difficult to secure, we assume the particular forms of earning function, distribution-of-ability function, and the utility function that were assumed by Atkinson (1973) in the original analysis without migration. Thus our earning function will be

$$f(n, S) = nS \qquad (9)$$

and we will use the Pareto distribution whose density function is written as

$$
\begin{aligned}
p(n) &= \mu n^{-\mu-1}, \quad \text{for } n \geq 1 \\
&= 0, \qquad \text{for } n < 1,
\end{aligned}
\qquad (10)
$$

where μ is parametrically assumed to exceed 2, and n_1 is assumed to equal unity.[18] It follows also from (6) that

$$n^* > \mu/(\mu - 1) = \bar{n}. \qquad (6')$$

The Optimal Choice of Tax Parameters

Our analysis then proceeds by first discussing the implications of individual optimizing behavior in this model, then deriving the feasibility locus between the tax parameters that this behavior implies in the presence of the restriction that the government's budget be balanced, and finally using this tax-feasibility locus to derive the optimal choice of the tax parameters, given the welfare criterion adopted.

Individual Optimization

The individual optimization implies that the nonmigrant will choose the length of education so as to maximize

$$I_d = A(\alpha + \beta nS)e^{-iS},$$

which, under the assumption that everybody spends some time on education, will result in

$$S = (1/i) - (\alpha/\beta n), \qquad (11)$$

$$nS = (n/i) - (\alpha/\beta), \qquad (12)$$

and

$$I_d = A\frac{\beta n}{i}\exp\left(\frac{\alpha i}{\beta n} - 1\right) = A\frac{\beta n}{ie}\exp\left(\frac{n_0}{n}\right), \qquad (13)$$

where $n_0 = \alpha i/\beta$.

Tax-Feasibility Loci

Next, given this individual-optimizing behavior, we can derive the *tax-feasibility locus*, reflecting additionally the government's budget constraint. Following Atkinson, we derive this for β and $n_0 = i\alpha/\beta$ (rather than α and β), where n_0 corresponds to the value of the ability index at which an individual ends his or her education. In a closed economy n_0 is smaller than unity if $\mu > 2$. This justifies the above assumption that everybody spends some time on education.[19] Thus we shall follow this assumption throughout the paper. Thus we note that the budget constraint (8) can be expressed as

$$\alpha \int_1^{n^*} p(n)\, dn = (1 - \beta) \int_1^{n^*} \left(\frac{n}{i} - \frac{\alpha}{\beta} \right) p(n)\, dn, \tag{8'}$$

where n^* itself is a function of α and β. Moreover, by substituting the Pareto distribution, we get

$$\alpha(1 - n^{*-\mu}) = (1 - \beta) \left\{ \frac{\bar{n}}{i}(1 - n^{*-\mu+1}) - \frac{\alpha}{\beta}(1 - n^{*-\mu}) \right\}.$$

Following Atkinson's procedures, we can then deduce the following, critical relationship:

$$\beta = 1 - \frac{n_0}{\bar{n}} \cdot \frac{1 - n^{*-\mu}}{1 - n^{*-\mu+1}} = 1 - \frac{n_0}{\bar{n}} h(n^*), \tag{14}$$

where $h(n^*) \equiv (1 - n^{*-\mu})/(1 - n^{*-\mu+1})$.

Now it is readily seen that if we were to "close" this economy and eliminate migration, $n^* \to \infty$ and $h(n^*)$ reduces to unity. The tax-feasibility loci for the "closed" (that is, without-migration) economy and for the "open" (that is, with-migration) economy, depicting the relationship between β ad n_0 from (14), are drawn in figure 5.2 with a straight line AC for the former case and with a curve AB for the latter.

Before proceeding to the last step of choosing the optimal tax parameters from this feasible set, however, we must investigate the properties of these loci. First, we must note that the closed-economy locus will be a straight line. Moreover because (as shown in the appendix, remark 1) $h(n^*) > 1$ for the relevant values of $n^* > 2$ and $\mu > 2$, the tax-feasibility locus for the open economy must lie below that for the closed economy (except when $n_0 = 0$).

Second, the slope of the tangent line for the tax-feasibility locus for the open economy can be shown everywhere to be steeper than the (unique) slope of the locus for the closed economy. That is to say (as per the

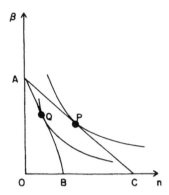

Figure 5.2

appendix, remark 3), we can show that

$$-\frac{d\beta}{dn_0} > \frac{1}{n}. \tag{15}$$

The Logarithmic Utility Function
Now we can turn to the optimal choice of the tax parameters, given these tax-feasibility loci. With Atkinson we will begin with the utilitarian welfare criterion, that is, we will maximize the average utility of TLBs.[20] Following Atkinson again, we will initially assume a specific utility function, that is, the logarithmic utility function. In this case the utilitarian objective is written as

$$\int_1^N \log\left\{\frac{\beta n}{ie}\exp\left(\frac{n_0}{n}\right)\right\} p(n)\,dn$$

$$= \text{const.} + \log\beta \int_1^N p(n)\,dn + n_0 \int_1^N n^{-1}p(n)\,dn. \tag{16}$$

The social indifference map for the population with ability between 1 and N can then be obtained by equating the above expression to a constant, and the indifference curves can then be drawn convex, as in figure 5.2. Moreover the slopes of the tangent lines to the indifference curves are identical for a given value of β or in other words the tangent lines are parallel along any horizontal line, because the slope

$$-\frac{d\beta}{dn_0} = \beta\frac{\int_1^N n^{-1}p(n)\,dn}{\int_1^N p(n)\,dn} \tag{17}$$

does not depend on the value of n_0.

We then arrive immediately at two important conclusions, noticing that the optimal tax parameters chosen by the TLBs will reflect the tangency of a social indifference curve with the tax-feasibility locus, that is, (15) with (17). First, the welfare level attained by the TLBs is strictly inferior to that in a closed economy, because the feasibility locus of an open economy is inside that for a closed economy.[21] Second, we see that the home country, pursuing the utilitarian objective on behalf of TLBs, will choose a *lower* marginal tax rate $(1 - \beta)$ if the economy is open rather than closed: the emigration possibility, in this sense, forces a less egalitarian policy on the home country. To see this, consider figure 5.2 again. If the economy is closed, point P will be chosen; if it is open, point Q will be chosen. Because the tangency slope of the indifference curves along the horizontal line through P is constant, and because the tangency slope of the opportunity curve for an open economy is steeper than for the closed economy as indicated by (15), the vertical coordinate of Q must be larger than that of P. Because the marginal rate of taxation equals $(1 - \beta)$, this amounts to choosing a lower marginal tax rate if the economy is open.

The Isoelastic Utility Function
We turn next to the more general case of an isoelastic utility function:

$$U = \frac{l_d^{1-\rho}}{1 - \rho}, \qquad \rho \geq 0, \qquad \rho \neq 1, \tag{18}$$

where ρ indicates the degree of inequality-aversion of society and, as is well known, this utility function converges to a logarithmic function when ρ approaches unity. The welfare of TLBs can then be expressed as

$$W = \frac{A'}{1 - \rho} \int_1^N \beta^{1-\rho} n^{1-\rho} \exp\left(\frac{(1 - \rho)n_0}{n}\right) p(n) \, dn, \tag{19}$$

where $A' = $ const. The marginal rate of substitution between β and n_0 can then be written as

$$-\frac{d\beta}{dn_0}$$

$$= \beta \int_1^N n^{-\rho} \exp\left(\frac{(1 - \rho)n_0}{n}\right) p(n) \, dn \bigg/ \left[\int_1^N n^{1-\rho} \exp\left(\frac{(1 - \rho)n_0}{n}\right) p(n) \, dn \right]. \tag{20}$$

Along a horizontal line, such that β is constant, this absolute slope of the indifference curve can be shown to be an increasing function of n_0 if $\rho < 1$, and a decreasing function of n_0 if $\rho > 1$ (cf. the appendix, remark 4). This has immediate consequences for the optimal choice of the tax parameters in our open economy vis-à-vis the closed economy.

Thus if $\rho < 1$, exactly the same argument as for the case of the logarithmic utility function applies and the open economy will be characterized by the choice of a lower marginal tax rate. (Note that when $\rho = 0$, we have the linear utilitarian criterion and we are maximizing average *income*.)

On the other hand if $\rho > 1$, that is, the inequality-aversion exceeds that in the logarithmic case, the tangency slopes to the indifference curves become steeper as one moves horizontally to the left of P. Hence we cannot assert now that the marginal rate of income taxation is necessarily less for the open economy.[22]

This paradoxical possibility when $\rho > 1$, however, can be shown to be ruled out in the extreme, Rawlsian case where, as is well known, we are dealing with the limiting case of the utilitarian welfare criterion when $\rho \to \infty$. In this extreme case of inequality-aversion, in which we maximize the discounted income of the individual with the lowest ability, we can write this discounted income because $n_1 = 1$, as

$$I_d = A \frac{\beta}{ie} e^{n_0},$$

so that we have the indifference curve

$$\beta e^{n_0} = \text{const.}, \tag{21}$$

with a marginal rate of substitution $-d\beta/dn_0 = \beta$, which is independent of n_0. Hence the argument can proceed exactly as with the logarithmic utilitarian case (that is, $\rho = 1$), and therefore the open economy would be characterized by a *lower* marginal tax rate.

Three Major Propositions

We can therefore summarize our results:

Proposition 1. The welfare level of the TLBs is definitely inferior in an open, via-à-vis the closed, economy.

Proposition 2. If the individual utility functon is isoelastic with $\rho \leqq 1$— the logarithmic function, with $\rho = 1$, and the linear function, with $\rho = 0$, being two special cases—then the criterion of maximizing the welfare of TLBs will lead to choice of a reduced marginal tax rate for an open economy.

Proposition 3. (1) If, however, $\rho > 1$, one cannot preclude the possibility that the open economy is characterized by an increased marginal tax rate. (2) For the extreme Rawlsian case, where $\rho \to \infty$, the open economy, however, will be characterized by a lower marginal tax rate.

Efficiency Implications

Our analysis has focused thus far on the effect of emigration on the choice of the tax parameters and the associated welfare impact on TLBs when the economy is open. In doing this we demonstrated the deterioration in the tax feasibility locus that the migration possibility entails. Now, however, we shift our focus to a related but distinct question: How precisely does efficiency get compromised in our open Atkinson economy?[23]

We must distinguish between *domestic* (that is, home-country) and *global* efficiency. By the former, we will mean the equalization of the relevant marginal rates of substitution (MRS) within the home country. By the latter, we will mean the equalization of the MRS within the home country and between the home and foreign countries.

But we will define global efficiency in a *restricted* fashion: the foreign country will be assumed to be behaving optimally vis-à-vis its own population, setting its own tax parameters correspondingly. Global efficiency will then be defined purely in the sense that the *home-country* migrants' decision to migrate must reflect the comparison of their gross, unadjusted productivities/returns.

Moreover we must note that domestic efficiency is not tantamount to maximization of domestic income because the latter would also reflect the distribution of world income among the two countries.

Domestic Efficiency
Now domestic efficiency requires the individual nonmigrant to choose the socially optimal amount of education. The corresponding first-order condition, necessary for a maximum, is yielded by maximizing[24]

$$\int_{S}^{S+R} f(n, S)e^{-it}\, dt = Afe^{-iS},$$

which yields

$$A\{-if + f_S\} = 0. \tag{22}$$

This condition is evidently not met in our Atkinson economy in which, it will be recalled, individuals optimize so as to satisfy

$A\{-i(\alpha + \beta f) + \beta f_S\} = 0.$ (2)

The equality of (22) and (2) would require that $\alpha = 0$ and $\beta = 1$, that is, the absence of income taxation!

If we consider next the migrants' income as part of domestic income, there is a similar failure of equality between the migrants' choice of the individually optimal length of education and the *socially* optimal choice thereof. The former will imply

$A\{-i(\alpha^* + \beta^* f^*) + \beta^* f_S^*\} + iC = 0,$ (2a)

whereas the latter will require

$A\{-if^* + f_S^*\} + iC = 0,$ (22a)

and (22a) and (2a) will not be equal unless $\alpha^* = 0$ and $\beta^* = 1$.

Global Efficiency
In addition to satisfying the preceding two first-order conditions, (22) and (22a), for a globally optimal choice (in the restricted sense as defined) of the educational length, global efficiency further requires that the decision to migrate depend on whether the following expression is positive or not:

$$\Gamma(n) = \int_{\hat{S}^*}^{\hat{S}^*+R} f^*(n, \hat{S}^*)e^{-it}\,dt - Ce^{-i\hat{S}^*} - \int_{\hat{S}}^{\hat{S}+R} f(n, \hat{S})e^{-it}\,dt$$

$$= \{Af^*(n, \hat{S}^*) - C\}e^{-i\hat{S}^*} - Af(n, \hat{S})e^{-i\hat{S}},$$ (23)

where $\hat{S}$ and $\hat{S}^*$ are the values of S and S^* satisfying (22) and (22a). However, the actual decision to migrate is made depending instead on whether (3) is positive or nonpositive. Unless therefore coincidentally $\beta = \beta^* = 1$ and $\alpha = \alpha^*$, the two conditions will be different. With only domestic income tax available as a policy instrument, the home country cannot affect the values of α^* and β^*, which are solely determined by the foreign government. Thus this third and final requirement for (restricted) global efficiency will not be met either.

Income Tax and Income Tax on Migrants in the Presence of Migration

Consider now a modification to the Atkinson, open economy. In addition to the (domestic) income tax, let us now utilize also an income tax on migrants. The effect of this is essentially to close the economy from the viewpoint of the budget constraint. This, however, will not restore in

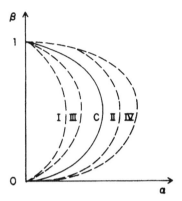

Figure 5.3

general the tax-feasibility locus of the closed economy without migration *even if* the income tax is uniformly applied to nonmigrants' domestic incomes and migrants' net-of-foreign-tax foreign incomes.

As long as (some) migrants' net-of-foreign-tax incomes exceed what the migrants could earn domestically corresponding to any educational level, this is tantamount to keeping the economy closed to migration but increasing the productivity of these "migrants." Hence evidently the tax-feasibility locus of the open economy with such utilization of the added policy instrument constituted by the income tax on migrants will dominate that for the closed economy confined only to the use of the (domestic) income tax, the latter in turn dominating of course the tax-feasibility locus for the open economy confined to the (domestic) income tax.

In figure 5.3 this is illustrated by the numbered tax-feasibility loci in terms of α and β referring to the open economies and the locus C referring to the closed economy. Locus *II* is the locus for the open economy with income tax on migrants' net-of-foreign-tax incomes at the same rates as the tax on nonmigrants' domestic incomes (assuming that these incomes exceed what the migrants would have earned (gross) domestically), that is, when

$$t = \alpha \quad \text{and} \quad \tau = \beta$$

in terms of (5). Locus *I*, on the other hand, is the tax-feasibility locus when the open economy cannot use the income tax on migrants. In fig. 5.3, locus *II* ⊃ locus *C* ⊃ locus *I*.

If the home country were to use "prohibitive" tax rates on migrants, *t* and *τ*, so that it pays migrants to stay home, we would revert of course to the closed-economy locus *C*. On the other hand the home country could set these tax rates t and τ "monopolistically" so as to extract the entire rent, if any, from the migrants' working abroad rather than at home, in which case the corresponding tax feasibility locus IV will be the "best" one; but it is likely to run afoul of explicit human-rights conventions.

On the other hand choosing the tax parameters t and τ at values that substantially reduce the migrants' tax liability to the home country will result in a shrinking-in of the tax-feasibility locus. In the limiting case of zero income tax on migrants it will revert to locus I, but will otherwise dominate it. However, it may be dominated in turn by the closed-economy locus, as illustrated in figure 5.3, where locus $I \subset$ locus $III \subset$ locus C.

Although all this is perfectly clear, it is not possible, without added restrictions, to say anything more than that the availability of the income tax on migrants generally permits the tax-feasibility locus to be improved over that in the open economy without this added policy instrument. Hence whether one maximizes TLB welfare more generally or takes the extreme Rawlsian case, it would be possible to improve welfare with the use of the income tax on migrants.[25]

At the same time it is important to note that the income tax on migrants can be used to correct the choice on migration to fulfill the global-efficiency requirement that the migrants choose to migrate when their gross, unadjusted incomes abroad exceed the gross, unadjusted incomes at home. However, it cannot obviously be used to correct the inefficiency of the choice regarding the length of education (which requires the use of the educational subsidy, as discussed in the preceding section).

All Three Policy Instruments: Global Efficiency and TLB Welfare Maximization

Now we know from the preceding section that an income tax on migrants can be used to correct the choice on migration but cannot correct for the inefficiency in the choice of educational length as required for domestic efficiency. At the same time it is evident that the use of an educational subsidy can help achieve domestic efficiency, but cannot correct for the socially inefficient (from the global viewpoint in the restricted sense discussed previously) choice on migration. It should be evident, therefore, that the use of both the educational subsidy and the income tax on migrants ought to enable us to achieve domestic and global efficiency.

An interesting problem for us to analyze, therefore, is the characterization of the optimal levels of these policy instruments. Moreover it would be important to ask whether, if the educational subsidy and the income tax on migrants were set in this way so as to achieve domestic and global efficiency, the tax-feasibility locus for this open Atkinson economy would lie outside the tax-feasibility locus for the open Atkinson economy which cannot use these policy instruments at all. In fact it will. Therefore, we can argue that the use of the income tax, the income tax on migrants, and the educational subsidy at appropriate values can both achieve domestic and global efficiency and improve the welfare of TLBs, vis-à-vis an economy that uses only the income tax and experiences migration. Indeed, we can go further and show that this global efficiency solution will also be characterized by virtual, full equity *and* will in fact be the first-best solution for TLB welfare.

Achieving Global Efficiency

Thus consider first the achievement of (restricted) global efficiency by a suitable use of the three policy instruments, by examining the three choices in our model: the choice of the educational lengths for nonmigrants and migrants, respectively, and the decision to migrate.

Choice of the Lengths of Education
As for the educational choice of the *nonmigrant*, it is easy to see that the first-order condition for a private maximum will be give by

$$A\{-i(\alpha + \beta f) + \beta f_s\} + G = 0, \tag{24}$$

as shown by Hamada (1974) for a closed economy, and where G is the educational subsidy. On the other hand we get from (22) the first-order condition for a social maximum as $A\{-if + f_s\} = 0$. Hence equality between (22) and (24) implies an educational subsidy such that

$$G = Ai\alpha = \alpha(1 - e^{-iR}). \tag{25}$$

By a similar reasoning, we can deduce the educational subsidy for the migrants. Thus the private-maximum first-order condition for potential migrants is readily shown to be

$$A\{-i(\alpha^* + \beta^* f^*) + \beta^* f_s^*\} + iC + G = 0, \tag{24a}$$

and for a social maximum it is

$$A\{-if^* + f_s^*\} + iC = 0, \tag{22a}$$

so that reconciling (24a) and (22a) yields the educational subsidy for the potential migrants as

$$G = \alpha^*(1 - e^{-iR}) - (1 - \beta^*)iC. \tag{25a}$$

The educational subsidy, however, must evidently be given uniformly to all individuals. Therefore (25) and (25a) should be equated so that we must have

$$\alpha^* = \alpha + \frac{i}{1 - e^{-iR}}(1 - \beta^*)C = \alpha + \frac{(1 - \beta^*)}{A(R)}C, \tag{26}$$

that is, if the migration cost C is negligible, the same intercept must be chosen for the (domestic) income tax, and the income tax on migrants' schedules.

Decision to Migrate

There remains now the problem of the choice between staying at home and going abroad. One therefore has to choose the tax scheme in such a way as to ensure the socially efficient choice in this regard. In fact we shall prove that the linear income tax on foreign income combined with educational subsidy and the domestic income tax, satisfies this requirement provided that β^* is set equal to β.

Now the condition for the globally efficient choice for deciding to emigrate is

$$\Gamma = \left[\int_{S^*}^{S^*+R} f^* e^{-it}\, dt - Ce^{-iS^*} \right] - \int_{S}^{S+R} fe^{-it}\, dt > 0, \tag{26'}$$

where both S and S^* are chosen to satisfy the marginal condition for securing the efficiency of the length of education. On the other hand individuals will migrate according to the (private) condition

$$\Gamma = \int_{S^*}^{S^*+R} (\alpha^* + \beta^* f^*)e^{-it}\, dt - Ce^{-iS^*} + G \int_{0}^{S^*} e^{-it}\, dt$$

$$- \left[\int_{S}^{S+R} (\alpha + \beta f)e^{-it}\, dt + G \int_{0}^{S} e^{-it}\, dt \right] > 0,$$

which, in view of (26), equals

$$\alpha \left[\int_{S^*}^{S^*+R} e^{-it}\, dt - \int_{S}^{S+R} e^{-it}\, dt \right]$$

$$+ \left[\int_{S}^{S^*+R} \frac{(1 - \beta^*)}{A} Ce^{-it}\, dt - (1 - \beta^*)Ce^{-iS^*} \right]$$

$$+ G\left[\int_0^{\hat{S}^*} e^{-it}\,dt - \int_0^{\hat{S}} e^{-it}\,dt\right]$$

$$+ \beta^*\left[\int_{\hat{S}^*}^{\hat{S}^*+R} f^* e^{-it}\,dt - Ce^{-i\hat{S}^*}\right] - \beta\int_{\hat{S}}^{\hat{S}+R} fe^{-it}\,dt > 0.$$

It is easy to see, however, that the second bracket vanishes. Moreover if we substitute here $G = \alpha(1 - e^{-iR})$, it can be seen that

$$\alpha\left[\int_{\hat{S}^*}^{\hat{S}^*+R} e^{-it}\,dt - \int_{\hat{S}}^{\hat{S}+R} e^{-it}\,dt\right] + G\left[\int_0^{\hat{S}^*} e^{-it}\,dt - \int_0^{\hat{S}} e^{-it}\,dt\right] = 0.$$

Therefore the criterion for the private decision on migration reduces to

$$\Gamma = \beta^*\left[\int_{\hat{S}^*}^{\hat{S}^*+R} f^* e^{-it}\,dt - Ce^{-i\hat{S}^*}\right] - \beta\int_{\hat{S}}^{\hat{S}+R} fe^{-it}\,dt > 0. \tag{27}$$

Therefore, if and only if β^* is set equal to β, permitting the fulfillment of (26) and (27) simultaneously, will the criterion for the optimal decision for emigration be satisfied.

The equalization of (26) and (27) therefore yields the condition for securing the globally efficient choice on the decision to migrate:

$$\beta = \beta^*. \tag{28}$$

Properties of the Globally Efficient Solution

Therefore setting the three policy instruments at appropriate values, that is, those that satisfy (26) and (28), will ensure global efficiency in our open Atkinson economy.

At the same time it is immediately obvious that setting $\beta = \beta^*$ virtually close to zero would again ensure, as argued by Hamada (1974), that full equity would be achieved alongside domestic (and, now restricted global) efficiency. Therefore we have a generalization of the closed-economy Hamada (1974) result to an open economy, thanks to the availability of one more instrument (that is, the income tax on migrants) when the economy is opened. Thus we can conclude

Proposition 4. By a combined, appropriate use of the (domestic) income tax, the income tax on migrants and the educational subsidy, (restricted) global efficiency can be achieved while the home country achieves both domestic efficiency and "almost" full equity. This requires that the marginal rate of taxation for the two income taxes be identical and virtually equal to unity, whereas the intercept for the income tax on migrants' schedule will differ from that for the (domestic) income tax schedule by virtue of the migration cost.

Now it is obvious that the tax feasibility locus for this globally efficient open economy will lie outside that for the inefficient open economy that cannot use the educational subsidy and the income tax on migrants, so that TLBs ought to *improve* their welfare. But we can go beyond the obvious and show something much stronger, namely, our generalized solution of efficiency *plus* virtually full equity constitutes also the first-best, that is, the welfare-*maximizing*, solution for TLBs. This is because global efficiency implies that world output, produced by both TLBs and migrants, is maximized provided that there is no distortion abroad. At the same time, $\beta^* \to 0$ implies that maximal revenue is being collected by the home country (α^* cannot be reduced below α without *both* disrupting the efficiency condition *and* eliminating migration altogether and therefore resulting in a closed economy, given $\beta = \beta^* \to 0$). Therefore TLB welfare ought to be at a maximum in this solution. Thus we can conclude

Proposition 5. The solution in proposition 4 is, at the same time, the welfare-maximizing first-best solution for TLBs.

Note finally that β^* is the marginal slope of the disposable income of the migrants *net* of both foreign-country and the home-country income taxes. How then are β and β^* to be equated by the home country given the fact that the foreign-country tax schedule is to be considered as exogenously determined? This equality can be achieved simply in the following way. First, let the home country extend its (domestic) income tax schedule to migrants. Second, as per double-taxation-avoidance arrangements, let the tax payments to the foreign country be made deductible as tax credits from tax liability to the home country. Third, to allow for the migration cost (C) complication already noted, let amount $(1 - \beta^*)iC$ be credited also against the tax liability of the migrants to the home country. The satisfaction of the first two conditions will then ensure that $\beta = \beta^*$, and satisfaction of the third will ensure that the required relationship between α and α^* (in (26)) will also be satisfied, *provided* the marginal income tax rate for the foreign country is less than that of the home country.[26,27]

Concluding Observations

Our main objective in this chapter has been to initiate a formal public-finance-theoretic analysis of an important policy issue that has come to attract attention from policymakers: namely, the exercise of home-country income tax jurisdiction over nationals working abroad.

Our main results have been developed by assuming that the home country maximized the welfare of TLBs. This social objective may appear reasonable to policymakers even though nationals who work abroad are part of the national population, especially if TLBs are at the lower end of unadjusted income distribution and the migrants at the upper end. Our welfare criterion can be regarded as an extension of the Rawls criterion, not applied to the individual with minimum income but to a predetermined band of individuals who are in lower income brackets. On the other hand one may well want to ask what happens to the migrants' welfare in our exercises in this chapter since policies that improve the welfare of the TLBs may well be worsening that of the migrants, resulting in a trade-off that may need to be addressed in policymaking.[28] To adapt our analysis to this newly defined objective function, which extends over the augmented and full set of nationals, we do not need to amend the derivation of the tax-feasibility loci in the analysis but rather to amend the (indirect) social indifference curves defined on the tax parameters. We hope to return to this task in another paper.

Appendix

This appendix is designed to prove some properties of the $h(n)$ function, the tax-feasibility locus, and the social welfare function. These properties are used in the text, as noted at appropriate places. We define, as in the text,

$$h(n^*) \equiv (1 - n^{*-\mu})/(1 - n^{*-\mu+1}).$$

Remark 1.   If $n^* > 1$, and $\mu > 1$, then $h(n^*) > 1$.

Proof.

$$h(n^*) - 1 = \frac{n^{*-\mu+1} - n^{*-\mu}}{1 - n^{*-\mu+1}} > 0, \quad \text{for } n^* > 1.$$

Remark 2.   If $n^* > \mu/(\mu - 1)$, then $h'(n^*) < 0$.

Proof.

$$h'(n^*) = \frac{-(\mu - 1)n^{*-\mu-1}\left\{n^* - \dfrac{\mu}{\mu - 1}\right\} - n^{*-2\mu}}{(1 - n^{*-\mu+1})^2} < 0.$$

Remark 3. The slope of tangent line to the opportunity locus expressed by (14) in the text is steeper than $1/\bar{n}$ as long as the opportunity locus is downward-sloping.

Proof. Totally differentiating (14), taking account of the fact that n^* depends on β and n_0, one obtains

$$d\beta = -\frac{dn_0}{\bar{n}} h(n^*) - \frac{n_0}{\bar{n}} h'(n^*)\left(\frac{\partial n^*}{\partial \beta} d\beta + \frac{\partial n^*}{\partial n_0} dn_0\right).$$

Therefore

$$\frac{d\beta}{dn_0} = -\frac{1}{n}\left\{h(n^*) + n_0 h'(n^*)\frac{\partial n^*}{\partial n_0}\right\} \bigg/ \left\{1 + \frac{n_0}{\bar{n}} h'(n^*)\frac{\partial n^*}{\partial \beta}\right\}. \tag{A1}$$

When the opportunity locus is downward-sloping, the denominator in the brace is positive. (If the denominator changes its sign from positive to negative, then the opportunity locus becomes tangent to a vertical line at some value of β and tilts into an upward-sloping locus. However, this upward-sloping locus does not interest us because the point on this portion of locus can never be efficient.)

On the other hand, from (11), (13), and the definition of n_0, one obtains

$$I_d = \frac{An}{ie} \beta \exp\left(\frac{n_0}{n}\right).$$

It is easy to notice that a marginal change in n_0 shifts the I_d schedule just β/n^* times as the change of β shifts it. Therefore, by applying the same reasoning as used to derive (5) (cf. fig. 5.1), one obtains

$$\frac{\partial n^*}{\partial n_0} = \frac{\beta}{n^*}\frac{\partial n^*}{\partial \beta}. \tag{A2}$$

Therefore

$$\left\{h(n^*) + n_0 h'(n^*)\frac{\partial n}{\partial n_0}\right\} \bigg/ \left\{1 + \frac{n_0}{\bar{n}} h'(n^*)\frac{\partial n^*}{\partial \beta}\right\}$$

$$= h(n^*)\left\{1 + \frac{\beta}{n^* h(n^*)}\left(n_0 h'(n^*)\frac{\partial n^*}{\partial \beta}\right)\right\} \bigg/ \left\{1 + \frac{1}{n}\left(n_0 h'(n^*)\frac{\partial n^*}{\partial \beta}\right)\right\}. \tag{A3}$$

Because $h(n^*) > 1$, $\beta < 1$, and $n^* > \bar{n}$, we get

$$\frac{\beta}{n^* h(n^*)} < \frac{1}{\bar{n}}. \tag{A4}$$

Because $n_0 h'(n^*)(\partial n^*/\partial\beta)$ is negative, and because the denominator is assumed to be positive, one can conclude from (A4) that the right side of (A3) is larger than $h(n^*)$, because the brace in the numerator is larger than the brace in the denominator, which itself is positive. Therefore we can conclude from (A1) and (A3) that

$$\frac{d\beta}{dn_0} < -\frac{1}{\bar{n}},$$

which is in fact (15).

Remark 4. The absolute slope of the indifference curve is an increasing function of n_0 along a horizontal line if $\rho < 1$, and a decreasing function of n_0 if $\rho > 1$.

Proof. The Schwarz inequality says (see, for example, Royden 1968, p. 210): Let g_1 and g_2 be integrable functions with respect to dF. Then

$$\left|\int g_1\, dF\right| \cdot \left|\int g_2\, dF\right| \geq \left|\int g_1 g_2\, dF\right|^2.$$

Let us write, for economy of space

$$\int_1^N n^{-\rho} \exp[(1-\rho)n_0/n]p(n)\, dn \equiv \int n^{-\rho},$$

$$\int_1^N n^{1-\rho} \exp[(1-\rho)n_0/n]p(n)\, dn \equiv \int n^{1-\rho},$$

and so forth.
 Then

$$\frac{\partial}{\partial n_0}\left[-\frac{d\beta}{dn_0}\right] = \beta\frac{\partial}{\partial n_0}[\int n^{-\rho}/\int n^{1-\rho}]$$

$$= \beta(1-\rho)\frac{[\int n^{-1-\rho}][\int n^{1-\rho}] - [\int n^{-\rho}]^2}{[\int n^{1-\rho}]^2}$$

$$\begin{cases} > 0, & \text{if } \rho < 1, \\ < 0, & \text{if } \rho > 1. \end{cases}$$

This is because by the Schwarz inequality applied to $dF = \exp[(1-\rho)n_0/n]p(n)\, dn$

$$[\int n^{-1-\rho}][\int n^{1-\rho}] \geq [\int n^{-\rho}]^2$$

and the equality does not hold because the integrands are not proportional to each other.

Notes

This paper is a significantly revised and augmented version of an earlier, unpublished paper (Bhagwati and Hamada 1974). Thanks are due to NSF Grant no. SCS-80-25401, to the Ford Foundation and to the German Marshall Fund for financial support of the research underlying this chapter. The stimulating atmosphere at the SSRC Workshop on Public Economics at Warwick, England, 1978, also must be gratefully acknowledged by Koichi Hamada. We are also indebted to Peter Diamond, William Baumol, Assar Lindbeck, John Wilson, and other participants at the New Delhi Conference in January, 1981, for their helpful suggestions. The excellent comments of two referees have led to substantial improvements in this chapter.

1. This tax proposal has been explored from the viewpoint of its economic rationale, its revenue implications, and its legal (constitutional, tax, and human rights) implications by Bhagwati and Partington (1976). This chapter can be seen as developing a yet further rationale for such a tax (in the version where the tax proceeds accrue to the country of emigration).

2. For a review of these and other brain-drain models in recent theoretical writings, see Bhagwati and Rodriguez 1975.

3. Note that lump-sum taxation to redistribute income is not being permitted; if it were, the conflict between efficiency and equity naturally would disappear! The conflict between efficiency and equity in the presence of factor mobility has also been mentioned by Cooper (1973, p. 54).

4. Our model does not allow for nonmigrants to earn foreign income or for migrants to earn domestic income, for simplicity. Therefore an income tax on nonmigrants' income is the same as an income tax on domestically earned income.

5. The United States, the Philippines, and (in theory) Mexico tax citizens who work abroad, regardless of length of residence or legal migration status. Therefore the "income tax on migrants" discussed in this chapter is a well-established, international tax-legal policy instrument as long as migrants do not change their nationality. Under *current* international practices, therefore, if migrants change their nationality, the "income tax on migrants" would become an infeasible instrument. For a lucid tax-legal discussion of these issues, see the valuable papers by Oldman and Pomp (1975, 1977, 1979).

6. George Psacharopoulos has pointed out to us that although it is plausible to write earnings as a function of innate ability, the econometric attempts at isolating this relationship have not been particularly successful so far.

7. We could have assumed instead that only a fraction of those who could earn more abroad would choose to migrate, with this fraction being an increasing

function of the difference between income earned by migrating and domestic income. However, our assumption simplifies the analysis without sacrificing anything critical.

8. Note that the linearity of the income tax on migrants is assumed here, parallel to Atkinson's income tax, but is not a necessary feature of the proposal in Bhagwati 1972.

9. This criterion would seem more consistent with the view that many migrants do not change their nationalities today and hence are, from a legal *and* sociological viewpoint, members of the home country (cf. Bhagwati 1979).

10. Wilson's illuminating chapter 4, based on the leisure-work choice model of Mirrlees (1971), studies the effect of migration on the optimal linear tax rate, assuming that the only policy instrument is the income tax (on domestic residents).

11. The optimality will reflect the precise choice of the objective function of course.

12. Alternatively we may assume that the total length $(S + R)$ of life, instead of R, is constant. However, this does not change our main results, as indicated by Hamada (1974). In fact it even simplifies some expressions. For example, the optimal subsidy formula becomes $G = \alpha$ instead of $G = Ai\alpha$.

13. The analysis of the more general possibility where migration is feasible over the entire interval of ability endowment is considerably more complex (cf. chapter 4).

14. With given values α^* and β^*, n^* is determined by

$$I_d(\alpha, \beta, n^*) - I_f(\alpha^*, \beta^*, n^*) = 0.$$

Therefore

$$\frac{\partial I_d}{\partial \alpha} \cdot d\alpha + \frac{\partial I_d}{\partial \beta} \cdot d\beta + \frac{\partial I_d}{\partial n^*} \cdot dn^* - \frac{\partial I_f}{\partial n^*} \cdot dn^* = 0.$$

Thus

$$\frac{\partial n^*}{\partial \alpha}\bigg|_{\beta=\text{const.}} = \frac{\partial I_d}{\partial \alpha} \bigg/ \left\{\frac{\partial I_f}{\partial n^*} - \frac{\partial I_d}{\partial n^*}\right\}$$

$$\frac{\partial n^*}{\partial \beta}\bigg|_{\alpha=\text{const.}} = \frac{\partial I_d}{\partial \beta} \bigg/ \left\{\frac{\partial I_f}{\partial n^*} - \frac{\partial I_d}{\partial n^*}\right\}.$$

Now from the expressions of I_d and I_f we have

$$\frac{\partial I_d}{\partial \beta} \bigg/ \frac{\partial I_d}{\partial \alpha} = f(n, S).$$

Moreover because the assumption underlying relation (4) presupposes that

$[(\partial I_f/\partial n) - (\partial I_d/\partial n)]$ is positive in the neighborhood of n^*, it follows that both $\partial n^*/\partial \alpha$ and $\partial n^*/\partial \beta$ are positive.

15. And we would have an ill-defined problem! (Cf. Hamada 1975.)

16. This requirement is in fact stronger than needed. If we solve the problem following the procedure discussed below for an arbitrary N, and if the resulting optimal tax parameters α and β do not give rise to n^* smaller than N, then our analysis is completely legitimate.

17. Recall that $I_d(n, \alpha, \beta)$ is the discounted value of income stream for individuals with ability n and with disposable income $\{\alpha + \beta f(n, S)\}$.

18. So long as the Pareto distribution is assumed, the restriction on n_1 does not change the value of the optimal tax rate in a closed economy. We owe this observation to Tony Atkinson. (Cf. Atkinson 1973.)

19. See Atkinson 1973 (p. 100 n2). Because the optimal n_0 in an open model is smaller then the optimal n_0 in the corresponding closed model (cf. fig. 5.2, and proposition 3(2)), we can justify this assumption in an open model as well.

20. In Atkinson's analysis the economy is closed of course. Our analysis of the open economy, on the other hand, applied the utilitarian criterion to TLBs alone.

21. This was shown also by Hamada (1975).

22. The deviation from $1/n$ of the slope of the tax feasibility locus is independent of the deviation of the tangency slope of indifference curves from the slope at P. Therefore one may get the paradoxical situation in the text if $h(n^*)$ is very close to unity, that is, the possibility of emigration is very small.

23. This question is pertinent to our analysis in the section on global efficiency and TLB welfare maximization.

24. For the individual productivity maximization over time to coincide with the socially optimal choice, we need to use the correct discount rate. As discussed by Hamada (1972), the correct discount rate should be the biological rate of interest, that is, the growth rate of the population (plus the positive rate of labor-augmenting technical progress).

25. We have therefore not elevated this simple but important conclusion into a proposition in the text. Note also that we *could* say something more if we were to attempt a solution to the very difficult analytical problem of choosing α, β, t, and τ so as to secure the best tax feasibility locus in the "monopolistic" case discussed in the text.

26. As Hamada (1978) has noted, this proviso is generally satisfied for migration from the developing to the developed countries. The extension of domestic tax schedules to migrants, with double-taxation relief, was proposed there as a device to restore global efficiency in a two-country world.

27. Of course one cannot actually *recommend* this first-best solution without reservations. In the real world the threshold of perception or incentives may be quite high. Moreover the administrative cost of redistribution may not be negligible. Our analysis in this section only shows that there is a *structure* implied in the model of income taxation deployed such that the conflict between equity and efficiency can be undone by a combination of proper instruments.

28. The delicate issue of comparing the welfare of different groups of people, in an environment where equity and efficiency considerations interact, is beautifully analyzed in chapter 7 by Baumol.

References

Atkinson, A. B. 1973. How progressive should income tax be? In *Essays in Modern Economics*, ed. M. Parkin. London: Longman.

Bhagwati, J. 1972. The United States in the Nixon era: The end of innocence. *Daedalus.*

Bhagwati, J., ed. 1976. *The Brain Drain and Taxation: Theory and Empirical Analysis.* Amsterdam: North Holland.

Bhagwati, J. 1979. International migration of the highly skilled: Economics, ethics and taxes. *Third World Quarterly* 1: 17–30.

Bhagwati, J., and K. Hamada. 1974. The brain drain, international integration of markets for professionals and unemployment: A theoretical analysis. *Journal of Development Economics* 1; reprinted in revised version in Bhagwati (1976).

Bhagwati, J., and M. Partington, eds. 1976. *Taxing the Brain Drain: A Proposal.* Amsterdam: North-Holland.

Bhagwati, J., and C. Rodriguez. 1975. Welfare-theoretical analyses of the brain drain. *Journal of Development Economics* 2; reprinted in Bhagwati (1976).

Cooper, P. N. 1973. Economic Mobility and National Economic Policy. Stockholm: Almquist and Wicksell International.

Hamada, K. 1972. Lifetime equity and dynamic efficiency on the balanced growth path. *Journal of Public Economics* 1: 379–396.

Hamada, K. 1974. Income taxation and educational subsidy. *Journal of Public Economics* 3: 145–158.

Hamada, K. 1975. Efficiency, equity, income taxation and the brain drain: A second best argument. *Journal of Development Economics* 2: 281–287.

Hamada, K. 1978. Taxing the brain drain: A global point of view. Ch. 5. In *The New International Economic Order: The North-South Debate*, ed. J. Bhagwati. Cambridge, Mass.: MIT Press.

Harris, J., and M. Todaro. 1970. Migration, unemployment and development: A two-sector analysis. *American Economics Review* 60: 126–142.

McCulloch, R., and J. Yellen. 1975. Consequences of a tax on the brain drain for unemployment and income inequality in the LDCs. *Journal of Development Economics* 2; reprinted in Bhagwati (1976).

Mirrlees, J. A. 1971. An exploration in the theory of optimum income taxation. *Review of Economic Studies* 38: 175–208.

Oldman, Oliver, and Richard Pomp. 1975. The brain drain: A tax analysis of the Bhagwati proposal. *World Development* 3; reprinted in Bhagwati (1976).

Oldman, Oliver, and Richard Pomp. 1977. Consideration of policy issues at the international level, legal and administrative aspects of compensation, taxation and related policy measures: Suggestions for an optimal policy mix. Paper for the Intergovernmental Group of Experts Meeting at UNCTAD, Geneva, UN doc. TD/B/C.6/AC.4/7, Geneva.

Oldman, Oliver, and Richard Pomp. 1979. Tax measures in response to the brain drain. *Harvard International Law Journal* 20, winter.

Rawls, John. 1971. *A Theory of Justice*. Cambridge, Mass.: Harvard University Press.

Rodriguez, D. 1975. Brain drain and economic growth: A dynamic model. *Journal of Development Economics* 2.

Royden, H. L. 1968. *Real Analysis*. 2d ed. New York: Macmillan.

6

Optimal Linear Income Taxation in the Presence of Emigration

John Douglas Wilson

Introduction

In this chapter I examine how potential emigration changes the optimal linear income tax. By using a model that is essentially a special case of the model I used in chapter 4 to study the same question, I conclude that the presence of potential emigration lowers the optimal marginal tax.

In chapter 4 a single consumption good is produced by one type of labor, using a linear technology. Individual differences are described by a parameter called ability, and income is increasing in ability. To redistribute income, the home-country government uses a linear income tax consisting of a constant marginal tax on income and a uniform poll subsidy. It taxes the incomes of residents, but is unable to tax emigrants. The optimal tax maximizes a social welfare function that includes as arguments the utilities of both residents and emigrants. The contribution of an individual's utility to social welfare is independent of whether he or she emigrates.

Potential emigration in this model may either raise or lower the optimal marginal tax. This ambiguity is present because a change in the tax from its optimal value may cause any pattern of residential population changes across ability levels. Simply stated, the elimination of residential population changes at low or high ability levels raises the optimal marginal tax, whereas their elimination at intermediate ability levels lowers the optimal marginal tax. The exact statement of this result involves a comparison of optimal taxes in open and closed economies.[1]

A problem with this result is that the meanings of "low," "high," and "intermediate," are not made clear. In this chapter I construct a model in which residential population changes always occur at ability levels that are low or high enough to guarantee that prohibiting them must raise the optimal marginal tax. Thus this chapter yields some information about what constitutes "low" and "high."

The crucial feature of the model is that there exists a unique ability level, depending on the home country's tax policy, that separates emigrants from residents. This feature is the result of two assumptions: (1) the utility that individuals obtain from a given consumption-labor vector does not depend on where they live, and (2) the budget constraint faced by individuals is linear both at home and abroad (that is, the home and foreign income tax schedules are both linear, rather than nonlinear). Under these assumptions, if the home-country net wage rate is below (above) the foreign net wage rate, then emigrants all have higher (lower) ability levels than residents. Thus this model may be viewed as approximating a situation in which emigrants are concentrated at relatively high (low) ability levels or, because income is increasing in ability, at relatively high (low) income levels.

Under this specification the residential population changes caused by a small tax change are completely described by the resulting small change in the ability level that separates emigrants from residents. Thus these residential population changes occur only at ability levels close to the minimum or maximum ability level possessed by residents before the tax change. It is this property of the model that is responsible for the main result.[2]

The main result is that closing an open economy raises the optimal marginal tax and poll subsidy. This result gives an exact meaning to the statement that potential emigration reduces the optimal marginal tax and poll subsidy. The definition of a closed economy used here is originally from chapter 4. A closed economy is formed by taking an open economy with its tax set optimally and imposing the constraint that no individual may change his or her residence in response to changes in the tax. Thus individuals who are emigrants (residents) in the open economy when the tax is optimal remain emigrants (residents) in the closed economy.

In chapter 5 Bhagwati and Hamada use an alternative definition of a closed economy that is perhaps more natural: the economy is closed when no individual is allowed to emigrate. They are able to show that closing the economy in this way raises the optimal marginal tax. Their model is similar to my model in that a unique ability level separates emigrants from residents. (They consider only the case in which the emigrants have high ability levels.) However, they specify particular forms of the utility function and the distribution-of-ability function. In the second part of this chapter I isolate the crucial implications of these assumptions that are responsible for their results. This allows identification of a reason why closing the economy in the sense of Bhagwati and Hamada may actually lower the optimal marginal tax.

The plan of this chapter is as follows. The next section describes the open economy, and the section following describes the closed economy. Then I show that closing the economy raises the optimal marginal tax. In the fifth section I consider the alternative definition of a closed economy used by Bhagwati and Hamada. Concluding remarks are made in a final section.

The Open Economy

Let us consider an economy composed of a home country and a foreign country (the rest of the world). This economy contains a continuum of individuals who are called home residents if they live in the home country and emigrants if they live in the foreign country. They are indexed by ability levels N_1 to N_2. The home government imposes a linear income tax on the incomes of home residents but is unable to tax emigrants. The income tax is optimal if it maximizes social welfare, which is a function of the utilities of both home residents and emigrants. Each individual's treatment in the measurement of social welfare is independent of his or her choice of residence. There may exist individuals who are not classified as home residents of emigrants (for example, foreign citizens). But they are assumed not to affect the optimal income tax, either because they are not subject to taxation while in the home country or because they are not allowed to enter the home country. Thus they are ignored in the following analysis.

The utility function for an individual with ability level n is $u(x, z, n)$, where x is consumption and z is labor.[3] We assume that utility is increasing in x and declining in z. With n interpreted as ability, it is natural to assume that the marginal rate of substitution between z and x, $s = -u_z/u_x$, is declining in n: $s_n < 0$. Let us make this assumption. It allows us to conclude that an individual's chosen labor supply is increasing in n. We also make the natural assumption that utility is increasing in n at all x and z under consideration.

A home resident with ability level n maximizes $u(x, z, n)$ subject to the budget constraint

$$x = a + qz,\tag{1}$$

where a and q are the poll subsidy and net wage rate in the home country. The economy is competitive, so the gross wage rate p^h equals the marginal product of labor in the home country. Then $q = (1 - t)p^h$ where t is the marginal tax. We assume that the technology is linear, implying that p^h is fixed.

For simplicity we assume that emigrants also face a linear budget constraint. Also preferences for consumption and labor do not depend on residence. Thus an emigrant with ability level n maximizes $u(x, z, n)$ subject to the budget constraint $x = a^f + q^f z$, where a^f and q^f are the poll subsidy and net wage rate in the foreign country. We assume that a^f and q^f are fixed. The interpretation of this assumption is that the home country is small in the sense that emigration has only a negligible impact on a^f and q^f.

Individuals reside where they can obtain the highest utility. Let $v(n, a, q)$ be the utility that an n-person obtains under poll subsidy a and net wage rate q. If a and q are the home poll subsidy and home net wage rate, and if $v(n, a, q)$ is greater (less) than $v(n, a^f, q^f)$, then the n-person is a home resident (emigrant). For the case in which q differs from q^f, the following lemma implies that there is one and only one interval of ability levels possessed by home residents.

Lemma 1. Given any (a', q') and (a, q), where $q' > q$, there exists an $n_1 \in [N_1, N_2]$ such that, for each $n \in [N_1, N_2]$,

$$v(n, a', q') \gtrless v(n, a, q) \qquad \text{as} \quad n \gtrless n_1.$$

Proof. If the tax change from (a, q) to (a', q') increases (reduces) utility at each ability level between N_1 and N_2, then clearly $n_1 = N_1$ ($n_1 = N_2$). Suppose that some utilities decline and others rise. Because $q' > q$, there exists a $\bar{z} > 0$ such that $a' + q'z \gtrless a + qz$ as $z \gtrless \bar{z}$. Then the lemma holds because labor supply rises with n. As illustrated by figure 6.1 (where indifference curves for three individuals are drawn), n_1 is the unique ability level at which the tax change does not alter utility. Q.E.D.

Consider an open economy in which some individuals are home residents and others are emigrants. Let $[n_s, n_h]$ denote the interval of home residents' ability levels. Lemma 1 implies that $N_1 < n_s < n_h = N_2$ when the home net wage rate is above q^f, and $N_1 = n_s < n_h < N_2$ when the home net wage rate is below q^f.[4]

Turning to the government, we assume that there are no public expenditures.[5] Thus the government budget is balanced when tax revenue net of poll subsidy payments equals zero:

$$\int_{n_s}^{n_h} (tz(n, a, q) - a)f(n)\, dn = 0, \tag{2}$$

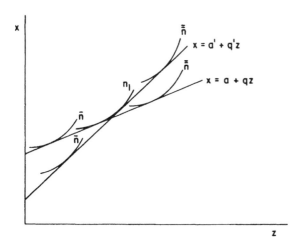

Figure 6.1

where $f(n)$ is the density function for the distribution of individuals across ability levels.[6] Note that n_s and n_h are functions of the tax (given the fixed home gross wage rate and the fixed a^f and q^f).

We call an individual a taxpayer if his or her net tax payment in the home country is positive $(tz(n, a, q) - a > 0)$. If the net tax payment is negative, we call the individual a tax recipient. A tax balances the government budget only if there are both taxpayers and tax recipients in the home country. Because $z(n, a, q)$ is increasing in n, we have the following lemma:

Lemma 2. Suppose that $[n_s, n_h]$ is the interval of ability levels possessed by home residents at a tax (a, t) where $t > 0$. If (a, t) balances the government budget, there exists an $n_2 \in (n_s, n_h)$ such that

$$tz(n, a, (1 - t)p^h) - a \gtreqless 0 \qquad \text{as} \quad n \gtreqless n_2.$$

The income tax is chosen subject to (2) to maximize a social welfare function that takes the form

$$W = \int_{N_1}^{\bar{n}} G(u(x, z, n))f(n)\, dn, \qquad G' > 0. \tag{3}$$

In chapter 5 Bhagwati and Hamada assume that $\bar{n}$ is sufficiently low to guarantee that no emigrants get included in the social welfare function at the taxes under consideration. We will also make this assumption in the discussion of their results. But to prove theorem 1, $\bar{n}$ may take any value.

In particular all individuals may be treated equally in the measurement of social welfare ($\bar{n} = N_2$). The important restriction for theorem 1 is that an individual's treatment does not depend on where he or she resides.

The Closed Economy

One way to study the effect of potential emigration on the optimal linear income tax is to ascertain how the optimal tax is changed by closing the economy. But there is more than one interesting way to close the economy. We use the definition of a closed economy from chapter 4. A following section examines how the results change when Bhagwati and Hamada's definition is used.

To construct the closed economy, first suppose that the tax is set at its optimal value in the open economy, denoted (a^*, t^*). With individuals residing where their utility is highest under (a^*, t^*), suppose that institutions are formed to prevent them from changing residence in response to any tax change. The economy is then said to be closed.

Some important comparisons between the open and closed economies are now made.[7] Closing the economy does not alter the manner in which social welfare depends on individual utilities. But by restricting migration, it does alter the utilities some individuals receive at particular values of a and t. Consequently it changes the relation of social welfare to a and t. Denote this relation by the function $W(a, t)$ for the open economy and by the function $W^c(a, t)$ for the closed economy. Clearly each of these functions increases with a and declines with t. Until the tax is changed from (a^*, t^*), nobody in the closed economy is prevented from migrating. Thus

$$W^c(a^*, t^*) = W(a^*, t^*). \tag{4}$$

Because the prevention of migration can only lower the level of social welfare at a given tax, we also have

$$W^c(a, t) \leqq W(a, t) \qquad \text{at all} \quad (a, t). \tag{5}$$

The tax (a^*, t^*) balances the government budget in the open economy. It must also balance the government budget in the closed economy because closing the economy has no effect on an individual's residence until the tax is changed from (a^*, t^*). Letting $G(a, t)$ and $G^c(a, t)$ denote net tax revenue at (a, t) in the open and closed economies (see (2)), we have

$$G^c(a^*, t^*) = G(a^*, t^*) = 0. \tag{6}$$

Conditions (4), (5), and (6) will all be used in the succeeding arguments. Lemmas 1 and 2 from the previous section will also be used. Clearly they hold for both open and closed economies.[8]

We will assume that the optimal marginal tax for the closed economy is positive. This assumption appears to be rather weak. But Sheshinski (1972) is able to prove it for Mirrlees's (1971) optimal income tax model only after assuming that labor is a nondecreasing function of the net wage rate. Using a model in which labor supplies are not perfect substitutes, Carruth (1982) presents computations where the optimal marginal tax is negative.

The Optimal Tax Comparison

Consider an open economy in which there are some home residents and some emigrants when the tax is optimal. We now prove that the optimal marginal tax and poll subsidy for this economy, t^* and a^*, are both less than the optimal marginal tax and poll subsidy for the corresponding closed economy, t^{**} and a^{**}.

Theorem 1. $t^* < t^{**}$ and $a^* < a^{**}$.

Proof. Under the assumption that both home residents and emigrants are present at (a^*, t^*), closing the economy prevents residential population changes from occurring in response to small tax changes from (a^*, t^*). As a result, it can be shown that there exist small feasible tax changes from (a^*, t^*) in the closed economy that increase social welfare.[9] This means that t^{**} differs from t^*, and changing the tax from (a^*, t^*) to (a^{**}, t^{**}) raises social welfare in the closed economy. Then by (4) and (5), this tax change also raises social welfare in the open economy. Thus (a^{**}, t^{**}) cannot be feasible in the open economy, because (a^*, t^*) is optimal there. We shall now assume that t^{**} is less than t^* and show that (a^{**}, t^{**}) must then be feasible in the open economy. This contradiction allows us to conclude that t^{**} is greater than t^*. By the optimality of (a^{**}, t^{**}), a^{**} is then greater than a^*.

Let $[n_s^*, n_h^*]$ denote the interval of home resident ability levels at the tax (a^*, t^*) in the open economy (and at any tax in the closed economy).[10] Either all emigrants at (a^*, t^*) have ability levels above n_h^*, or they all have ability levels below n_s^*. We first consider the former case.

To begin, note that lemma 1 and the assumption that t^{**} is below t^* imply that the tax change from (a^*, t^*) to (a^{**}, t^{**}) increases (reduces) the home utilities of all individuals with ability levels above (below) some n_1. Because this tax change must make some home residents better off in the

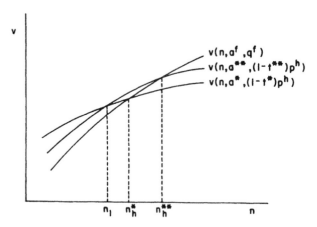

Figure 6.2

closed economy (because (a^{**}, t^{**}) is optimal there), n_1 is less than n_h^*. As illustrated in figure 6.2, this implies that the tax change increases the highest ability level of home residents in the open economy to some n_h^{**}. Because (a^{**}, t^{**}) balances the government budget in the closed economy, lemma 2 implies the existence of an n_2 between n_h^* and n_h^* with the property that all individuals with ability levels above (below) n_2 are taxpayers (tax recipients) at (a^{**}, t^{**}). Thus all individuals with ability levels between n_h^* and n_h^{**} are net taxpayers at (a^{**}, t^{**}). It follows that the rise in the highest ability level possessed by home residents from n_h^* to n_h^{**} increases net tax revenue at (a^{**}, t^{**}). Because (a^{**}, t^{**}) is feasible in the closed economy, where residential population changes do not occur, it must also be feasible in the open economy. This establishes the desired contradiction.

The second and final case to consider is that in which the emigrants at (a^*, t^*) have ability levels below n_s^*. Making the assumption that t^{**} is less than t^*, we first show that the tax change from (a^*, t^*) to (a^{**}, t^{**}) must make some home residents worse off. In other words the ability level n_1 in lemma 1 is above n_s^*. Suppose that this is not the case. Then, as shown in figure 6.3, there exists an $a' \leqq a^{**}$ such that the tax change from (a^*, t^*) to (a', t^{**}) raises (lowers) the home utilities of all individuals with ability levels above (below) n_s^*. In other words this tax change raises each home resident's home utility and lowers each emigrant's home utility. Thus nobody in the open economy changes residence in response to the tax change, and nobody's utility declines. Because (a', t^{**}) is feasible in the closed economy, it must then also be feasible in the open economy.[11] But this contradicts the optimality of (a^*, t^*). We can conclude that $t^{**} < t^*$ implies $n_1 > n_s^*$.

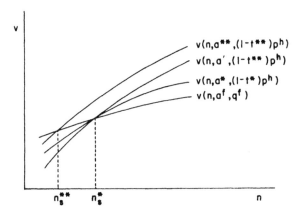

$v(n, a^{**}, (1-t^{**})p^h)$
$v(n, a', (1-t^{**})p^h)$
$v(n, a^*, (1-t^*)p^h)$
$v(n, a^f, q^f)$

n_s^{**} n_s^* n

Figure 6.3

Because $n_1 > n_s^*$, the tax change from (a^*, t^*) to (a^{**}, t^{**}) raises the lowest ability level of home residents in the open economy to some n_s^{**} (see fig. 6.4). Recall that all individuals with ability levels below (above) some $n_2 > n_s^*$ are tax recipients (taxpayers) at (a^{**}, t^{**}). If $n_2 \leqq n_s^{**}$, all home residents in the open economy at (a^{**}, t^{**}) are taxpayers. Then (a^{**}, t^{**}) is feasible in the open economy, which establishes the desired contradiction. Suppose n_2 is greater than n_s^{**}. Then all individuals with ability levels between n_s^* and n_s^{**} are tax recipients at (a^{**}, t^{**}). Thus the emigration of these individuals from the home country must raise net revenue at (a^{**}, t^{**}). Because (a^{**}, t^{**}) is feasible in the closed economy, where residential population changes do not occur, it is then feasible in the open economy. Thus we have the desired contradiction.

Having considered all cases, we can conclude that t^{**} is greater than t^*. This completes the proof.

The Bhagwati-Hamada Closed Economy

An economy has been called closed if individuals must reside where they would if the economy was open and the tax was optimal. Henceforth we refer to such an economy as a W-closed economy. Unfortunately it may not correspond to the normal concept of a closed economy. Specifically not only are some individuals required to remain home residents, but others must remain emigrants. This observation can be given a rather unrealistic interpretation. Suppose that all individuals included in the measurement of social welfare are born in the home country, but each decides at the start

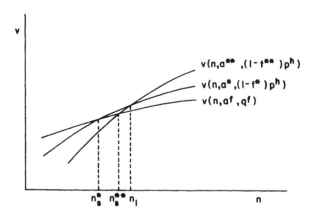

Figure 6.4

of his or her life whether to be a home resident or to emigrate. Then some individuals are required to emigrate when the economy is W-closed.

The natural alternative to a W-closed economy is to suppose that once the economy is closed, *all* individuals must remain in the home country, regardless of their chosen residences in the open economy under an optimal tax. Bhagwati and Hamada in chapter 5 study how the optimal marginal tax is changed by closing an open economy in this manner. They are able to show that the optimal marginal tax rises, but only after assuming specific forms of the utility function and distribution-of-ability function. They also assume that the emigrants in an open economy with an optimal tax are all individuals with ability levels above some n_h. In my model this corresponds to the case in which the home net wage rate is less than the foreign net wage rate. For this case we will now derive conditions under which the optimal marginal tax for Bhagwati and Hamada's closed economy (the BH-closed economy) is greater than the open economy optimal marginal tax. Bhagwati and Hamada's model satisfies these conditions. We will see, however, that there are other reasonable models in which one of the conditions fails to hold, and therefore closing the economy in the BH sense may quite possibly lower the optimal marginal tax.

Throughout the analysis we will impose Bhagwati and Hamada's assumption that emigrants are given zero weight in the measurement of social welfare. More precisely the maximum ability level of those individuals who are included in the social welfare function ($\bar{n}$ in (3)) is below the minimum ability level of emigrants in the W-closed economy. This assumption is important. If emigrants were given positive weight, then the social indifference curves on (a, t)-space would be more steeply sloped in the BH-closed economy than in the W-closed economy. In other words the poll subsidy would have to rise more in the BH-closed economy than in the W-closed economy to keep social welfare constant following an increase in the marginal tax.[12] The reason is simple. Changing the economy from W-closed to BH-closed returns high-ability individuals to the home country. Having returned, their utilities are lowered by a tax change involving increases in the poll subsidy and marginal tax that keep social welfare constant in the W-closed economy (recall lemma 1). Consequently their return must raise the increase in the poll subsidy needed to keep social welfare constant following a rise in the marginal tax. This increased steepness of social indifference curves provides a reason for why closing the economy in the BH sense may lower the optimal marginal tax. We will ignore this reason and concentrate on changes in the optimal marginal tax that stem from the effect of closing the economy on the set of feasible taxes.[13]

The analysis is conducted by breaking the change in the tax from its open economy optimal value to its BH-closed economy optimal value into three separate changes. These changes are illustrated in figure 6.5, where the optimal taxes for the open, W-closed, and BH-closed economies ((a^*, t^*), (a^{**}, t^{**}), and (a^b, t^b)) are depicted as tangencies between a social indifference curve and the tax possibility frontier (TPF) for the relevant economy. (The tax (a^{be}, t^{be}) is discussed below.) To begin, let us close the open economy in the W sense. We know that the resulting change in the optimal tax involves an increase in the marginal tax. With the economy W-closed, all individuals with ability levels above some n_h are emigrants. If we bring them back into the home country, the economy becomes BH-closed. This generates a budget surplus at (a^{**}, t^{**}) because these high-ability individuals are taxpayers at (a^{**}, t^{**}) (by lemma 2). Thus the TPF rises above (a^{**}, t^{**}), changing the optimal tax to (a^b, t^b). In figure 6.5 t^b lies above t^{**}. To obtain conditions under which this is the case, we break the move from the W-closed economy to the BH-closed economy into two separate changes. First, the emigrants are returned to the home country, but at the same time revenue is taken away from the home government to keep the government budget balanced at (a^{**}, t^{**}). In other words the government is required to undertake expenditures at a level, denoted e, that keeps the TPF passing through (a^{**}, t^{**}).[14] Figure 6.5 shows that the slope of the TPF at (a^{**}, t^{**}) rises, and the optimal tax changes to (a^{be}, t^{be}), where $t^{be} > t^{**}$. We will uncover below a very reasonable assumption under which the optimal marginal tax must indeed rise. To conclude the move to the BH closed

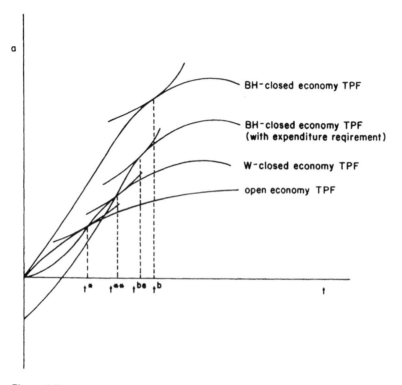

Figure 6.5

economy, the home government is given back the revenue that was taken away. As a result the optimal tax moves from (a^{be}, t^{be}) to (a^b, t^b).

To say that t^b is at least as great as t^{be} is to say that the imposition of an expenditure requirement does not raise the optimal marginal tax. This is the first of two conditions that together imply that t^b is greater than t^{**} and hence greater than t^*. Because it is the most controversial of the two, it is discussed at length below.

The second condition is the condition for t^{be} to be greater than t^{**}. To state it, let $T(n, t)$ denote an n-person's net tax payment at the tax $(a_{be}(t), t)$, where $a_{be}(t)$ is the function describing the TPF for the BH-closed economy after the imposition of the expenditure requirement described previously $(a_{be}(t^{**}) = a^{**})$:

$$T(n, t) = tz(n, a_{be}(t), (1 - t)p^h) - a_{be}(t). \tag{7}$$

Consider a small tax change that takes place along this TPF and involves an increase in the marginal tax. The resulting marginal change in an n-

person's net tax payment is

$$\frac{\partial T(n, t)}{\partial t} = z + t\frac{\partial z}{\partial q}(-p^h) + t\frac{\partial z}{\partial a}a'_{be}(t) - a'_{be}(t). \tag{8}$$

The appendix shows that t^{be} is greater than t^{**} if this marginal change is increasing in n:

$$\frac{\partial^2 T(n, t)}{\partial t\partial n} > 0. \tag{9}$$

This assumption is reasonable because the tax change under consideration involves an increase in the marginal tax on income, and incomes are increasing in n. Because the effects of the tax change on the choice of labor may differ across ability levels, the assumption need not hold. However, its failure appears to be an unlikely occurrence. An example of a utility function that must satisfy (9) is the familiar Cobb-Douglas utility function. For this function the marginal effects of t and a on z are independent of n.

To summarize, we have found that $t^{**} > t^*$, and we have established conditions under which $t^{be} > t^{**}$ and $t^b \geq t^{be}$. Combining the results, we have the following theorem.[15]

Theorem 2. Consider the case in which the home net wage rate is less than the foreign net wage rate at (a^*, t^*) and the social welfare function does not include the individuals who are emigrants in the open economy at (a^*, t^*). Suppose that (a) $\partial^2 T(n, t)/\partial t\partial n > 0$, and (b) the imposition of a positive government expenditure requirement in the BH-closed economy does not raise the optimal marginal tax.

Then $t^b > t^*$ and $a^b > a^*$.

The importance of (b) is easily understood. Moving from the W-closed economy to the BH-closed economy returns high-ability emigrants to the home country, thereby raising the TPF. Because a reduction in government expenditures also raises the TPF, one can guess that the effect of this reduction on the optimal marginal tax should be a major determinant of how the return of emigrants alters the optimal marginal tax. Of course it is not the sole determinant. Even if the return of emigrants was accompanied by an increase in government expenditures that kept the height of the TPF at a given marginal tax from changing, the slope of the TPF at this tax would still generally change. Under (a) the slope would increase, that is, a greater increase in the poll subsidy could be obtained from a given increase in the marginal tax.

It is perhaps appropriate to label the tax change from (a^{be}, t^{be}) to (a^b, t^b) as the income effect of emigration. Under (b) income redistribution is a normal good in the sense that an increase in the revenue available for redistribution does not lower the optimal marginal tax ($t^{be} \leqq t^b$). In chapter 5 Bhagwati and Hamada present an interesting special case of Mirrlees's (1971) optimal income tax model in which (b) holds.[16] But Stern (1976) provides numerical calculations in which (b) is violated. He considers closed economies in which the government not only uses income taxation to redistribute income but also to raise revenue to finance an exogenously determined level of public expenditures. All of his calculations show that the imposition of a positive expenditure requirement raises the optimal marginal tax. Thus the failure of condition (b) appears to be quite possible. If closing the economy generates a sufficiently negative income effect, meaning t^b is sufficiently below t^{be}, then closing the economy will lower the optimal marginal tax. Intuitively the additional revenue generated by the return of high-ability emigrants to the home country may make increases in the marginal tax less desirable.[17]

Concluding Remarks

The main conclusion from this chapter is that the optimal poll subsidy and marginal tax for an open economy are lower than they would be if residential population changes did not occur in response to changes in the tax from its optimal value. This result gives a specific meaning to the claim that the presence of potential emigration prevents the optimal tax from being more egalitarian. The property of my model that is crucial for this result is that a small tax change causes residential population changes only among individuals with incomes close to either the minimum or maximum income level of home residents before the tax change. In chapter 4 I show that closing the economy can lower the optimal marginal tax when residential population changes take place at intermediate income levels.

I have also argued that the definition of a closed economy used here should be distinguished from the alternative definition used by Bhagwati and Hamada in chapter 5. For the case in which emigrants have higher ability levels than home residents, I have isolated interesting conditions under which the prevention of all emigration raises the optimal marginal tax. But I have also argued that there are situations in which the optimal marginal tax may actually decline. In particular this possibility exists where income redistribution is an "inferior good," meaning an increase in the revenue available for redistribution lowers the optimal marginal tax. Stern's numerical calculations demonstrate that this situation is not unlikely. Consequently if the tax possibility frontier is raised significantly because a large number of high-income individuals are forced to remain in the home country, then the optimal marginal tax may quite possibly decline. Where such "income effects" are not important, the prevention of all emigration lowers the optimal marginal tax.

Appendix

Consider the case in the section on the BH-closed economy in which emigrants have higher ability levels than home residents have and are not included in the social welfare function. A claim made in that section is now proved.

Claim. If $\partial^2 T(n, t)/\partial t \partial n > 0$, then $t^{be} > t^{**}$.

Proof. Let $a_w(t)$ be the equation for the W-closed economy TPF, and let $a_{be}(t)$ be the equation for the TPF for a BH-closed economy with an expenditure requirement, denoted e, that balances the government budget at $(a^{**}, t^{**})(a_{be}(t^{**}) = a^{**})$. For t^{be} to be less than or equal to t^{**} (contrary to the case illustrated in fig. 6.5), there must exist a $\bar{t}$ where

$$a_{be}(\bar{t}) = a_w(\bar{t}) \quad \text{and} \quad a'_{be}(\bar{t}) \leqq a'_w(\bar{t}). \tag{A1}$$

It is now shown that this cannot happen.

By the definitions of $a_{be}(t)$ and $a_w(t)$, we have, for all t,

$$\int_{N_1}^{N_2} T(n, t) \, dn = \int_{N_1}^{N_2} (tz(n, a_{be}(t), (1 - t)p^h) - a_{be}(t))f(n) \, dn = -e \tag{A2}$$

and

$$\int_{N_1}^{n_h} (tz(n, a_w(t), (1 - t)p^h) - a_w(t))f(n) \, dn = 0, \tag{A3}$$

where n_h is the highest ability level of home residents in the W-closed economy. Suppose (A1) holds at some $\bar{t}$. By totally differentiating (A2) and (A3) and evaluating the resulting expressions at $\bar{t}$, we obtain

$$(a'_{be}(\bar{t}) - a'_w(t)) \int_{N_1}^{n_h} \left(1 - \bar{t} \frac{\partial z(n, a_w(\bar{t}), (1 - \bar{t})p^h)}{\partial a} \right) f(n) \, dn$$
$$= \int_{n_h}^{N_2} \frac{\partial T(n, \bar{t})}{\partial t} f(n) \, dn. \tag{A4}$$

But (A2) implies

$$\int_{N_1}^{N_2} \frac{\partial T(n, \bar{t})}{\partial t} f(n)\, dn = 0. \tag{A5}$$

It follows from (A5) and the assumption that $\partial T/\partial t$ increases with n that the right side of (A4) is positive. Because the integral on the left side is positive,[18] $a'_{be}(\bar{t})$ is greater than $a'_w(\bar{t})$, which contradicts (A1). This completes the proof.

Notes

This chapter is a significantly revised version of a paper presented at the conference The Exercise of Income Tax Jurisdiction over Citizens Working Abroad, under the auspices of the National Institute of Public Finance and Policy, New Delhi, January, 1981. I would like to thank J. Bhagwati, P. Diamond, K. Hamada, J. Mirrlees, N. Stern, and two anonymous referees for helpful comments and suggestions.

1. See chapter 4 (propositions 1 and 2).

2. These criteria for "low" and "high" ability levels were not recognized in chapter 4.

3. We assume that $u(x, z, n)$ is quasi-concave in (x, z) and continuously differentiable in (x, z, n).

4. For the case in which the home and foreign net wage rates differ, we arbitrarily suppose that those individuals who are indifferent between residences do not emigrate. This assumption is inconsequential because these individuals form a set of measure zero.

5. If there is a positive level of public expenditures, a tax may not be feasible even when all home residents are taxpayers. (Lemma 2 may be violated.) Consequently theorem 1 may not be true for the case in which the home net wage rate is above the foreign net wage rate. But a positive expenditure level does not upset any other result in this chapter.

6. The function f is assumed to be continuous and positive at each n belonging to (N_1, N_2).

7. The closed economy considered here is a special case of the partially closed economy considered in chapter 4.

8. In lemma 2 the interval of home resident ability levels at (a, t) and the feasibility of the tax (a, t) must be in reference to the same economy.

9. See chapter 4 for a discussion of the welfare effects of small tax changes from (a^*, t^*).

10. If we assume that the home government in the open economy can choose the residence of any individual who is indifferent between residences, then the home

and foreign net wage rates can be shown to differ at both (a^*, t^*) and (a^{**}, t^{**}). Then by lemma 1 the sets of home-resident ability levels at (a^*, t^*) and at (a^{**}, t^{**}) in the open economy are well-defined intervals under the convention given in note 4.

11. We assume here and everywhere else that a reduction in the poll subsidy raises net tax revenue in the closed economy. Then (a', t^{**}) is feasible because (a^{**}, t^{**}) is feasible. This assumption necessarily holds if leisure is a normal good.

12. Of course, the social indifference curves for the open and W-closed economies also differ. However, because they differ in the way prescribed by (4) and (5) in the text, it is possible to prove theorem 1.

13. The more egalitarian the social welfare function, the less the return of high-ability emigrants to the home country affects social indifference curves. Suppose, for example, that social welfare is given by the function

$$W = (1/\alpha) \int_{N_1}^{\bar{n}} u^\alpha f(n)\, dn,$$

where a reduction in α signifies an increase in egalitarianism. Then for the case in which $\bar{n} = N_2$, there exists an $\bar{\alpha}$ such that, if $\alpha < \bar{\alpha}$, theorem 2 continues to hold.

14. By interpreting the reduction in income available for income redistribution as an expenditure requirement (and this is no more than an interpretation), we are assuming that any expenditures undertaken by the government do not directly affect the optimal tax in the BH-closed economy. More precisely expenditures may affect utility, but then the utility function is separable in expenditures: $u(x, z, n) + k(n, e)$.

15. Assumption (a) need only hold at marginal taxes between t^{**} and t^{be}. Assumption (b) need only hold for the particular change in expenditures described in the text. Finally, note that a^b is greater than a^* because t^b is greater than t^*. (Otherwise (a^*, t^*) would give a higher level of social welfare than (a^b, t^b), which would contradict the optimality of (a^b, t^b).)

16. Their assumptions include the form of the utility function and the distribution-of-ability function. Furthermore (b) holds only if the parameters of the utility function are chosen so that the index of relative risk aversion is less than or equal to one.

17. I know of no calculations of the difference between t^b and t^*. Stern (1982) and Carruth (1982) go part way by presenting calculations in which t^b is significantly less than t^{**}. Their models contain two types of labor, skilled and unskilled. Stern calculates, for example, that a rise in the skilled portion of the population from 25 to 50 percent lowers the optimal marginal tax from 0.6939 to 0.4263. Unfortunately, their calculations are not directly applicable to my analysis because skilled and unskilled labor are not perfect substitutes in production in their models. An increase in the skilled portion of the population raises the unskilled gross wage rate.

18. Note 11 applies here.

References

Atkinson, A. B. 1973. How progressive should income-tax be? In *Essays in Modern Economics*, ed. M. Parkin. London: Longmans.

Carruth, A. 1982. On the role of the production assumptions for optimum taxation. *Journal of Public Economics* 17: 145–155.

Mirrlees, J. A. 1971. An exploration in the theory of optimal income taxation. *Review of Economic Studies* 38: 175–208.

Sheshinski, E. 1972. The optimal linear income tax. *Review of Economic Studies* 39: 297–302.

Stern, N. 1976. On the specification of models of optimum income taxation. *Journal of Public Economics* 6: 123–162.

Stern, N. 1982. Optimum taxation with errors in administration. *Journal of Public Economics* 17: 181–211.

7

The Income Distribution Frontier and Taxation of Migrants

William J. Baumol

Introduction

The profession's interest in the possibility of using a program of transnational taxation of skilled migrants from less developed countries (LDCs) as a means to influence income distribution and resource allocation has been stimulated by illuminating writings of Bhagwati (see, for example, Bhagwati 1979). Many of Bhagwati's papers have dealt with the subject discursively, focusing largely on the practicalities of the issue. Writings on the theory of the subject were, until recently (with the appearance of the papers of Bhagwati and Hamada, Mirrlees, and Wilson), rather scarcer, and it is to that area that this chapter is devoted. It will rely on a construct—the income distribution frontier—recently used for other purposes by myself and Dietrich Fischer (Baumol and Fischer 1979). This graph will, I believe, make somewhat clearer the nature of the choices that are involved.

First, it is appropriate to summarize briefly the proposal to be discussed. It has been believed for some time that an LDC bears an unacceptable burden when it invests heavily in the training of the most capable members of its population only to find many of them attracted away by the prospect of higher income in the industrialized economies. It is believed that this is unfair to their country of origin, which receives little or nothing in return for its outlays. Aside from that, because those who migrate may include many who would be earners of relatively high incomes even if they remained at home, their departure deprives their native country of a significant source of taxation, and thus also of the means to provide some redistribution of income. Finally, it is suggested that some resource misallocation may be caused by disparities between tax rates in the migrant's country of origin and place of residence, a misallocation that a tax upon the incomes of migrants can, perhaps, reduce.

In all this it is proposed to confine the tax to those who have decided to retain citizenship in their native countries, even after moving abroad. This is of course what makes the proposal practicable, because it is hard to imagine how taxes would be collected from those who have cut off all ties with their country of origin.[1]

By and large my results will prove consistent with those of Bhagwati and Hamada. Specifically we will see that at the level of abstraction with which we are dealing, (a) those who wish to remain at home will be better off, at least potentially, if migration is prohibited than if it is permitted and the incomes of the migrants are untaxed; (b) with a tax on migrants' incomes, however, nonmigrants are potentially better off still; (c) the migrants themselves may be expected to prefer no constraints on migration *and* no taxes by their home country (but we will encounter an interesting and not altogether implausible externalities case in which freedom of migration along with taxation of migrants is preferred by all groups); (d) in the absence of externalities, efficiency requires identity of tax arrangements at home and abroad. As a result if tax rates in the country of residence of the migrants are higher than the rates in their originating countries, a tax on migrants will contribute to international efficiency. On the other hand if relative tax rates show the reverse pattern, then taxation of migrants is likely to aggravate inefficiency. (e) Finally, maximization of global welfare does not yield a unique solution because there is no unique and unambiguous criterion of distributive preferability.

The Income Distribution Frontier: Brief Review

Modern literature on optimal taxation has made much good use of the concept of a linear tax on income. Bhagwati and Hamada show in chapter 5 how this approach can be used fruitfully to examine the consequences of a tax on migrants, and Mirrlees in chapter 8 and Wilson in chapter 6 have carried the analysis further in a most felicitous manner. But the approach does have one shortcoming when applied to a subject such as ours, in which judgment and intuition about practical implications must play a substantial role. Because the results are most easily expressed in terms of the values of the parameters of the optimal tax they do not lend themselves easily to heuristic examination. Because they do not indicate directly who gets what and how this distribution is affected by the imposition of a tax on migrants, the approach is not as helpful to the intuition as it is to rigorous deductions about the choice of values of the tax parameters.

The income distribution frontier serves as a complement to the optimal tax analysis. Whereas it may be less tractable under rigorous analysis, it leaves little doubt about interpretation and therefore serves as a useful bridge to policy formulation in practice.

The income distribution frontier is a simple concept. Assuming that one can define a single variable y_i that measures the real income of individual i, the frontier $f(y_1, \ldots, y_n) = 0$ is defined as the solution to the program

$\max y_1$ subject to

$y_i \geq k_i$ $(i = 2, \ldots, n)$,

$\phi(y_1, \ldots, y_n) \leq 0$,

where ϕ is presumably derivable from the available production set, the pertinent institutional arrangements, and the other circumstances constraining the production and distribution of income. In other words $f(\cdot) = 0$ is the boundary farthest from the origin in any given direction of the set of available income distribution vectors and so constitutes the efficient frontier of the set.

Figure 7.1 describes a typical income distribution frontier for the two-person case. It begins with some initial vector y^* determined by the general-equilibrium solution of the model describing the workings of the economy, given its initial tax arrangements.

Several attributes of the frontier may usefully be noted:

1. The frontier is not expressed in terms of subjective utilities but in terms of some objective measure of real income that, to some degree of approximation, can presumably be observed. Although one can raise obvious objections to this attempt to expunge utility from the analysis, it gets us out of intractable problems of interpersonal comparison, it permits useful constructs such as the 45° line that becomes the locus of points of equality, and it deals with observable incomes, which after all are used by non-economists as their criterion of the degree of equality.

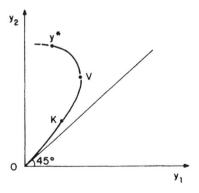

Figure 7.1

2. Little seems to be known about the shape of the curve in the direction of the axis nearest the initial point, that is, as one moves in the direction of increased inequality. That is why the upper left end of the curve is not drawn in.

3. On the other hand if income taxes and transfers are the means used to equalize incomes, we do have an analytic basis that can be used to determine the shape of the frontier as it approaches the 45° line. As shown in the diagram, we can expect the curve to approach the 45° line gradually, the two meeting only at the origin. This means that the frontier will ultimately acquire a positive slope (below the vertical point V).[2] It also means that complete equality can never be achieved by taxes and transfers because there is no (positive-valued) point at which the curve crosses the 45° line.

The reason for this behavior of the curve is easy to explain intuitively. As one approaches the 45° line, the tax system is in effect *guaranteeing* a greater degree of equality. If it were to guarantee absolute equality, as is implied by a point on the 45° line, then all financial reward for labor must be eliminated. If labor has a negative marginal utility and output cannot be produced without labor, the result follows.[3]

As just described, the income distribution frontier applies to an economy in which labor is voluntary and supplies are provided through a free market. Work is supplied, preponderantly, only in exchange for wages and is not volunteered without compensation. The public sector can carry out at least some redistribution, but only by the usual means: progressive income taxes, welfare payments, provision of public services to the poor, and so forth.

In my analysis it will be desirable to complicate the construction somewhat. The reason is that the two-person (two-group) case is insufficiently rich for our purposes. We will find it useful to divide the relevant population into three groups: the very poor, who remain in the country of origin; those who are at least potentially wealthier and nevertheless choose not to emigrate; and the potentially wealthier persons who want to migrate or have already done so.

The Income Distribution Frontier with Three Groups

Figure 7.2 shows the income distribution frontier for an economy with the three groups, their incomes being represented on the three axes. The initial income vector y^* yields the highest (per capita) income $y_3 = By^*$ to the group associated with the vertical axis. That group (group III) will therefore

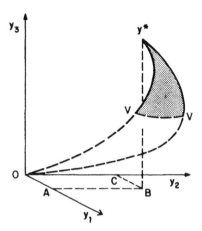

Figure 7.2

be taken to be composed of the actual (or potential) migrants. The two remaining groups receive, respectively, $y_1 = OA$ and $y_2 = OC$, where $OA < OC$, so that groups I and II will be interpreted, respectively, as the poorer and the more affluent nonmigrants.

The frontier itself curls toward the origin exactly as in the two-dimensional case and for precisely the same reasons—because it represents the opportunities for redistribution via taxation, increased equality can be achieved only at the cost of increased production disincentives that ultimately strangle production altogether. Here VV is the locus of vertical points (it is the locus whose projection on the y_1y_2 plane consists of the points in the projection of surface OVy^*V lying furthest from the origin along the rays in the y_1y_2 plane). Thus the shaded surface Vy^*V is clearly the efficient set—it is the income distribution frontier, and VV is one of its boundaries. The equality locus is now the ray OE, which goes through the midpoint M of the outer boundary of the unit simplex (fig. 7.3). As before the income distribution frontier of figure 7.2 cannot intersect ray OE except at the origin, and everywhere else OE will lie below the frontier.

The three-dimensional surface of figure 7.2 represents income distribution options when all three groups are simultaneously subjected to the redistribution process. We will also be concerned with the case in which redistribution takes place only between two of the three groups—specifically when there is no effort to distribute income from migrants to the groups that remain at home. In that case the relevant income distribution frontier is of course a curve in two-dimensional space. The relevant curve will look very much like that in figure 7.1, and it will lie in a plane

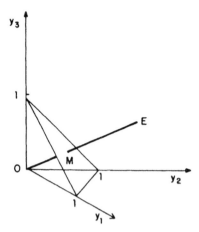

Figure 7.3

parallel to the floor of the diagram. We will find it convenient actually to project it to the floor.

Restrained and Unrestrained Migration

In the Bhagwati-Hamada models a world in which migration from the LDCs is prohibited is used as a standard of comparison. It is used to dramatize the undesirable consequences of failure to tax migrants, showing that those who remain behind may actually benefit from a prohibition of all migration compared with the situation in which migrants are permitted to escape the net of the tax authorities. I will now repeat the exercise trying to identify the source of the result.[4]

Where markets are imperfect and the other assumptions of the competitive model of general equilibrium are violated we cannot tell what will result from a restriction on freedom of migration. The theorem of the second best tells us that even though prohibition of migration imposes a constraint upon the economy, the fact that other constraints already impede its efficiency means that the added constraint may conceivably even improve matters.

Only in a world in which the competitive mechanism would otherwise produce optimality are the results unambiguous. There the ban on migration is the one constraint on what would otherwise be an unconstrained optimal solution. The result can only be a reduction in aggregate income. Specifically labor will not be able to find its way into those activities and

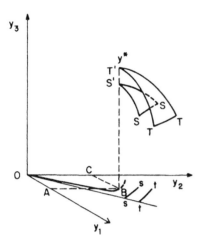

Figure 7.4

to those geographic locations where it can make its maximal marginal contribution. The income distribution frontier must consequently shrink toward the origin. Everyone therefore stands to lose in the process.

This is why the Bhagwati-Hamada result appears so surprising. Why in these circumstances does the outcome seem to favor those who do not migrate, even in a competitive world?

Figure 7.4 shows us the situation and helps to remove the paradox. Confining itself to the efficient locus (the region of the surface in figure 7.2 in which all partial derivatives are nonpositive) we see two such surfaces, SSS' and TTT'. The latter represents the case in which migration is unrestricted, and the former corresponds to that in which migraton is prohibited. Thus for reasons just indicated, TTT' lies further from the origin than SSS' along any ray that intersects them both. Points S' and T' represent the distributions that will be attained without any intervention aside from the prohibition of migration. As drawn, T' lies directly above S', though this need not always be so, even approximatey. Such a juxtaposition is consistent with the obvious conclusion that the ban on migration of the very skilled (group III) can be expected to reduce the incomes of those individuals. (Otherwise in such a simplified model why would it be necessary to do anything to prevent them from migrating?) But the relative position of S' and T' means more than this. It implies that the forced retention of the potential migrants in the domestic labor force does nothing to affect the incomes of others in the economy in a free market equilibrium. Although this premise is not necessary for my argument, it is a very convenient simplification. And such an outcome is certainly not impossible. All that is required is a balancing of two countervailing forces—the complementarity between the skills of the potential migrants with those of their fellow citizens who choose to remain at home can increase the productivity of the latter when the former are forced to stay in their native land, and this can overcome the depressing effect on real wages of the increased labor supply in that country.[5]

We are now in a position to proceed to the comparison we are after. We want to determine what can be done for groups I and II (the two nonmigrant groups) when group III goes abroad and is exempted from taxation by the country of origin. This is to be compared with what can be achieved for the members of groups I and II if the members of group III are forced to remain at home and remain subjected to the full redistributive powers of the government in their native country. Second, these arrangements are to be compared with free migration along with taxation of migrants.

The story of the first of these cases starts off at point T'—the free market distribution with unrestricted migration. Now groups I and II find themselves at point B on the floor of the diagram. Any redistribution that affects them must be arranged between themselves alone because, by hypothesis, nothing can be extracted from group III to contribute to their incomes. This means that the possible distributions are bounded by an income distribution frontier in two-dimensional space—like that in figure 7.1. This is shown on the floor of figure 7.4 and more clearly in figure 7.5, which depicts only the floor of the preceding graph. Here we see that the relevant locus is OB, which encompasses the initial distribution point B for groups I and II and gradually approaches the 45° line as it nears the origin.[6]

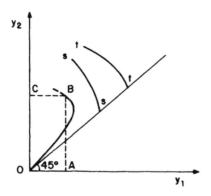

Figure 7.5

This then is what can be yielded for groups I and II by a policy of unrestricted migration without taxation.

On the other hand with migration prohibited, the story focuses on surface SSS' in figure 7.4. True, this locus lies inside the corresponding free migration locus, TTT'. But now, instead of confining themselves to a single point T', the policymakers retain the freedom to range over the entire surface SSS'. In particular they can select points on SS—the rightmost bound of the surface SSS' corresponding to VV, the locus of vertical points in figure 7.2.

The projection of SS on the floor of figure 7.4 is ss (see also fig. 7.5), which becomes the income distribution frontier for groups I and II under restricted migration. We see that despite the inefficiency of the prohibition of migration, ss lies outside point B and with it curve OB on the floor of the graph. What this tells us is that from the point of view of groups I and II restriction of migration is more efficient than freedom of migration because both I and II can be made better off by preventing group III from leaving.[7] And this is so despite the inefficiency of impediments to migration from the global point of view.

Another feature of the restricted migration case is noteworthy. It will be observed that unlike OB, curve ss, the output distribution frontier for this case, can reach the 45° line on the floor of the diagram. This means that so long as there is no attempt to enforce universal equality, it is indeed possible to use taxes and transfers to achieve full equality among particular groups, or a first approximation to it, without reducing output to zero.[8] The cost in output forgone may still be substantial, but it is not necessarily prohibitive.[9] In other words the restricted migration case may not only benefit all classes of those who would remain behind in any event—it may also permit a degree of equalization in their incomes that otherwise might not be attainable.

The Role of Taxation of Migrants

So far rather than explaining the paradox, I may seem only to have confirmed it. But it is now quite easily dispelled. The basic source of the potential advantages to groups I and II of the prevention of migration is that with it the government retains for itself full freedom of action in its distributive policy. In particular it retains the right to tax the members of group III, the high-income group. Restricted migration is potentially helpful to groups I and II because in this comparison the government, as it were, ties its hands behind its back when migration is permitted. The government permits itself to redistribute income to the poor, but takes it only from the fairly poor and leaves the more affluent to escape altogether. Thus the original Bhagwati-Hamada contention is perfectly consistent with this interpretation. Taxation of migrants may be desirable simply because it gives the government access to the incomes of those who can best afford to contribute to the welfare of the poor.

Interpreted in this way there is no longer any mystery to the matter. Obviously the poor can benefit even if the pie is smaller, if the government simultaneously assumes the authority to cut the poor a much larger slice of that smaller pie.

More explicitly we can use our diagram to compare the effects of a tax on the incomes of migrants in a world with freedom of movement with the outcomes in the cases we have already examined. For this purpose we need merely note that once taxation of migrants is instituted, in principle all of surface TTT' becomes attainable.[10] This means that TT, the rightmost end of the surface, becomes just as real a possibility as SS. And because the T surface lies everywhere further from the origin than the S surface, curve SS will lie to the left of TT. Thus tt, the projection of TT on the floor of the figure, now becomes the income distribution frontier, and its relation to the other two frontiers ss and OB will be as shown in figure 7.5. From the point of view of groups I and II, tt will be superior to both other frontiers, and in addition it may share with ss the possibility of an intersection with the 45° line. But the superiority of tt now has a very simple explanation—the fact that it corresponds to a more efficient arrangement from the viewpoint of all groups in the economy, together with willingness by the government of the country of origin to make full use of instruments of redistribution that place the wealthier migrant class within the scope of its authority. With both efficiency and effective government policy potentially on the side of members of groups I and II, it is hardly surprising that they stand to gain from a policy of taxation of migrants.

Taxation of Migrants and Allocative Efficiency

From the atmosphere of mystery that hung over the initial description of the relation of restricted migration to the welfare of the nonmigrating members of the community we seem to have swung over too far in the opposite direction. Now matters seem excessively simple—taxation of rich migrants can help the poor only because it takes from the rich.

But centuries of economic analysis have trained us to resist leaving the story in this state. We are led to look for opportunities for mutual gains, for aspects of such a problem that are not zero sum. One reason for this, if no other, is that it is politically easier to institute a change that benefits all groups than one that helps some groups at the expense of others. Is there any way in which a tax on migrants can benefit all the groups involved? This is not as farfetched as it may sound at first. We all know how, for example, Pigouvian taxes upon detrimental externalities, which are paid to some extent by all of us, can be beneficial to everyone. There are ways in which this can also occur here.

One possibility has already been mentioned. I have already noted that inequalities in tax rates from country to country can lead to a misallocation of resources, with some individuals induced to migrate to jurisdictions in which taxes are low even though they do not make a maximal contribution to value of output by that choice of residence.

It is conceivable that where this occurs, a supplementary tax on migrants' income by their home country's government may act as a corrective and hence may contribute mutual gains via the resulting improvement in allocative efficiency.

But even where this is true, it is hard to believe that the improvement in allocation of the world's resources resulting from the proposed tax would produce results that were readily noticeable by any particular group of individuals. It does not seem plausible that it could compensate the members of group III for the loss in disposable income imposed by the supplementary tax on their income.

Yet there is another avenue for mutual gains from such an arrangement— one that *is* quite plausible and potentially significant. Recently there has been a spate of writings on externalities and the desirability of income redistribution (see, for example, Hochman and Rodgers 1969). The argument, in oversimplified form, can be illustrated by an arbitrary choice of one of its facets. It is widely held that poverty is a stimulus of crime and that much of this crime is directed against the wealthy. This means that wealthy persons will benefit indirectly from some reduction in income inequality from that which would result without government intervention. Similarly in an international setting peace and progress in the long run may require a reduction in the disparities between rich and poor nations. Thus there is reason for the rich to favor *some* income redistribution, even though it occurs at their own expense.

This illustration involves no element of altruism, but altruistic redistribution motives can be analyzed in similar terms. If poverty offends the consciences of wealthier persons and improvement in the circumstances of the poor gives them pleasure they may rationally (and in some ultimate sense, self-interestedly) choose voluntarily to support a program of taxation that takes money from the rich and gives it to the poor.

Why a program of taxation? Why not do the job through individual philanthropy? This is where the externalities side of the matter enters and plays a crucial role. First, no one wealthy individual acting alone can hope to make a significant contribution to reduction in poverty generally. Only by joint action, with simultaneous commitment by all those in a position to contribute, is there any hope of effective action.

Furthermore suppose there are many well-to-do individuals who are likely to derive psychic pleasure from a reduction in poverty. Then any one contributor's efforts will yield fruits that are enjoyed by other wealthy persons, who thereby unavoidably become free riders. As we know, particularly when large numbers are involved, the presence of a free-rider problem means that inadequate resources will be allocated to production of the benefit in question.

In these circumstances it will be rational for any individual acting alone to be extremely sparing in the contribution he or she is willing to make toward improvement in the conditions of the poor. Yet it may simultaneously be rational for that same individual to vote for a tax law that forces both himself and others in similar circumstances to contribute substantially for the same purpose. Only such a law may be able to provide the assurance that no one who can afford to pay will be permitted to ride free[11] (on this analysis, see Baumol 1952).

It is easy to provide casual evidence suggesting strongly that such considerations can be relevant for the taxation of migrants from the LDCs, and that it may indeed be a significant source of mutual gains.

There is a long tradition of emotional connection of migrants with their homelands. Persons who have migrated and been successful in their own careers have often devoted enormous effort seeking to help their less fortunate compatriots. Virtually every ethnic group has some history of such devotion, and there is every reason to believe that it is equally characteristic of successful migrants from the LDCs. Indeed it is not irrelevant to note that some of the most avid supporters of the taxation of migrants from the LDCs are themselves members of this group!

Distributive Criteria for the Full Set of Participants

If the externalities described in the preceding section are sufficiently great, it is clear that *some* nonzero level of taxation of migrants will be optimal— institution of such a tax will represent a (near) Pareto improvement.[12] But

how large a tax will then be called for still remains an open issue, for even
with considerable altruism on the part of the migrants it is plausible that the
amount of income they will want to give up to those who remain behind
will be rather less than the amount the latter will want them to contribute.

In any event the analysis should be capable of dealing with the case in
which altruism is a rather scarce commodity, so that taxation of migrants
does *not* offer mutual gains. In that circumstance the distributive interests
of the migrants and the other citizens of their native country are likely, for
all practical purposes, to be diametrically opposed.

Unfortunately here there exists no unique criterion that can settle these
differences, and so one cannot say in general what level of taxation is called
for *optimally*. Indeed we cannot even say that a nonzero tax level is to be
considered desirable.

There are two sources of difficulty. First, in judging optimality of distribution we normally want to take account of other differences characterizing
the individuals concerned: Did the government spend a good deal on their
education? Are they contributing to the productivity of the economy of
their native country? These and other such questions *should*, it is generally
agreed, be taken into account. But there is no universally accepted procedure for their inclusion. Second, because there is a tradeoff between
degree of equalization and the size of total output, some sort of compromise will have to be reached, particularly if it is true that absolute equality
can virtually preclude all production—that perfect equality is achievable
only in the graveyard. But *what* compromise then recommends itself? Here,
as we know, our problem is not the absence of a criterion, but rather the
profusion of criteria that have been offered.[13]

There have been many discussions undertaking to summarize some of
these criteria. Those generally listed include, among others, the utilitarian
criterion, the Rawls criterion, the income-maximization criterion, and a
compromise criterion assigning positive weights to both output and degree
of equality. A brief return to the income distribution frontier in the two-
person case will indicate the degree of ambiguity introduced by the availability of such a variety of standards.

In figure 7.6 three families of indifference curves are indicated. First
consider the family labeled H, which consists of lines each having a slope
of -1. Each such line satisfies the equation $y_1 + y_2 = k$ for some value of
the constant k and consequently represents a constant level of total income
for the two members of the community. The higher the line in this family,
the higher the combined incomes of the members of the community;
consequently, the optimal distribution on the maximal total income cri-

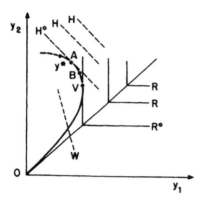

Figure 7.6

terion is the point of tangency A between the income distribution frontier Oy^* and H^0, one of this family of indifference curves. This criterion is not at all egalitarian, because it assigns the same value to an increment in the income of a poor person and to an equal increase in that of a wealthy one. Consequently it is not surprising to find its optimal point relatively far from the $45°$ line along the income distribution frontier. Yet it is noteworthy that it need not lie to the left of the market equilibrium point y^*. That is to say, some degree of income equalization may well stimulate output rather than inhibit it.[14]

The Rawlsian criterion, on the other hand, is a lexicographical ordering of increments in income, with the poorest member of the community assigned first priority. This is the most egalitarian of the criteria we will consider. Graphically it is represented by the family of L-shaped indifference curves labeled R, whose vertices all lie on the $45°$ line. That is to say, on the Rawlsian criterion a change in the vector of outputs is considered an improvement if it increases the absolute income of the poorest person (any rightward move from a point to the left of the $45°$ line) regardless of what it does to the incomes of others. Strongly egalitarian though it is, however, even the Rawlsian criterion does not insist on complete equality. It, too, sensibly accepts a compromise in which the output cost of increased equalization becomes unacceptably great. In figure 7.6 the optimal Rawlsian point is given by point V, where the income distribution frontier is vertical.[15] Thus the Rawlsian point can be expected to lie well to the right of the total income maximization point A, but to the left of the $45°$ line.

To avoid complicating the figure, only one of the parallel indifference curves, W, of the weighted average criterion has been indicated. This criterion assigns constant weights to total output and to degree of equality.[16] The absolute slope of these indifference curves is intermediate between the unit slope of the income maximization curves and the "infinite slope" of the relevant portion of the Rawlsian curves, because the weighted average criterion assigns a higher social value to an income gain by a poor person than it does to an equal gain by a rich one, but it assigns a positive value to each of them.[17] Consequently its optimal solution point B on the income distribution frontier will, not surprisingly, fall somewhere between A and V.

These three criteria are all I need to make my point.[18] For what the discussion has confirmed is that once we take into account the desires and interests of the migrants, we are in no position to calculate an optimal solution. True, any particular criterion does give us an answer that is generally unique, but that really assumes away the problem. Perhaps candor calls for us to proceed the other way—to select the point on the frontier that appeals to us most and then to formulate the criterion that justifies that choice. Such an exercise is not the pure rationalization it may appear to be at first glance. Its value is that it forces us to face up explicitly to the ethical standards implicit in our initial choice. For once we become aware of its implicit underpinnings we may well be led to reconsider that choice.

Concluding Comment

This of course is not the end of the matter. Formal analysis always forces simplifications on us and sometimes important considerations are consequently omitted from the calculations. Migration and the taxation of migrants have other significant effects on the welfare of both the migrants and those who remain behind. For example, success of the migrants in foreign lands may inspire an increased desire for education among the remainder of the homeland population, and this may well redound to the benefit of the community. On the other hand failure to tax migrants may induce an undesirably large level of migration and may thus contribute to scarcity of teachers in the country of origin. Perhaps at least as much to the point are the administrative complexities certain to beset any such tax proposal in practice. In his various writings on the subject, Bhagwati has listed many more such issues, and there is nothing to be gained here by an attempt to recapitulate the discussion. We merely have to recognize the existence of such supplementary issues and the possibility that they are of enormous and perhaps even overriding importance.

Nevertheless my analysis does offer some substantial conclusions that must of course be considered presumptive rather than categorical. Specifically the analysis has confirmed the superiority from the viewpoint of the nonmigrants of a tax upon the incomes of the migrants. Here the main contribution of the discussion has been its explanation of the source of this superiority. Aside from that the discussion has offered an externalities argument (which, in my view, has considerable plausibility) indicating the likelihood of mutual gains from such an arrangement. The persistence of the discussion of this issue and the identity of the advocates of such taxation is perhaps the main piece of evidence of the significance of this externality phenomenon.

Notes

I am grateful to the Sloan Foundation whose grant was exceedingly helpful in completion of this chapter, and am indebted to James Mirrlees and Pulin Nayak for their useful comments on the manuscript.

1. This exemption, however, must be recognized as another possible source of misallocation of resources. The difference between the taxes paid by citizens and noncitizens of their native countries may well induce people to switch their allegiances, particularly if the tax on migrants is substantial. That, in turn, may reduce the numbers who later return to work in their country of origin either temporarily or permanently. The assumption that there is a zero tax elasticity of citizenship retention simply is unsafe.

2. Actually, in the region where the curve is positively sloped, although it does continue to bound the feasible region, it no longer constitutes part of the income distribution frontier, which includes only the northeast boundary of the feasible region. A point such as K in the positively sloping segment of the curve, involves incomes for both parties below those at V, so that K is clearly not in the efficient set.

3. For a more careful argument, see Baumol and Fischer 1979. The shape of the curve has been recognized previously (see, for example, Phelps 1973). However, as Dr. Nayak has emphasized, if people prefer some labor to none, or will do *some* work out of altruism, then the 45° line can be reached at a point inside the nonnegative orthant.

4. In this exercise it is useful to use as a base point the (real) situation in which free migration is possible and the migrants have already identified themselves by departing. The case of prohibition of departure can then be taken as a conceptual experiment in which we see what would have happened if those *known* to constitute group III, the migrants, had been forced to stay at home. We proceed in this way because otherwise it would be impossible to distinguish the potential migrants

from the members of the other two groups. I am grateful to Professor Mirrlees for calling this issue to my attention.

5. Of course if our three groups operate in labor markets that are totally independent, the configuration of S' and T' must be precisely as shown in figure 7.4. However, that is hardly plausible. The potential migrants who otherwise would be engineers or doctors in foreign countries are likely to become engineers or doctors at home if they cannot leave, and that means they will be rivals of those who otherwise would have performed those jobs at home—presumably the members of group II.

6. This does involve an analytical complication. A rise in the rate at which skilled nonmigrants are taxed may induce some of them to become migrants, and that will change the composition of our three groups of individuals; that is, the composition of the groups at different points of OB will be different.

7. We can see now why it is convenient but not necessary to assume that point S' lies directly below T' so that B is their common projection on the floor of the diagram. For we know that SS lies to the right of S' so that ss must lie further from the origin than B, which gives us our conclusion. But even if T' were not directly above S', the result is plausible. Certainly it must hold if the projection of T' is closer to the origin than that of S' (strong complementarity in production of group III with groups I and II). But even if the reverse is true, it is clearly possible for our result to hold. So long as the projection of T' lies somewhere between B and ss, our argument remains vaid.

8. Note that with nondiscriminatory taxes and transfers based only on the taxpayers' income it is impossible to make a person who is richer than another before the tax payment become the poorer individual after the tax payment. Hence even if SS reaches the 45° line, it cannot cross it. I am indebted to David Bradford and Peter Diamond for pointing out an error on this issue in a previous draft of this paper.

9. An example in practice occurs when welfare payments yield income levels comparable with those obtained by very unskilled laborers. There are many who have commented with some disapproval on the resulting inducement to inefficiency, but few have claimed that the economy as a whole must inevitably totter as a result.

10. However, a change in the tax rate on the incomes of migrants or of the skilled nonmigrants may well lead to changes in the membership of those groups, an issue with which the analysis cannot readily deal explicitly.

11. It is not difficult to translate these circumstances into formal terms. Let us assign an index i to each individual in the community that increases with the magnitude of the person's income y_i, so that $y_i \leqq y_{i+1}$. Let i's utility function be

$$u_i = U^i(x_{i1}, \ldots, x_{in}, y_1, \ldots, y_{i-r}) \qquad (1 \leqq r < i), \qquad (1)$$

where x_{ij} is i's consumption of good j.

Let i seek to maximize his or her utility subject to a budget constraint

$$\sum p_j x_{ij} \leqq y_i - T_i, \tag{2}$$

where T_i is a tax paid by i to be distributed to lower-income persons, in accord with some formula

$$y_k = f(y_k^*, T_i) \qquad \partial y_k / \partial T_i > 0 \qquad (k \leqq k^*, \text{ for some } k^* \leqq i - r), \tag{3}$$

where y_k^* is k's initial income.

In general if the partial derivatives of U^i with respect to y_k ($k \leqq i - r$) are all positive we should expect a utility maximizing solution for i to yield $T_i > 0$. That is, i will then *want* some redistribution to occur at his or her expense.

Next suppose, as is true of reality, that if such a redistributive tax is imposed on i, it will also be imposed at the same time upon other persons, particularly everyone wealthier than i. In that case we would expect the tax rate that maximizes i's utility to increase because every such increase will lead to a rise in poor person k's income larger than before, and hence, given $\partial U^i / \partial y_k$, it will contribute more to i's utility.

To describe this case, we replace (2) by

$$\sum p_j x_{ij} \leqq y_i - tT_i^* \qquad (T_i^* \text{ constant}), \tag{2'}$$

and (3) by

$$y_k = f(y_k^*, t \sum T_w^*)$$

$$\tag{3'}$$

$\forall k \leqq k^*$ (for some $k^* \leqq i - r$), $\qquad \forall w \geqq w^*$ (for some w^* with $k^* < w^* \leqq i$).

These tell us, clearly, that now k benefits not only from i's contribution, tT_i^*, but also from the contribution of everyone else with income no less than y_w.

A glance at (2') indicates that t may formally be considered as one of i's consumption goods whose price is T_i^*. Moreover substituting (3') for y_k in (1), i's utility function can be rewritten

$$U^i(\cdot) \equiv V^i(x_{i1}, \ldots, x_{in}, t, y_k^*, y_{k+1}^*, \ldots, y_{i-r}^*).$$

A rise in the ratio of $\sum T_w^*$ to T_i^* can be taken to be equivalent to a decrease in the price of t. If this is valid, our result follows from the Slutsky theorem: an increase in the number of persons who are subject to the redistributive tax will, considering only the substitution effect, increase the tax rate that i considers optimal.

12. A *near* Pareto improvement because in a case such as this, even if the bulk of the migrants are happy to pay some tax, it is hardly likely that *all* of them will feel that way. After all the Pareto criterion was formulated in large part to make it possible to take account of the preferences of individuals rather than having to judge matters in terms of the (indefinable) preferences of entire groups in which opinions do not happen to be unanimous.

13. The new fairness analysis associated with the work of Foley (1967), Varian (1974, 1975), and others may at first blush seem to have escaped these sources of ambiguity, letting the preferences of the individuals involved determine whether a particular distribution of outputs is fair or unfair. As in the classic problem of fair

division of a cake, a distribution is judged to be fair if no one participant envies the holdings of any other. But this argument holds only in the absence of the two considerations just mentioned in the text. It is precisely because those considerations cannot be ignored when we turn from a study of pure exchange to an analysis of production that the new fairness analysis runs into great complications when it deals with production.

14. One may argue that in the absence of externalities a regime of universally perfect competition will maximize the value of the community's total output, so that these points, y^* and A, will coincide. But then monopoly can aggravate inequality *and* reduce value of output, thus showing how equalization can sometimes contribute both to equality and to aggregate income. Perhaps more to the point is the contrast between economies in which workers are offered a direct stake in the introduction of labor-saving innovation (as in Japan or on a kibbutz in Israel) and communities in which the labor force regards every such innovation as a threat. Empirical evidence seems to confirm the a priori judgment that such a sharing process in the long run contributes both to output and to equality.

15. It will be noted that on this argument the Rawlsian solution in figures 7.3 and 7.4 must lie either on ss or on tt, depending on whether emigration is or is not permitted.

16. Actually there is no reason to make these indifference curves either linear or parallel. One may, for example, wish to posit a diminishing marginal rate of substitution of progress toward either one goal as an offset for decreased achievement in terms of the other. But even the choice of measure of equality can impart a nonlinearity to the indifference curves. However, this obviously does not affect the substance of our discussion.

17. We would expect this slope to be steeper than it would be otherwise if the more well-to-do derive external benefits from increased equality, other things being equal. For in that case the loss in utility suffered by wealthy individual 2 from a given reduction Δy_2 in his income is partly offset by the rise in his utility resulting from the associated gain Δy_1 in the poorer person's income. Consequently a rise in y_1 smaller than it would have been in the absence of the externalities will be required to compensate for the loss in welfare produced by any given decline in y_2. In short $\Delta y_2 / \Delta y_1$ will be increased in absolute value by the externalities. Consequently the optimal solution will tend to move rightward toward greater equality, as we would expect intuitively.

18. Although the utilitarian criterion has been mentioned, it is not dealt with here because more information is required before it can be represented in my diagram. To find the utilitarian solution point we must have some information about the utility functions of the affected individuals. Some, notably Professor Lerner, have taken the position that in the absence of such information a Bayesian viewpoint must lead us to interpret the utilitarian criterion as a call for equalization of incomes. But with an income distribution frontier having the shape indicated in the figures, it is hard to take that conclusion literally. And if, like the Rawlsian solution, a Bayesian utilitarian is to accept some compromise taking into account the cost of

income forgone, one is apparently left with no guidance to lead us to that compromise which is to be considered the best of the (regrettable) choices that are available. In any event, as Sen (1973) has emphasized, the utilitarian criterion is not so unambiguously egalitarian once differences in the utility functions of different individuals are taken into account. Once some individual i is known to derive more pleasure than another person j from an additional dollar of income, the utilitarian criterion calls for more money to go to i than to j because the former is the more effective pleasure-producing machine. Thus even though an equal distribution will leave i happier than j, a utilitarian optimum calls for a still-greater disparity in relative well-being. Furthermore if wealth gives its possessor on-the-job training in the enjoyment of consumption, the optimal disparities in income distribution may well grow with the passage of time in a utilitarian world, taking the solution point further and further to the left on the income distribution frontier! Note that most of this was recognized by Edgeworth as early as 1877: "Unto him that hath greater capacity for pleasure shall be added more of the means of pleasure" (Edgeworth 1877, p. 43, as quoted in Creedy 1979).

References

Baumol, W. J. 1952. Welfare Economics and the Theory of the State. London: Longman. 2d ed., 1965. Cambridge, Mass.: Harvard University Press.

Baumol, W. J., and Dietrich Fischer. 1979. The output distribution frontier: Alternatives to income taxes and transfers for strong equality goals. *American Economic Review* 69: 514–525.

Bhagwati, J. N. 1979. International migration of the highly skilled: Economics, ethics and taxes. *Third World Quarterly* 1: 17–30.

Creedy, J. 1979. The early use of Lagrange multipliers in economics. Working paper no. 27, Department of Economics, University of Durham, England.

Edgeworth, F. Y. 1877. New and Old Methods of Ethics. London: James Parker and Company.

Foley, Duncan. 1967. Resource allocation and the public sector. *Yale Economic Essays* 7.

Hochman, Harold M., and James D. Rodgers. 1969. Pareto optimal redistribution. *American Economic Review* 49: 542–557.

Phelps, E. S. 1973. Taxation of wage income for economic justice. *Quarterly Journal of Economics* 87: 331–354.

Sen, Amartya. 1973. On Economic Inequality. Oxford: Clarendon Press.

Varian, H. R. 1974. Equity, envy and efficiency. *Journal of Economic Theory* 9: 63–91.

Varian, H. R. 1975. Distributive justice, welfare economics, and the theory of fairness. *Philosophy and Public Affairs* 4: 223–247.

8   Migration and Optimal Income Taxes

James A. Mirrlees

Migration

High tax rates encourage emigration. The resulting loss of tax revenue is widely believed to be an important reason for keeping taxes down. If, as Bhagwati (1980) has proposed, the emigrants' foreign incomes were taxed, there would be two advantages to the domestic government: emigrants would contribute to tax revenues, and tax rates could be higher. There are also implications for other taxes and subsidies. In particular education would become a better investment for the state, and should therefore be subsidized to a greater extent. In chapter 5 Bhagwati and Hamada show, in a simple model, that foreign and domestic incomes should be taxed at the same rate, namely (nearly) 100 percent. The assumptions of that model lead perhaps too directly to the conclusion. Income is the outcome of education in the same way that a firm's profits are the outcome of its investments, consumers wishing to maximize discounted net income less education costs. Thus nearly full taxation of the return and nearly full subsidization of the capital cost induces individuals to do what the state would like, with essentially all costs and benefits accruing to the state. Fundamental reasons for less than full taxation are absent from the model, and one wonders whether the conclusion that the same tax rates should be levied on domestic and foreign incomes would hold in a more realistic model.

The model also ignores the possibility of emigrants severing themselves completely from their country's tax system. One might perhaps think it obvious that this is a reason for reducing the foreign-income tax rate relative to domestic tax rates, a point possibly too obvious to be worth exploring formally.

In this chapter I examine the optimal taxation of foreign incomes by LDCs (less developed countries) in models that may be a little more realistic than the Bhagwati-Hamada model. Although only special cases are solved explicitly, the results for these cases tend to support the case for high taxation of foreign earnings. It should be emphasized that the arguments apply only to LDCs with governments whose expenditures benefit the generality of the population. As a preliminary, the third section is devoted to the theory of optimal taxation when foreign earnings are not taxed.

It should be emphasized at the outset that the income taxes and subsidies appearing in the models correspond to all taxes on incomes *and expenditures* in the real world. If it were desirable to tax foreign earnings at the same rate as domestic earnings, the foreign-income rate should include an element corresponding to such taxes as sales tax, value-added tax, and import duties.

A second simplification I have allowed is to ignore all intertemporal $considerations, and even to pretend that individuals either earn income at home or abroad but not both. These are not satisfactory assumptions, but models allowing migration to be temporary or permanent and to take place part of the way through the working life seem to become complicated very quickly. In the fourth section, where the discussion is conducted heuristically, it is possible to allow for partial migration.

Criteria

Three different criteria occur to people thinking about migration, depending on the group whose welfare is to count. The first criterion attempts to restrict the group to those who do not migrate. This is hardly satisfactory. Some of those who do not migrate may have wished to do so; some who do migrate may do a great deal for their country of origin, such as sending home remittances. It is therefore hard to see how a loyalty criterion could be implemented. The fact that many countries do so little to tax emigrants, temporary or permanent, suggests that governments are not guided by a loyal-citizen criterion. Because it is morally unattractive, we should be pleased to be able to reject it. An alternative interpretation of the criterion is that the government should restrict taxation (and benefits) to voters. That opens the question: Who should be voters? But, whether the voters are all nationals, or one colonel, we should be prepared to argue that they ought to vote in the interests not only of one another, but of others, if that seems to be right.

The second criterion defines the relevant group as that of nationals, whether working in the country or not. "Nationals" had better be understood in a nonlegal sense because the group is otherwise endogenous, the extent to which people change nationality being influenced by economic variables. Perhaps the best definition is nationality at birth, though even that is not always well-defined. With this criterion, like the first, it is unclear how to classify immigrants. Strictly speaking, they are excluded; but I hope few of us believe that is morally right. Yet the alternative of including all who would or might like to immigrate is not consistent with the spirit of the criterion.

The third main possibility is to include all humans. Criteria that do so are surely morally defensible, but they may be thought not to be what an adviser to a democratic state is expected to be guided by. The network of double-tax agreements and the allowances for foreign-income tax provided by many countries suggest that the conclusion is too hasty. Totally to neglect the welfare of citizens of other countries is not acceptable as explicit policy motivation.

In the case of an LDC one might reduce possible conflict between the national and world welfare functions by insisting that marginal incomes for those living in the countries to which emigrants go have a negligible weight in the world welfare function because of their high incomes. Specifically it would then be permissible to neglect the effect on their incomes of changes in their governments' tax revenue, brought about by changes in emigration. These effects are in principle substantial and can be neglected only if there is some reason to regard the welfare change as negligible. One can also often neglect immigration as negligible, simply because incomes are too low to encourage it. In this chapter effects on foreigners are neglected on these grounds. But it is not always permissible to do so. Doctors and engineers may migrate from one poor country to another. There are LDCs where the use of government revenue would not need to be assigned more weight than government revenue in a typical industrial country.

No Tax on Foreign Incomes

The easiest theory of optimal income taxation is that for an economic model in which individuals' productivity—here identified with their wage—is identifiable and fixed, though their inclination to migrate is unknown. An individual of productivity n receiving after-tax income $x(n)$ has utility

$$v(n) = u(x(n), n). \tag{1}$$

The number of such individuals who remain in the economy is $f(v(n), n)$, an increasing function of v. A small change in $x(n)$, δx, induces a few people more or less to emigrate, but they are almost indifferent between staying and going. Assuming that this indifference correctly reflects what they will or would experience, the effect on total utility is

$$u_x \delta x \cdot f(v(n), n).\tag{2}$$

Notice that this argument neglects the effects on those living in the foreign economies of resulting changes in tax revenue there.

The effect of δx on tax revenue in the domestic economy, because we assume marginal productivities do not change, is a reduction by

$$\delta x \cdot f(v(n), n) + (x - n)f_v \cdot u_x \cdot \delta x.\tag{3}$$

For optimality (2) and (3) must be in constant proportion as n varies. Thus

$$u_x f = \lambda f + \lambda(x - n)f_v u_x\tag{4}$$

for some constant λ. The constant is to be determined by the economy's budget constraint. Information about propensities to migrate is conveniently expressed by the *elasticity of numbers with respect to after-tax income*:

$$\eta = \frac{x f_v u_x}{f}.\tag{5}$$

With this notation (4) can be rewritten as

$$\frac{n - x}{x} = \frac{1}{\eta}\left(1 - \frac{u_x}{\lambda}\right).\tag{6}$$

The left side is tax as a proportion of after-tax income.

In general η is a function of n as well as x, so that (6) is not an explicit formula for the optimal tax rates. When η is constant, it is easily solved. For example, if

$$\eta = 0.5, \qquad u = t(n) - \frac{1}{x},\tag{7}$$

then (6) becomes

$$n = 3x - \frac{2}{\lambda x}.\tag{8}$$

Thus writing $\lambda = 12/a$,

$$x(n) = \tfrac{1}{6}[n + (2a + n^2)^{1/2}]$$

and

$x/n \to \frac{1}{3}$ $(n \to \infty)$.

In this case x is a convex function of n. There is a minimum consumption level, depending on the resource constraint, and the marginal tax rate falls from 5/6 on the lowest incomes to 2/3 on the highest. This example suggests that rather high tax rates are justifiable even if the propensity to migrate is quite large. Of course other sources of labor supply elasticity have been neglected.

To help intuition about η, consider the following situation. Denote foreign earnings, net of foreign tax, by m, and suppose that m, n are jointly distributed in the population with density $g(m, n)$. (One might well suppose that a nonzero proportion of people with home wages n have no foreign opportunities, that is, $m = 0$; but it is simpler to neglect that here, for it makes no essential difference to the analysis.) Suppose furthermore that working abroad involves the same disutility of labor for anyone as working at home and is equivalent to multiplying after-tax income by $\gamma < 1$: that is, an (m, n)-person who works abroad has utility $u(\gamma m, n)$.

Then the number of n-people who decide not to migrate is

$$f(v, n) = \int_0^M g(m, n) \, dm, \tag{9}$$

where $M = M(v, n)$ is defined by

$$u(\gamma M, n) = v. \tag{10}$$

From (9) we have

$$f_v = g(M, n) M_v = \frac{g(M, n)}{\gamma u_x(\gamma M, n)}.$$

In formula (5), η is defined in terms of $u_x(x, n)$, where x is after-tax income of an n-person, satisfying $u(x, n) = v$. By (10), $\gamma M = x$. Consequently

$$\eta = \frac{x f_v u_x}{f} = \frac{xg}{\gamma f} = Mg(M, n) \Big/ \int_0^M g(m, n) \, dm. \tag{11}$$

It is to be expected that under any tax schedule, and in particular the optimum, η will vary to a substantial extent with n. To explore this, it is worth analyzing another specific example. Let

$$u(x, n) = u_1(x) + t(n). \tag{12}$$

Let $\log m$ and $\log n$ be distributed according to a binormal distribution with means zero and variances σ_m^2 and σ_n^2 and correlation coefficient ρ, so that $g(m, n)$ is proportional to

$$\frac{1}{mn} \exp\left[-\frac{\mu^2 - 2\rho\mu\nu + \nu^2}{2(1 - \rho^2)} \right],$$

where

$$\mu = \frac{\log m}{\sigma_m}; \qquad \nu = \frac{\log n}{\sigma_n}.$$

The restriction to zero means is no real restriction: different means can be accommodated by varying the parameter γ.

With a little manipulation, we find using (11) that

$$\eta = \frac{1}{\alpha} \frac{1}{\psi(\zeta)}; \qquad \alpha = \sigma_m \sqrt{1 - \rho^2}, \tag{13}$$

where we define

$$\psi(\zeta) = e^{(1/2)\chi^2} \int_{-\infty}^{\zeta} e^{-(1/2)z^2} \, dz, \tag{14}$$

$$\zeta = \frac{\mu - \rho\nu}{\sqrt{1 - \rho^2}} = \frac{1}{\sqrt{1 - \rho^2}} \left[\frac{\log M}{\sigma_m} - \frac{\rho \log n}{\sigma_n} \right]. \tag{15}$$

ψ is an increasing positive function, approximately $1/(1 - \zeta)$ for $\zeta < -3$ ($\psi(-3) = 0.305$), and approximately $\sqrt{2\pi} e^{(1/2)\chi^2}$ for large ζ.

The optimal-tax formula (6) for this case is

$$\frac{n}{x} - 1 = \alpha\psi(\zeta) \cdot (1 - u_1'(x)/\gamma). \tag{16}$$

Recollect that by (10), $M = x/\gamma$, and this should be substituted in (15):

$$\zeta = \frac{1}{\alpha} \log(xn^{-\tau}\gamma); \qquad \tau = \rho\sigma_m/\sigma_n. \tag{17}$$

To gain some qualitative insight, we shall analyze the implications of (16) for small and large n in turn. But notice first that if we define x_0 by

$$u_1'(x_0) = \gamma, \tag{18}$$

(16) is satisfied when $x = x_0$ and $n = x_0$. Thus

$$x(x_0) = x_0. \tag{19}$$

By concavity of u, $x < n$ for $n > x_0$ (income taxation) and $x > n$ for $n < x_0$ (income subsidization).

As $n \to 0$, one expects that x tends to a positive limit. I can show that it does, provided that $\lim_{x \to 0} u_1 = -\infty$. This seems a reasonable assumption to make, and it will be assumed. If $\lim x$ is positive as $n \to 0$, the left side of (16) tends to -1. Also, by (17), $\zeta \to \infty$, and ψ therefore tends to infinity. It follows from (16) that $u_1'/\gamma \to 1$ as $n \to 0$, that is,

$$x(0) = x_0. \tag{20}$$

Before further comment on the joint significance of (19) and (20), consider n large. To avoid a lengthy analysis, assume that ζ tends to a limit, possibly $\pm\infty$, and consider the three possibilites:

(1) $\zeta \to -\infty$. Then $\psi \sim -1/\zeta$, and (16) implies that

$$-\alpha \log \frac{xn^{-\tau}}{\gamma} \cdot \left(\frac{n}{x} - 1\right) \to 1$$

if $x \to \infty$ or is bounded above in any case. Because $xn^{-\tau} \to 0$, $n/x \to 1$. These two statements can be consistent only if $\tau > 1$, and then we have

$$x \sim n - \frac{1}{\alpha(\tau - 1)\log n}. \tag{21}$$

(2) $\zeta \to \bar{\zeta}$. Then $x \sim \gamma e^{\alpha \bar{\zeta}} n^{\tau} \to \infty$, and from (16),

$$\frac{x}{n} \to [1 + \alpha\psi(\bar{\zeta})]^{-1}. \tag{22}$$

These statements can be consistent only if $\tau = 1$, and then we have

$$[1 + \alpha\psi(\bar{\zeta})]\gamma e^{\alpha \bar{\zeta}} = 1. \tag{23}$$

(3) $\zeta \to \infty$. Again $x \to \infty$, and (16) implies that $n/x \to \infty$. With $xn^{-\tau} \to \infty$, this requires $\tau < 1$. We have $\psi \sim \sqrt{2\pi} e^{(1/2)\kappa^2}$ as $\zeta \to \infty$. Therefore

$$\sqrt{2\pi}\alpha \frac{x}{n}\exp\left[\frac{1}{2\alpha^2}\left\{\log\left(\frac{xn^{-\tau}}{\gamma}\right)\right\}^2\right] \to 1.$$

Taking logarithms,

$$\frac{1}{2\alpha^2}\left\{\log\left(\frac{xn^{-\tau}}{\gamma}\right)\right\}^2 + \log\left(\frac{x}{n}\right) \to -\log(\alpha\sqrt{2\pi}).$$

Because $\log(x/n) = \log(xn^{-\tau}) - (1 - \tau)\log n$, and $xn^{-\tau} \to \infty$, we deduce on dividing by $\{\log(xn^{-\tau}/\gamma)\}^2$ that

$$\frac{(1 - \tau)\log n}{\{\log(xn^{-\tau}/\gamma)\}^2} \to \frac{1}{2\alpha^2}.$$

Taking square roots we obtain

$$x \sim \gamma n^\tau \exp(\alpha\sqrt{2(1 - \tau)\log n}). \tag{24}$$

In summary we have shown that $x/n \to 1$ and the marginal tax rate therefore tends to zero when $\rho\sigma_m/\sigma_n = \tau \geq 1$, but that $x/n \to 0$ and the marginal tax rate tends to one when $\rho\sigma_m/\sigma_n < 1$. The latter case is perhaps the most realistic. In the lower range of n, where incomes are subsidized, we have found that $x = x_0$ both at $n = 0$ and at the zero-tax level. Thus x is a *decreasing* function of n near $n = 0$. In the setting of the problem it was supposed unreasonably that it would be possible, if desirable, to have after-tax income a decreasing function of before-tax income. Because we have found that it is optimal to exploit this freedom in a model with no elasticity of labor supply other than through migration, we should really modify the problem at least by requiring x to be a nondecreasing function of n. If we do so, it is optimal to have x constant for an initial range of n. In this model it is optimal to have a marginal tax rate of 100 percent on the lowest range of incomes.

The Foreign-Income Tax: General Considerations

From the point of view of the worker, domestic labor and foreign labor are substitutes. Therefore if one is taxed, both should be. From the general theory of nonlinear taxation (see, for example, Mirrlees 1976) we know that the marginal rate of tax on one commodity should be greater than the marginal rate on another if the marginal rate of substitution of the first for the second increases with ability. The result is independent of the distribution of ability, but it does depend on the assumptions (among others) that ability can be characterized one-dimensionally, and that individual consumers use some of each of the commodities. We therefore cannot apply the theorem automatically. It is plausible that more able people find it easier to substitute a dollar of foreign earnings for a dollar of home earnings, and therefore plausible that foreign income should be taxed at a higher rate than domestic income. But this is not a strict implication of the theorem. In particular one may well wonder whether the presence of opportunities for earning untaxed foreign income may not affect the marginal rate of substitution between taxed foreign income and home income so as to greatly weaken the result.

This issue is worth exploring formally, despite the highly restrictive assumption that abilities in the population can be characterized by a single real variable. Consider then a model in which a typical consumer has utility function $u(x, y, y', z, n)$, where

x = income after tax;

y = foreign earnings net of tax, subject to domestic tax;

y' = foreign earnings net of tax, not subject to domestic tax;

z = domestic earnings before tax.

Recollect that in this kind of model one identifies earnings, before deduction of the taxes that are to be determined, with labor supplied by the consumer. With foreign tax rates being fixed throughout the analysis, we can use variables for foreign income that are net of tax collected by foreign governments. n is the consumer's "ability."

The tax policy of the domestic government makes x a function of y, y', and z of the form

$$x = c(y, z) + y'.$$

We know from the theorem alluded to above that in a model in which there is no untaxable commodity, the difference between the marginal tax rates on two income sources (as a proportion of before-tax income from the source) has the opposite sign to the partial derivative with respect to n of the ratio of the marginal utilities of the two income sources. In the present model that means that foreign income is taxed at a higher marginal rate than domestic income under the optimal system if

$$\frac{\partial}{\partial n} \frac{u_y(x, y, z, n)}{u_z(x, y, z, n)} < 0. \tag{25}$$

This is the correct result when there is no untaxed commodity. We can deduce the corresponding result when the untaxed income source y' is introduced. The consumer chooses y' to maximize

$$u(c(y, z) + y', y, y', z, n).$$

Denoting the maximized utility by $\bar{u}(c, y, z, n)$, the above result now applies to the utility function $\bar{u}$. By the envelope theorem,

$$\bar{u}_y = u_y(c + y', y, y', z, n),$$

$$\bar{u}_z = u_z(c + y', y, y', z, n),$$

where y' is the function of c, y, z, n defined by the fact that it maximizes u. Define

$$s(c, y, y', z, n) = u_y/u_z.$$

We have to consider the partial derivative of s with respect to n, taking account of the dependence of y' on n. Thus foreign income should be taxed more highly at the margin than domestic income if

$$s_n + s_{y'} \frac{\partial y'}{\partial n} < 0. \tag{26}$$

It seems likely that the willingness s to substitute home for foreign earnings would have a negative partial derivative with respect to n: $s_n < 0$. It also seems plausible that y' would increase with n, given y and z and c. But it does seem reasonable that y' should have the opposite effect on s from n, that $s_{y'} > 0$. In this case the presence of an untaxed source of income does seem to be a good reason for having a lower marginal tax rate on the source for which it is a closer substitute.

The case for supposing that the partial derivative of s with respect to untaxable foreign income y' is positive is by no means overwhelming. One way of thinking about this question is to consider the special case

$$u = u_0(x) + u_1(z/n) + u_2(y/n) + u_3(y'/n), \tag{27}$$

where u_1, u_2, and u_3 might be thought of as utility arising from labor activity in successive subperiods of the consumer's life. In this particular case it is evident that s, being the ratio of the derivatives of u_1 and u_2, is independent of y'. Consequently by (26) the condition for higher tax on foreign income is simply that s_n be negative, a condition that, as I have remarked, seems quite plausible. The form (27) may not seem particularly plausible, with consumption separated from labor and allocated over the lifetime independently of labor. An additively separable utility function for consumption and labor is quite commonly used and is at least not evidently absurd. The implicit assumption of a rather perfect capital market is much more unrealistic, but there is no reason to think that a more detailed treatment of intertemporal consumption would affect the presumption about $s_{y'}$ one way or the other. One influence neglected by the additive form (27) is the way that experience of working abroad may make the transition to complete independence from the home country, severing the tax link, more palatable. Like all intertemporally additive utility functions, it supposes that the influence of recent circumstances is no different from the influence of earlier experiences. The best case for supposing that $s_{y'}$ is positive is that working abroad may tend to make the home country, its needs, and the obligations it imposes, less vivid and compelling.

For the more general case in which consumers differ in more than one dimension of ability—for example, their earning capacity may not be highly correlated with their earning capacity at home—no result as conveniently applicable as (25) is available. A simple generalization of the Atkinson-Stiglitz theorem (Atkinson and Stiglitz 1976) tells us that foreign and home income should be taxed at the same rate if the consumer's utility function takes the form

$$u(\phi(x, y, z), x, n_1, n_2, \ldots).\tag{28}$$

In this case the marginal rate of substitution between y and z is the same for everyone who has the same x, y, and z. Unfortunately (28) is not a particularly plausible form in our context. That does not imply that the two sources of income should be taxed at different rates. It does not seem to be worth pursuing the impact of a nontaxable income source y' on the Atkinson-Stiglitz result in the present context, interesting though the question is, more generally.

From a heuristic discussion like this, one should not draw firm conclusions. But I think it shows that the commonsense belief that taxes on foreign income ought to be low because it is easy to change citizenship, or cheat, is not very well founded. There may be other offsetting arguments for taxing foreign income at a higher rate. In any case escape to nontaxed status, whether legally or illegally, may often be as easily available to the home earner as to the foreign-income earner. Escape routes do often provide a case for lower tax rates. One must assess their bearing on different kinds of earnings rather carefully before concluding that they provide a case for low foreign-income tax rates.

A Model of Foreign-Income Taxation

The rather general model indicated in the previous section is, it seems, hard to get detailed results from. Qualitative results are quite interesting, but quantitative ones are a better basis for policy discussion, however preliminary. In this section I extend the model used in the third section to the case in which foreign income can, sometimes, be taxed by the home country. From the previous analysis we found that it might be optimal, under special circumstances, to have a tax system under which after-tax domestic earnings decrease with earnings, whereas foreign after-tax earnings increase. That is a mildly interesting curiosity, but hardly realistic. The model omitted labor-supply elasticity, which surely exists. One simple way of bringing it in is to introduce the possibility of untaxed labor, as in the preceding section. The model is therefore generalized as follows.

Imagine a country whose citizens can choose to stay in the country as income-tax payers; to work abroad, report their incomes to the home government, and pay income tax at a different rate; or not to pay income taxes to the home government. They vary in their abilities to earn income in these three categories and in their willingness to sever legal connections with the home country. This conception is expressed by supposing that people of given income-earning ability would choose the one of the two taxable possibilities that provides greatest utility, but that a proportion depending on the utility thus available would prefer nontaxable status. We then have to identify the tax policies that maximize total utility, subject to the home government's budget constraint.

The next few pages are devoted to the mathematical analysis of this problem. Conditions characterizing the optimum for nicely-behaved situations are stated as the solution at the end of the section. These take the form of a pair of differential equations and corresponding initial conditions. The equations are not as readily interpretable as (6), although a sympathetic eye would see a resemblance to the previous equation (particularly in the specialized form (16)). Numerical solution would be possible, though there are difficulties that will be alluded to below. Rather than pursue that approach, we turn in the final section to the analysis of special cases for which substantial information may be obtained.

In this section, notation is first established, then a Lagrangian for the problem set up. The Lagrangian is a double integral in the space of home and foreign incomes. First-order conditions are obtained by considering the subpopulation with a particular home income and choosing the utility level for those who choose to be taxable at home with due regard to the effects on migration. This procedure yields an equation for the derivative with respect to utility of the taxable foreign income of someone indifferent about migrating. A similar procedure yields another equation for the derivative of home income with respect to utility. These conditions provide the two differential equations. The initial conditions are obtained by careful attention to those who have the lowest foreign-income earning ability.

An individual who works at home in an occupation that attracts tax has productivity n. If he or she worked abroad with taxable status, the income net of foreign tax would be m. Taxes exist—and are to be chosen optimally—that provide utility $u_h(n)$ if he or she stays at home, $u_f(m)$ if he or she works abroad. This formulation embodies the assumption that the government cannot know what an individual's income would have been had he or she gone abroad instead of staying at home, or vice versa. An individual of type (m, n) who chooses to remain a taxpayer gets utility

$$v = \max\{u_h(n), u_f(m)\}. \tag{29}$$

In equilibrium $f(m, n, v)$ of such people choose to remain taxable, the others emigrating for good and severing their tax liability to the home government or indulging in other untaxable activities with greater utility. To be more precise, f is a density function for m and n.

The after-tax earnings that people require to achieve specified levels of utility are given by convex increasing functions:

$$y(m) = Y(u_f(m)),$$
$$z(n) = Z(u_h(n)), \tag{30}$$

where y refers to foreign earnings after deduction of home tax, and z to home earnings, net of tax. Notice that this notation differs from that used in the previous section, where y and z referred to earnings before deduction of home tax.

Let H be the set of (m, n) for which $u_h \geq u_f$, and F the set for which $u_h < u_f$. Then the state's tax revenue is

$$T = \iint_H [n - z(n)]f(m, n, u_h(n)) \, dm \, dn$$
$$+ \iint_F [m - y(m)]f(m, n, u_f(m)) \, dm \, dn. \tag{31}$$

This formulation assumes that the indifferent stay at home. One would suppose that they form a set of measure zero, so that the convention is of no significance.

The total utility of (m, n)-people who leave the tax system is

$$\int_v^\infty w f_w(m, n, w) \, dw = \Omega(m, n, v) \tag{32}$$

as a definition. Welfare will be measured by total utility. The welfare of the whole relevant population is

$$W = \iint_H [\Omega(m, n, u_h) + u_h f(m, n, u_h)] \, dm \, dn$$
$$+ \iint_F [\Omega(m, n, u_f) + u_f f(m, n, u_f)] \, dm \, dn. \tag{33}$$

Our problem is to find how to maximize W subject to the government budget constraint, for which a multiplier λ is introduced. Thus we seek to maximize $W + \lambda T$ by choice of the functions u_h and u_f. It is convenient to write $W + \lambda T$ in the form

$$L = \iint_H \phi(m, n, u_h(n))\, dm\, dn + \iint_F \psi(m, n, u_f(m))\, dm\, dn, \tag{34}$$

where

$$\phi(m, n, v) = \Omega(m, n, v) + [v + \lambda(n - Z(v))]f(m, n, v),$$
$$\psi(m, n, v) = \Omega(m, n, v) + [v + \lambda(m - Y(v))]f(m, n, v). \tag{35}$$

The inverse utility functions Z and Y are central to the analysis. It is assumed that, offered the same after-tax income at home and abroad, anyone would choose to remain in his or her own country, which is equivalent to

$$Y(v) > Z(v), \qquad \text{for all } v. \tag{36}$$

A further reasonable assumption is that

$$Y'(v) \geqq Z'(v), \qquad \text{for all } v. \tag{37}$$

The problem to be solved is not immediately of standard type, since the region of integration is divided up in a rather inconvenient way. Necessary conditions for maximization will be found by first considering the choice of the function u_h, given that u_f has already been chosen, and afterward reversing the role of the two functions. Before doing that we shall make one further modification in the problem. When considering a model with taxation only of domestic incomes, we found that, under optimal taxes, it might be the case that utilities decrease with productivity over certain ranges. We noted that such an arrangement is not likely to be feasible. In the model we are now considering, it would also be somewhat intractable to allow utility to decrease with income. Let us therefore constrain u_f and u_h to be nondecreasing functions. Let us also make the reasonable (and justifiable) assumption that they are continuous functions.

Define a function M inverse to u_f. Specifically,

$$M(v) = \max\{m: u_f(m) \leqq v\}. \tag{38}$$

Like u_f, M has to be a nondecreasing function. The region of (m, n)-space that we call H, where people would choose to work in the home country, can now be defined by the inequality

$$m \leqq M(u_h(n)). \qquad (39)$$

It follows that we can write the integral L as $\int L(n) \, dn$ with

$$L(n) = \int_0^{M(u_h(n))} \phi(m, n, u_h(n)) \, dm + \int_{M(u_h(n))}^{\infty} \psi(m, n, u_f(m)) \, dm. \qquad (40)$$

We must choose the functon u_h as the nondecreasing function that maximizes L. It would be nice if we could, for each n, choose $u_h(n)$ so as to maximize $L(n)$ given in (40) and then find that the resulting u_h is a nondecreasing function of n. It turns out that my model is simple enough for this to be true. I shall not take the space to prove this rigorously. Another point is worth making rigorously. We can show that

$$u_h(0) > u_f(0). \qquad (41)$$

To prove this we simply have to show that it is never desirable to have $M(u_h(n)) = 0$. We see from the definitions (35) that

$$\phi(m, n, u) - \psi(m, n, u) = \lambda f(m, n, u)(Y - Z - m + n) \qquad (42)$$

is positive when $m = 0$. Therefore small positive M in (40) always yields a larger value of $L(n)$ than having $M = 0$. This proves (41). We may therefore define the minimum utility level by

$$\omega = u_h(0). \qquad (43)$$

People with m less than $M(\omega)$ never work abroad and pay tax. We define

$$m_0 = M(\omega). \qquad (44)$$

Below this level of m the choice of u_f has no effect, and we can therefore restrict attention to the choice of the function for $m \geqq m_0$.

The first-order condition for the choice of $u_h(n)$, when M is differentiable at that value of u, is obtained from (40) by differentiation:

$$[\phi(M(u), n, u) - \psi(M(u), n, u)]M'(u) = -\int_0^{M(u)} \phi_u(m, n, u) \, dm. \qquad (45)$$

Notice that we have used the fact that $u_f(M(u)) = u$. The statement that (45) holds at $u = u_h(n)$ can be expressed equivalently as the statement that it holds when $n = N(u)$. In an exactly similar way, we get the first-order condition for $u_f(m)$ when the function N inverse to u_h is differentiable at

$u = u_f(m)$ and u_f is strictly increasing in m:

$$[\phi(m, N(u), u) - \psi(m, N(u), u)]N'(u) = \int_0^{N(u)} \psi_u(m, n, u)\,dn. \tag{46}$$

This holds when $m = M(u) > m_0$. As in the previous case, it turns out that u_f is strictly increasing in the relevant range $m \geq m_0$, and the constraint that it be nondecreasing is therefore satisfied.

Finding conditions that determine the numbers ω and m_0 is the familiar task of finding terminal conditions in calculus of variations problems. It is most straightforward if ϕ and ψ do not vanish when $n = 0$, nor do their derivatives and difference. A heuristic derivation is as follows.

Consider small changes in the u_f function near m_0. The effect is to move a few marginal people with $n = 0$ into or out of the domestic economy: the change in L is proportional to $\phi(m_0, 0, \omega) - \psi(m_0, 0, \omega)$. At the optimum this expression must be zero. Using (42), this implies

$$m_0 = Y(\omega) - Z(\omega). \tag{47}$$

With little trouble it can be shown that this is also a valid condition when f tends to zero as n tends to zero.

Now consider the effect of changing $u_h(0)$ by a small amount while leaving other utility levels the same (except, necessarily, for n very close to zero). The effect on L is proportional to

$$\int_0^{m_0} \phi_u(m, 0, \omega)\,dm, \tag{48}$$

which therefore must vanish. It would vanish automatically if ϕ_u were zero when $n = 0$, but it is then possible to get an essentially similar condition, which will be noted below.

It only remains to replace the functions ϕ and ψ by their definitions (35). We have

$$\phi_u = [1 - Z'(u)]f + \lambda[m - Z(u)]f_u \tag{49}$$

and a similar expression for ψ_u. Using these, we have the solution.

Solution. The functions M and N are given by

$$(N - M - Z + Y)fM'(u)$$
$$= -\{\rho - Z'(u)\} \int_0^M f\,dm - (N - Z) \int_0^M f_u\,dm, \tag{50}$$

$$(N - M - Z + Y)fN'(u)$$

$$= \{\rho - Y'(u)\} \int_0^N f\,dm + (M - Y) \int_0^N f_u\,dn, \tag{51}$$

which hold for $u > \omega$, with

$$M(\omega) = Y(\omega) - Z(\omega), \quad \text{called } m_0,$$

$$N(\omega) = 0, \tag{53}$$

$$\frac{\rho - Z'(\omega)}{Z(\omega)} = \lim_{n \to 0} \left\{ \int_0^{m_0} f_u(m, n, \omega)\,dm \middle/ \int_0^{m_0} f(m, n, \omega)\,dm \right\}.$$

The optimal relationships between income before and after taxes, $z(n)$ and $y(m)$, are deduced from the equations

$$z(N(u)) = Z(u); \quad y(M(u)) = Y(u).$$

Equations (50) and (51) are translations of (45) and (46), using (42) and (49). The number ρ is $1/\lambda$ and is determined by the resource constraint. Eq. (53) is given in the more general form that is valid when f and f_u vanish at $n = 0$. (Essentially this comes from the principle that the multipliers in a calculus-of-variations problem of Pontrjagin type should tend to zero as rapidly as possible.)

Notice that because of the initial conditions, (50) and (51) yield expressions of the form "0/0" for $M'(\omega)$ and $N'(\omega)$. These initial derivatives have to be found by l'Hôpital's rule. This makes general analysis of the solution difficult. But there is a class of examples that is more amenable and seems to be general enough to be interesting.

A Special Case

Define

$$F(M, N, u) = \int_0^M \int_0^N f(m, n, u)\,dm\,dn. \tag{54}$$

Unfortunately this function has no very natural economic interpretation: it is the number with earning ability $(m, n) \leqq (M, N)$ who would choose to remain taxable if all of them were offered the same utility u. Using the definition, we have

$$F_M = \int_0^N f\,dn, \quad F_N = \int_0^M f\,dm, \quad F_{Mu} = \int_0^N f\,dn,$$

$$F_{Nu} = \int_0^M f_u \, dm, \qquad F_{MN} = f,$$

which allow us to write the basic equations (50) and (51) a little more briefly.

The real advantage of this new function emerges if it takes the special form

$$F(M, N, u) = F(G(M, N), u). \tag{55}$$

Using the notation F for both functions should cause no confusion. The new F may be taken to be increasing in G, which is increasing in M and N. Equations (50) and (51) can now be written

$$(N - M - Z + Y)fM' = -[(\rho - Z')F_G + (N - Z)F_{Gu}]G_N, \tag{56}$$

$$(N - M - Z + Y)fN' = [(\rho - Y')F_G + (M - Y)F_{Gu}]G_M. \tag{57}$$

From these it follows that

$$(N - M - Z + Y)f\frac{dG}{du}$$

$$= -[(Y' - Z')F_G + (N - M - Z + Y)F_{Gu}]G_M G_N,$$

which can be rewritten

$$(N - M - Z + Y)\left(f\frac{dG}{du} + F_{Gu}G_M G_N\right) = -(Y' - Z')F_G G_M G_N. \tag{58}$$

We know that G is an increasing function of u and that G_M, G_N, F_G, and F_{Gu} are all positive. (Note that $F_{Gu}G_M = F_{Mu} > 0$.) Furthermore $Y' \geq Z'$. Equation (58) therefore implies that

$$N - M - Z + Y \leq 0,$$

that is,

$$N(u) - Z(u) \leq M(u) - Y(u). \tag{59}$$

This proves the following:

Proposition. If F can be written in the separable form (55), the tax optimally paid by a person who earns taxed income at home is not greater than that paid by a person of equal utility who earns taxed income abroad.

The point of the separability condition is that it is general enough to allow a greater propensity to leave the tax system for people with high foreign earning power m, compared with those with realtively high home earning power n. This can be done by making G more sensitive to variations in M than in N, but we are then forced to make possibly unacceptable assumptions about the underlying distribution of m and n. The condition is however strongly sufficient.

A further result is obtained by going back to (56) and (57). It is convenient to define

$$\gamma = F_G/F_{Gu}. \tag{60}$$

Corollary.   Under the above assumptions,

$$N \geqq Z + \gamma(Z' - \rho), \tag{61}$$

$$M \geqq Y + \gamma(Y' - \rho). \tag{62}$$

These conditions place lower bounds on the optimal tax rates if we are prepared to estimate the magnitudes of ρ and γ.

It will be evident from the above discussion that in one very special case it is easy to calculate optimal tax schedules, namely when

$$Z(u) = Y(u) - K \tag{63}$$

for some constant K. Equation (63) means that migration is equivalent to a constant income-loss K, independent of income levels. This assumption presumably seriously overstates the relative willingness of the rich to migrate. It implies that $Z' = Y'$. Then the inequalities (59), (61), and (62) just derived become equalities, and the optimal taxes are defined by

$$N = Z + \gamma(Z' - \rho), \tag{64}$$

$$M = Y + \gamma(Y' - \rho) = N + K, \quad \text{by (63)}. \tag{65}$$

From these equations we can deduce that a home earner should pay more than a foreign earner with the same income. Because at equal utility $M > N$, equal income implies that the home earner is better off: $u_h > u_f$. Therefore by concavity of utility, which is equivalent to convexity of Z and Y, $Z'(u_h) > Z'(u_f) = Y'(u_f)$. With $N(u_h) = M(u_f)$ in (64) and (65), we then have

$$Z(u_h) < Y(u_f), \tag{66}$$

showing that the home earner pays more tax at all levels of income. It will be appreciated that this result depends on the extreme assumption that $Y(u) - Z(u)$ is constant. If instead it is an increasing function of u, the tax on the foreign earner can be greater even at equal incomes.

As an illustrative example suppose that

$$U_h(x) = -\frac{1}{x}, \qquad U_f(x) = -\frac{1}{x-K}, \qquad f(m,n,u) = h(m,n)(-u)^{-\eta}. \quad (66)$$

Easy calculations yield

$$\gamma = (-u)/\eta,$$

$$Z(u) = 1/(-u),$$

$$Y(u) = 1/(-u) + K.$$

From these equations we have

$$Z'(u) = Z^2, \qquad \gamma = 1/(\eta Z).$$

Substitution in (64) then tells us that $z(n)$ is given by solving

$$n = \frac{1+\eta}{\eta} z - \frac{\rho}{\eta} \frac{1}{z}. \quad (67)$$

Disposable income of foreign earners is given by

$$y(m) = z(m - K) + K. \quad (68)$$

To determine m_0 and ω, we use the auxiliary conditions in the solution above. From (53),

$$\frac{\rho - 1/\omega^2}{1/(-\omega)} = \frac{\eta}{-\omega},$$

which simplifies to

$$\omega = \left(\frac{1+\eta}{\rho}\right)^{1/2}. \quad (69)$$

The other condition yields

$$m_0 = Y(\omega) - Z(\omega) = K. \quad (70)$$

These results are consistent with (67) and (68), with

$$z(0) = y(m_0) = \left(\frac{\rho}{1+\eta}\right)^{1/2}. \quad (71)$$

From (67) it can be seen that the marginal tax rate

$$1 - z'(n) \rightarrow \frac{1}{1+\eta} \quad (72)$$

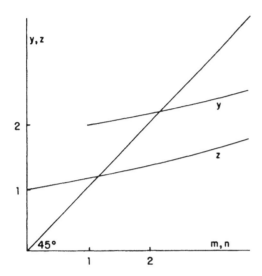

Figure 8.1

as $n \to \infty$. The same result holds for foreign incomes. Notice that the details of income distribution incorporated in the function h affect results only through ρ.

A numerical solution for the case

$$K = 1, \qquad \eta = \tfrac{1}{2}, \qquad \rho = \tfrac{3}{2}$$

is shown in figure 8.1

Conclusions

The final numerical example made several assumptions. One assumption very favorable to home taxes being higher than taxes on foreign income was that the cost of working abroad be equivalent to a reduction of income independent of income actually enjoyed. Another, which is probably favorable to the opposite conclusion, was that the distribution of incomes be described by a density function of the multiplicative form $h(m, n)q(u)$. This means that among people enjoying the same utility the propensity to migrate is the same for those with relatively high n as for those with relatively high m. The basic structure of the model used tends to have the latter work abroad, the former at home; it may seem that a change in prospective utility would be more likely to induce those working abroad to give up citizenship, either through taste or opportunity. Yet we have seen that a more general assumption works in much the same way, yielding the result that those working abroad pay higher taxes than people provided with equal utility working at home.

Taking these results with the general ideas presented in the opening section of this chapter, that an income tax on foreign earnings should include an element corresponding to expenditure taxes at home; and that the relative magnitude of the optimal taxes depends on the degree of substitutability of home and foreign taxable earnings with untaxed alternatives; it seems that it may well be desirable to institute substantial income taxes on foreign earnings, if only the narrowly economic considerations incorporated in my model are relevant.

Notes

This chapter is a revised version of "Optimal foreign-income taxation," a paper presented at the conference The Exercise of Income Tax Jurisdiction over Citizens Working Abroad, under the auspices of the National Institute of Public Finance and Policy, New Delhi, January, 1981.

I am grateful to the sponsors of the conference for providing the occasion for this paper. Valuable comments were provided by Peter Diamond and other participants in the New Delhi conference, and at a seminar in University College, London. I am particularly grateful to two referees who provided useful comments and identified serious errors in the previous version of this chapter.

References

Atkinson, A. B., and J. E. Stiglitz. 1976. The design of tax structure: Direct versus indirect taxation. *Journal of Public Economics* 6: 55–75.

Bhagwati, J. 1980. Taxation and international migration: Recent policy issues. Mimeo, Conference on U.S. Immigration Issues and Policies, Chicago.

Mirrlees, James A. 1976. Optimal tax theory: A synthesis. *Journal of Public Economics* 6: 327–358.

9

Optimal Income Taxation and Migration: A World Welfare Point of View

John Douglas Wilson

Introduction

The migration of professionals and technicians from developing countries (LDCs) to developed countries (DCs) has become an important phenomenon in recent years. Theoretical and empirical studies have documented the losses to LDCs (excluding emigrants) inflicted by this migration and the gains to DCs and emigrants.[1] Bhagwati has proposed a surtax on the earnings of the skilled emigrants from LDCs.[2] The arguments for this proposal have been based generally on equity considerations.

Taking a different approach, Hamada (1978) has considered the implications of efficiency considerations for the taxation of emigrants. In his model, taxation has no effect on individual behavior other than its possible effect on migration. Thus as a condition for Pareto optimality, taxation should not affect migration. Because migration decisions are based only on a comparison of after-tax incomes in Hamada's model, the total tax paid by an individual should not depend on where he or she lives. Hamada argues that tax rates over the range of incomes possessed by potential emigrants are generally higher in LDCs than in DCs.[3] Where this is the case, a surtax should be placed on emigrant incomes to equalize tax burdens.

The purpose of this chapter is to present a study of how taxation should depend on residence when governments must use a distortionary income tax to raise and redistribute revenue. In my model each individual provides labor in exchange for consumption and resides in the country where his or her utility is highest. There exist innate differences between individuals such as in skill or ability, and incomes therefore differ. Only income taxation is available.[4] But each individual's tax schedule, which gives his or her tax as a function of labor income, is allowed to be nonlinear and to depend on both citizenship and residence. The world tax system is the collection of these tax schedules. It is optimal if it maximizes world social welfare, which is an increasing function of the utilities of the world population. I focus on conditions for the maximization of any such function. Thus I follow Hamada by concentrating on conditions for "world efficiency."

I first show that although income taxation distorts consumption-labor decisions, migration decisions should not be distorted. Specifically, under an optimal world tax system, each individual's contribution to output is at least as great as it would be if he or she performed the same labor in any other country. This result depends critically on the assumption that an individual's preferences for consumption and labor do not vary with residence. In other words one migrates if doing so increases the net wage received for one's present supply of labor (net of taxes and migration costs), no matter how small the increase. Surprisingly my next major conclusion holds not only when preferences do not vary with residence, but also when there are variations that meet certain interesting restrictions. I show that social welfare is maximized by a world tax system in which each emigrant's tax is at least as high as the tax that would have been paid in his or her home country. In this sense it is optimal for an individual not to be able to escape taxation by emigrating. Unfortunately if the government of a particular country is concerned only with the welfare of its own citizens, then an optimal tax system from its viewpoint is likely to be inefficient from the viewpoint of world social welfare maximization.

The plan of this chapter is as follows. In the next section I present the basic model. Then I show that migration is efficient under an optimal world tax system, and in the following section some implications of this result for the optimal world tax system are given. I extend the model by allowing preferences for consumption and labor to vary with residence. My approach uses heavily Lancaster's "new approach to consumer theory" (1966). In the sixth section I show that the presence of these preference variations does not invalidate the fourth section's main conclusion about the optimal world tax system. Before concluding remarks, I look briefly at how a government that is concerned only with the welfare of its own citizens should tax those who emigrate.

The Model

Consider a world consisting of any number of countries. Each individual is a citizen of one country, and differences between individuals other than citizenship are described by a vector of attributes denoted n. Lump-sum taxes based on attributes are assumed not to be possible. However, the tax an individual pays may depend on income, citizenship, and residence. Each individual resides in the country where he or she can obtain the highest utility. But citizenship cannot be altered for tax purposes.

The Technology

The model is based on a model developed by Mirrlees (1976a) to study the optimal incentive structure in an organization. Competitive private firms in each country use labor and fixed factors to produce a single consumption good. There is a continuum of types of labor, and each individual chooses one type to provide. For simplicity, we suppose that the different types can be represented by a single variable z. In other words z is a measure of both the quantity and quality of work.

In the standard optimal income tax model developed by Mirrlees (1971), different types of labor are assumed to be perfect substitutes. Mirrlees (1976a) greatly generalizes the technology. Let $f^i(z)$ denote the number of individuals supplying type z labor in country i, and let y^i denote country i's output. For the case of perfect substitutes, this country's production function may be written (omitting fixed factors as arguments) as

$$y^i = H\left(\int \alpha(z) f^i(z)\, dz \right).$$ (1)

An example of a production function in which different types of labor are not perfect substitutes is the Cobb-Douglas production function, generalized to a continuum of inputs:

$$y^i = H\left(\int \alpha(z) \log f^i(z)\, dz \right).$$ (2)

Mirrlees (1976a) provides other examples.

We do not limit our attention to a particular form of the production function. But we do assume, as is the case in (1) and (2), that each country's output is a differentiable function of its labor inputs. This means that if f^i is a differentiable function of some parameter ε, then there exists a function $p^i(z)$ such that

$$\frac{dy^i}{d\varepsilon} = \int p^i(z) \frac{\partial f^i(z, \varepsilon)}{\partial \varepsilon}\, dz.$$ (3)

The value of p^i at a given z may be thought of as the marginal product of type z labor in country i. It is important to realize that $p^i(z)$ generally depends on how much of each type of labor is being performed in the country.

The relation between output and labor and fixed factors is assumed to exhibit constant returns to scale, implying that the value of output equals the value of all factors.[5] The returns to fixed factors are referred to as economic rents. Taxing these rents is a nondistortionary way to raise and redistribute revenue. We assume that economic rents are taxed at 100 percent, with income taxation being used to raise additional revenue (or disperse a revenue surplus) and to redistribute income. The significance of this assumption is discussed in the concluding remarks. An equivalent assumption is that the government owns all fixed factors. In either case an individual's net income consists of his or her gross wage minus the total tax on this wage (possibly negative).

Utility Maximization and Taxation

Individuals' preferences for consumption x and labor z depend on their attributes n and are represented by a well-behaved utility function, $u(x, z, n)$, which is increasing in x and declining in z.[6] For now, we assume that preferences do not vary with residence. But this assumption will be amended below.

Only income taxation is available (and 100-percent taxation of rents), but the tax schedule faced by individuals may be nonlinear and depend on their citizenship and residence. A citizen of country j (a j-citizen) residing in country i faces a net wage schedule denoted $w^{ji}(z)$ and a tax schedule denoted $t^{ji}(z)$. For a particular z, $w^{ji}(z)$ is calculated by subtracting both $t^{ji}(z)$ and the j-citizen's migration costs from his or her gross marginal product in country i (as defined in (3)). This way of including migration costs in the model is equivalent to assuming that the provision of z requires the expenditure of a certain amount of consumption that varies with citizenship and residence but has no direct effect on utility.[7] Consumption net of this expenditure is x. The j-citizen's net marginal product $p^{ji}(z)$ equals his or her gross marginal product minus the migration costs. We then have

$$w^{ji}(z) = p^{ji}(z) - t^{ji}(z). \tag{4}$$

The collection of net wage schedules for the citizens of each country residing in each country $\{w^{ji}\}$ is referred to as the world wage system. The collection of tax schedules $\{t^{ji}\}$ is the world tax system.

Each j-citizen chooses the commodity vector (x, z) that maximizes his or her utility subject to the constraint that x equals the maximum net wage for z over all residences:

$$x = w^j(z) = \max_i w^{ji}(z). \tag{5}$$

This citizen then resides where the maximum net wage can be obtained for the chosen labor supply.

The Optimal Tax Problem

Suppose that social welfare is some function of the utilities of the members of the world population, and that this functon is increasing in each utility. The problem is to find the world tax system that maximizes this function. It is not fruitful to let the world tax system be the "control variables" in this problem, because there may be more than one equilibrium associated with a given world tax system. Instead we let the control variables be the allocation of commodities (consumption and labor) across the world population and the allocation of the world population across residences. These two allocations constitute a commodity-residence (CR) allocation. A CR allocation is feasible if and only if it is a competitive equilibrium for some world tax system. The optimal tax problem consists of finding the CR allocation that yields the highest social welfare among all feasible CR allocations. Once such a CR allocation is found, a world tax system under which it is a competitive equilibrium can be specified. This world tax system is optimal.

The implicit assumption being made in this specification of the problem is that the tax authority can choose among multiple equilibria for a given world tax system.

We will find it useful to break the constraint that a CR allocation must be a competitive equilibrium for some world tax system into two separate constraints.[8] First, the total output net of migration costs produced using the labor available in each country must be at least as great as total consumption.[9] Second, there must exist a world wage system with the following property: each individual's commodity vector and residence give him or her the highest utility that can be obtained under the world wage system. Such a world wage system is said to support the CR allocation.[10] We are faced with a second-best allocation problem because a CR allocation is feasible only if it is supported by some world wage system. This constraint is present because only income taxation is available. Because the tax schedules may take any nonlinear form, it is possible to choose net wage schedules independently of marginal products.

The Efficiency Proposition

If income taxation must be used to raise and redistribute income, then consumption-labor decisions must be distorted. However, we now show that migration decisions should not be distorted. Specifically if a CR allocation is optimal, as previously defined, then the net marginal product of a j-citizen in his or her present residence is at least as high as it would be if he or she performed the same labor in any other country. In other words the optimal world tax system induces individuals to reside where their net marginal products are highest. This means that all j-citizens performing the same type of labor have identical net marginal products, regardless of whether they reside in different countries.

Proposition 1. Suppose preferences are independent of residence. If a CR allocation is optimal and type z labor is performed by j-citizens in country k, then $p^{jk}(z) \geqq p^{ji}(z)$ for all i.[11]

Proof. The key to this result is the observation that any world wage system that supports a feasible CR allocation can be replaced by another supporting world wage system under which each individual is indifferent between residences but receives the same net wage as before. We simply construct the world wage system so that each individual faces the same net wage schedule in every country. To elaborate, if $W = \{w^{ji}\}$ is the original supporting world wage system, we replace it by a new world wage system, $\overline{W} = \{\overline{w}^{ji}\}$, where $\overline{w}^{ji} = \max_k w^{jk}$ for each j and i. Clearly each individual's utility-maximizing labor supply and resulting net wage are the same under W and $\overline{W}$, and the net wage schedules in $\overline{W}$ are independent of residence.

Now suppose that an optimal CR allocation violates proposition 1. In particular suppose that there exists a country j and an interval of labor types Z such that each z in Z is provided by j-citizens who reside in country k, but for some l,

$$p^{jl}(z) > p^{jk}(z), \quad \text{for all } z \text{ in } Z.$$

Let us support this CR allocation by a world wage system $\overline{W}$ under which the net wage schedules faced by j-citizens do not depend on residence. At each z in Z, let us move a small portion of the j-citizens in country k, $\delta f^k(z)$, to country l. Let us give them the commodity vector they received in k. Because they face the same wage schedule in each country under $\overline{W}$ and are therefore indifferent between residences, the resulting CR allocation is also supported by $\overline{W}$. These residential population changes do not alter anyone's utility. Nor do they alter total consumption. But they increase total output net of migration costs by

$$\int_z (p^{jl}(z) - p^{jk}(z))\delta f^k(z)\, dz.$$

This excess output can be distributed in a way that makes everyone better off. We first define a new world wage system, $\overline{\overline{W}} = \{\overline{\overline{w}}^{ji}\}$, in which every net wage schedule is above the corresponding net wage schedule under $\overline{W}$ by the same small epsilon:

$$\overline{\overline{w}}^{ji}(z) = \overline{w}^{ji}(z) + \varepsilon; \qquad \varepsilon > 0.$$

For any positive epsilon, each individual's utility is clearly greater under $\overline{\overline{W}}$ than under $\overline{W}$. Also, each individual remains indifferent between residences under $\overline{\overline{W}}$. By choosing a sufficiently small epsilon, we can bring each individual's utility-maximizing commodity vectors under $\overline{W}$ and $\overline{\overline{W}}$ as close to each other as desired.[12] Thus because $\overline{W}$ supports a CR allocation under which there is excess output, epsilon can be chosen so that $\overline{\overline{W}}$ also supports a CR allocation under which consumption is no greater than net output. Because the latter CR allocation is feasible and gives each individual a higher utility than under the original CR allocation, the original CR allocation could not have been optimal. This contradiction establishes the proposition.   Q.E.D.

Proposition 1 essentially states that there should be aggregate production efficiency in world production. In other words production should take place on the frontier of the world production possibility set, which gives all possible combinations of labor and consumption that are technologically feasible when labor is completely mobile between countries. The desirability of aggregate production efficiency is a standard result from the optimal taxation literature. But it is usually expressed as a necessary condition for the optimal division of production between the private and public production sectors of a closed economy in which commodity taxes are optimal. We have chosen our assumptions so that if social welfare is an increasing function of the utilities of the world population, then aggregate production efficiency is a necessary condition for the optimal division of production between countries.

Optimal Income Taxation

An implication of proposition 1 is that there exists an optimal world tax system in which the tax schedules do not depend on residence:

for each j, $\quad t^{jk}(z) = t^{jl}(z)$, $\quad$ for any k, l, and z. $\hfill$ (6)

To see this, first observe that if countries k and l both contain j-citizens who perform type z labor, $w^{jk}(z)$ must equal $w^{jl}(z)$ and, by proposition 1, $p^{jk}(z)$ must equal $p^{jl}(z)$. These two equalities imply that $t^{jk}(z)$ equals $t^{jl}(z)$. For the case in which j-citizens perform z in k but not in l, $t^{jl}(z)$ may be arbitrarily set at any value where $w^{jl}(z)$ is no greater that $w^{jk}(z)$. In particular $t^{jl}(z)$ may be set equal to $t^{jk}(z)$, because proposition 1 implies that $p^{jl}(z)$ cannot be greater than $p^{jk}(z)$.

The issue of how tax schedules should depend on residence should be distinguished from the issue of how the tax an individual chooses to pay (by choosing a labor supply) depends on his or her residence. For example, when an LDC citizen migrates to a DC, he or she may face the same tax schedule but pay a lower tax because he or she chooses to work less. Suppose that a world tax authority wishes to design a world tax system to maximize a world social welfare function that is increasing in the utilities of both LDC and DC citizens. An interesting question is whether there exists an optimal world tax system (many tax systems may be optimal) in which any LDC citizens who emigrate to the DC do not reduce their tax burdens by doing so. Given the assumptions of the model, the answer is yes. More generally we have the following proposition, where z^{nji} is the labor supplied by a j-citizen with attributes n (an nj-citizen) when forced to reside in i.

Proposition 2. Suppose preferences are independent of residence. Then there exists an optimal world tax system $\{t^{ji}\}$ with the following property: If an nj-citizen resides in country k under this tax system, then

$$t^{jk}(z^{njk}) \geqq t^{ji}(z^{nji}) \quad \text{for all } i. [13]$$

Proof. From the previous section we know that an optimal CR allocation is supported by a world wage system in which the wage schedules faced by individuals are independent of their residence. Under such a world wage system an nj-citizen chooses the same z in each residence: $z^{njk} = z^{nji}$, for all i.[14] Thus the net wage is the same in each residence. The proposition then follows immediately from proposition 1. $\hfill$ Q.E.D.

Proposition 2 states that there always exists an optimal world tax system such that no individual escapes taxation by migrating. Under such a tax system all citizens of a particular country who possess the same attributes pay the same tax, regardless of where they reside.

Residence-Dependent Preferences

The assumption that an individual's preferences over consumption and labor do not vary with residence is quite strong. In this section preferences may depend on residence in a way that enables us to show that proposition 2 remains true, although proposition 1 normally no longer holds.

Let us follow Lancaster by "breaking away from the traditional approach that goods are the direct objects of utility and, instead, supposing that it is the properties or characteristics of the goods from which utility is derived" (Lancaster 1966, p. 133). In particular let us suppose that the two commodities, consumption and labor, produce two characteristics in amounts c_1 and c_2, and that each individual's utility is a function of c_1 and c_2 and increases with each.[15] (Utility may still depend directly on labor by letting one of the characteristics equal $-z$.)

A distinguishing feature of Lancaster's approach is that the relation between characteristics and commodities, called the consumption technology, is "determined by the intrinsic properties of the goods themselves and possibly the context of technological knowledge in the society" (1966, p. 135). This feature is preserved here by supposing that the consumption technology is the same for all citizens of a given country in a given residence, but possibly depends on citizenship and residence. The consumption technology for j-citizens residing in country i is described by the functions $c_1 = c_1^{ji}(x, z)$ and $c_2 = c_2^{ji}(x, z)$. These functions give the efficient levels of characteristics one and two that are attainable from given quantities of consumption and labor. Efficiency means here that it is not possible to obtain more of one characteristic from a given commodity vector without obtaining less of the other.

The assumption here that only one efficient characteristics vector is associated with each commodity vector is restrictive but necessary for the analysis.[16] We do not assume that a given characteristics vector can be obtained from only one commodity vector. However, we do assume that when we are given a commodity vector that an individual obtains under an optimal CR allocation, we can find some neighborhood of it that possesses the following property: if the individual is able to obtain a given characteristics vector (c_1, c_2) in some country by choosing a commodity vector from this neighborhood, then in *every* country there exists a commodity vector that gives him (c_1, c_2).[17] Because the consumption technology is allowed to depend on residence, this assumption makes sense only if the number of characteristics is no greater than the number of commodities. Hence we have been forced to restrict the analysis to only two characteristics.

Again following Lancaster, we suppose that "the personal element of consumer choice arises in the choice between the collections of characteristics only ..." (1966, p. 134). Specifically each individual's utility function on characteristics space $u(c_1, c_2, n)$ is assumed to depend only on attributes and not on residence. We assume that this function and the consumption technology for each individual in each residence yield a utility function on commodities space $u^{ji}(x, z, n)$ that is increasing in x and declining in z. It is a straightforward matter to show that if $u(c_1, c_2, n)$ is quasi-concave in (c_1, c_2) and if the functions c_1^{ji} and c_2^{ji} are concave, then the corresponding utility function on commodities space is quasi-concave. We make these assumptions.[18]

There are several interpretations of the model. For example, we may interpret one characteristic as "job prestige," which increases with z. Then the other characteristic could be called "basic consumption," which increases with x, but declines with z because an increase in z lowers the time available for consumption activities. It is reasonable to expect the production of each of these characteristics to depend on the individual's citizenship and residence. The characteristics model allows for both possibilities.[19]

Alternatively "basic consumption" may be assumed to be a function of x and a vector of "locational attributes," whereas the other characteristic equals $-z$. Here a locational attribute may be interpreted as a nonproduced commodity (for example, lakes, mountains, weather, distance of the emigrant from his or her home country) or a public good in the Samuelson sense (for example, national defense).[20] Assuming that these locational attributes are exogenously fixed in the model, we may write basic consumption as a function of only x. Differences across countries in levels of locational attributes cause this function to depend on residence.

The following lemma gives a common feature of these examples that is the essential property of this specification of taste differences.

Lemma 1. In the characteristics model, an optimal CR allocation is supported by a world wage system under which each member of the world population is indifferent between residences.

Proof. Consider an optimal CR allocation and let $\{w^{ji}\}$ denote a world wage system that supports it. This world wage system defines a collection of sets $\{A^{ji}\}$, where A^{ji} is the set of characteristics vectors that a j-citizen can obtain in country i with a commodity vector satisfying his or her budget constraint, $x \leqq w^{ji}(z)$. A j-citizen's characteristics vector under the CR allocation maximizes his or her utility subject to the constraint that it lie in A^{ji} for some i:

$$(c_1, c_2) \in A^j = \bigcup_i A^{ji}.$$

This citizen resides in a country where he or she can obtain this utility-maximizing characteristics vector while satisfying the budget constraint.

Now for each j let us define a subset of A^j consisting of every characteristics vector in A^j that j-citizens can obtain in any country from some combination of consumption and labor:

$$\bar{A}^j = A^j \cap B^j,$$

where

$B^j = \{(c_1, c_2 | \text{for each } i, \text{ there exists an } (x, z) \text{ such that}$

$$c_1^{ji}(x, z) = c_1 \quad \text{and} \quad c_2^{ji}(x, z) = c_2\}.$$

For a given j-citizen, let (c_1^*, c_2^*) be the characteristics vector that he or she obtains under the optimal CR allocation. Then (c_1^*, c_2^*) is his or her utility-maximizing characteristics vector in A^j. As assumed above, (c_1^*, c_2^*) lies in B^j. Thus it is also the j-citizen's utility-maximizing characteristics vector in $\bar{A}^j$. If the j-citizen is constrained to choose any characteristics vector in $\bar{A}^j$, regardless of residence, then (c_1^*, c_2^*) maximizes his or her utility in any residence; and he or she is indifferent about where to reside. In country i the net wage schedule under which (c_1^*, c_2^*) maximizes the j-citizens' utility is

$$\bar{w}^{ji}(z) = \max_x \{x | (c_1^{ji}(x, z), c_2^{ji}(x, z)) \in \bar{A}^j\}.$$

(Utility maximization occurs where the budget constraint $x \leqq \bar{w}^{ji}(z)$ holds with equality, because utility is assumed to increase with x and decline with z.) We can conclude that the world wage system $\{\bar{w}^{ji}\}$ supports the optimal CR allocation and leaves each member of the world population indifferent between residences. This completes the proof.

Optimal Taxation in the Presence of Residence-Dependent Preferences

For the model in which references do not vary with residence, proposition 2 states that there exists an optimal world tax system under which individuals reside where they pay the greatest taxes. In other words no individual's tax declines when he or she emigrates from the home country. This result remains valid for the characteristics model. The basic argument is sketched and then a more detailed proof is presented.

By lemma 1 an optimal world tax system can always be designed so that individuals' utilities do not depend on where they reside. Suppose that we start with a world tax system with this property. But suppose that some individuals do not reside where their taxes are as high as the taxes they would pay elsewhere. Then we can always alter this tax system so that all utilities remain unchanged in equilibrium, but some of these individuals are induced to migrate to countries where they pay higher taxes. The additional tax revenue can be distributed in a way that makes some individuals better off without making anyone worse off. Thus the original world tax system could not have been optimal. We can conclude that there always exists an optimal world tax system under which each individual resides where he or she pays the greatest tax.

A more formal proof is now provided.

Proposition 2'. In the characteristics model there exists an optimal world tax system $\{t^{ji}\}$ with the following property: if an nj-citizen resides in country k under this tax system, $t^{jk}(z^{njk}) \geqq t^{ji}(z^{nji})$ for all i.[21]

Proof. Consider an optimal world tax system and let $\{p^{ji}\}$ denote the set of net marginal product functions associated with it. Lemma 1 implies that there exists a supporting world wage system $W = \{w^{ji}\}$, which leaves all individuals indifferent between residences. Let (x^{nji}, z^{nji}) denote the commodity vector that an nj-citizen would choose under W if forced to reside in country i. By definition,

$$t^{ji}(z^{nji}) = p^{ji}(z^{nji}) - x^{nji}. \tag{7}$$

Now suppose that some j-citizens reside in country k. But suppose, contrary to the proposition, that there exists a set of n's (with a positive measure) and a country i where $t^{jk}(z^{njk}) < t^{ji}(z^{nji})$. Let N denote this set. For each n belonging to N, let us move a small portion of the nj-citizens in country k, $\delta f^k(z^{njk})$, to country i and give them the commodity vector (z^{nji}, z^{nji}). Because each individual being moved is indifferent between residences under W and is given a commodity vector that maximizes his or her utility under W, W supports the resulting CR allocation. These residential changes raise output net of migration costs by

$$\int_N (p^{ji}(z^{nji}) - p^{jk}(z^{njk}))\delta f^k(z^{njk})\,dn.$$

They raise consumption by

$$\int_N (x^{nji} - x^{njk})\delta f^k(z^{njk})\, dn.$$

Recognizing (7), we find that the second CR allocation is characterized by an excess of net output over consumption.

This excess output can be distributed in a way that makes everyone better off. Consider a new world wage system $\overline{W} = \{\overline{w}^{ji}\}$, where

$$\overline{w}^{ji}(z) = w^{ji}(z) + \varepsilon^{ji}(z); \qquad \varepsilon^{ji}(z) > 0.$$

By arguments similar to those in the proof of lemma 1, we can choose each of the $\varepsilon^{ji}(z)$ functions so that the resulting world wage system $\overline{W}$ leaves all individuals indifferent about where to reside.[22] With everyone indifferent, $\overline{W}$ supports a third CR allocation in which everyone has the same residence as under the second CR allocation, in which there is excess output. The $\varepsilon^{ji}(z)$ functions with this property can be made small enough at each z to ensure that total consumption under the third CR allocation remains no greater than total net output.[23] Then by definition the third CR allocation is feasible. Because it clearly raises everyone's utility, the original CR allocation could not have been optimal. This contradiction establishes the proposition.   Q.E.D.

Conflicts between National and World Social Welfare Maximization

We have looked at tax policies that achieve world efficiency under the constraint that optimal lump-sum taxation is impossible. Unfortunately there are likely to be great practical difficulties in implementing such policies. Here an example is given to illustrate the problems involved.

Let us consider a world consisting of two countries, an LDC and a DC. Some citizens of the LDC emigrate to the DC, where they are subject to the DC tax system. (The DC tax system treats these emigrants and the DC citizens equally.) We initially suppose that the assumptions of the first model hold; namely, that utility does not depend directly on residence, and therefore that LDC citizens live where their net wages are highest.

Suppose that the DC government allows the LDC government to collect a surtax on the incomes of emigrants. The LDC is assumed to be small in the sense that its government does not believe that emigration affects the wages emigrants receive net of DC taxes. Also the LDC government cares about the welfare of both emigrants and residents, but not about the welfare of DC citizens. Its optimal tax system maximizes an individualistic social welfare function.

Given these assumptions, the LDC government should choose a tax system under which its citizens reside where their net marginal products minus DC tax are highest.[24] The reasoning is similar to the reasoning behind proposition 1. However, this is not the policy for world efficiency described in proposition 1. That policy says individuals should reside where their net marginal products are highest. Because the LDC government cares only about the welfare of its own citizens in the present case, the net marginal product of an emigrant from its point of view is the actual net marginal product (net of migration costs) minus the DC tax. For this reason, the LDC's tax policy can easily lead to world inefficiency.

For example, suppose that it is optimal from the LDC government's viewpoint for each type of labor in some interval Z to be provided by both LDC residents and emigrants. Then for each z in Z, the net marginal product of z in the LDC should equal the net marginal product in the DC minus the DC tax. If the DC tax is positive, this implies that the net marginal product of z is higher in the DC than in the LDC. In this sense there are too few emigrants providing z in the DC. Both countries could be made better off if the LDC changed its taxation of emigrants so that more citizens providing the labor types in Z emigrated. But for social welfare in both countries to rise, the DC would then have to compensate the LDC, perhaps by giving the LDC some of the tax revenue collected from the additional emigrants. International agreements of this type are hard to imagine.

Now suppose that preferences vary across residences in the manner described by the characteristics model. By a proof similar to the proof of proposition 2, it can be shown that there exists an optimal tax system for the LDC in which each LDC citizen resides where the tax that he or she pays to the LDC government is highest. In contrast proposition 2' implies that there exists an optimal world tax system in which each individual resides in the country where the *sum* of his or her taxes to the DC and LDC governments is highest. Again we see that the institutional arrangement described here for taxing emigrants is not likely to be conducive to world social welfare maximization.

Concluding Remarks

It is perhaps enlightening to rephrase one of the main results in a slightly different way. Consider a feasible world tax system (consisting of income tax schedules that depend on citizenship and residence) that satisfies the condition for world efficiency; namely, there does not exist another feasible world tax system that makes one portion of the world population better off without making another portion worse off. Proposition 2' implies that there exists another feasible world tax system in which everyone receives the same utility as in the first world tax system, but each emigrant pays at least as great a tax on his or he income as if he or she had remained in the home country.[25] This result is an implication of proposition 2', because proposition 2' holds for any world social welfare function that is increasing in utilities. It lends some support to Bhagwati's proposed surtax on emigrant incomes in instances in which individuals would otherwise lower their tax payments by emigrating.

I now note three important limitations to the analysis. First, proposition 2' does not give necessary conditions for an optimal world tax system. There may exist other optimal world tax systems in which individuals reside where their tax payments are lower than elsewhere.

Second, 100-percent taxation of rents has been assumed. An alternative assumption is that each fixed factor can be taxed at any rate between zero and 100 percent, but that the rates cannot depend on the residences of factor owners. In this case, propositions 1, 2, and 2' still hold.[26] They may not hold, however, when the tax rates on rents can vary with the residences of factor owners. Because the ownership of fixed factors is an innate attribute of individuals in this model, making tax rates depend on residence is equivalent to instituting a tax or subsidy on migration that depends on this attribute. Such taxes or subsidies may be desirable.

Third, proposition 2' is based on the assumption that preferences for commodities vary with residence in a special way. Specifically, the relation between commodities and characteristics differs across residences, and utility ultimately depends on characteristics. There exist, however, other interesting types of preference variations under which lemma 1, on which proposition 2' is based, need not hold. For example, individuals may possess skills for performing labor that are specific to residence: an $\{n^i\}$-person possesses utility function $u(x, z/n^k)$ in country k.

It is interesting that the characteristics model does not place restrictions on how an individual's elasticity of substitution between consumption and labor differs across residences. Stern (1976) has produced numerical calculations showing the optimal linear income tax in closed economies to be quite sensitive to this elasticity. But one can easily produce special cases of the characteristics model in which it is optimal for income tax schedules to be identical across residences, although elasticities greatly differ across residences. Stern's results appear to be inapplicable here because the tax schedules for different countries must be chosen under the constraint that individuals will not reside where their utility is lower than elsewhere.

Notes

This chapter is a revised version of a paper presented at the conference The Exercise of Income Tax Jurisdiction over Citizens Working Abroad, under the auspices of the National Institute of Public Finance and Policy, New Delhi, January, 1981. I would like to thank J. Bhagwati, P. Diamond, K. Hamada, J. Mirrlees, and N. Stern for helpful comments.

1. Bhagwati 1976 contains some of the better work in this area.

2. This proposal is described by Bhagwati and Partington (1976). For a discussion of the legal aspects, see Oldman and Pomp 1975 and Pomp and Oldman 1979.

3. See Hamada 1978, pp. 143–147.

4. Also assume that all economic rents on fixed factors go to the government, either through direct ownership or a 100-percent tax. This assumption is discussed in the concluding section.

5. This is not vey restrictive, because decreasing returns to scale activities can be dealt with by defining certain factors as the property rights to such activities.

6. We assume that $u(x, z, n)$ is quasi-concave in (x, z) and continuously differentiable in (x, z, n).

7. Other "costs" of providing labor are accounted for by the form of the utility function. However, they cannot vary with residence in this model, because the form of the utility function is independent of residence.

8. This approach is taken by Mirrlees (1976b) to study optimal nonlinear commodity taxation (see especially pp. 333–335).

9. Three points should be made here. First, this condition refers to the *maximum* total net output that can be obtained from the labor available in each country under the CR allocation, since competitive firms in each country use labor efficiently. Inefficiencies result from not having an optimal allocation of labor across countries. Second, assuming free disposal, we do not have to assume an equality between net output and consumption, because any excess net output can be purchased by the government and thrown away. Third, this condition can be generalized in an obvious way to allow for the production of fixed supplies of public goods.

10. For simplicity we require that each net wage schedule of a supporting world wage system be continuously differentiable everywhere except at a finite number of z, where it may have a jump discontinuity.

11. More accurately this statement holds for all but a finite number of z (a set of measure zero). To elaborate, let $f^{ji}(z)$ denote the number of j-citizens who supply type z labor in country i. We assume that under the optimal CR allocation, $p^{ji}(z)$ and $f^{ji}(z)$ are defined and continuous for each j and i at all but a finite number of z. Then proposition 1 is proved for those z where these continuity assumptions hold. If proposition 1 fails to hold at one of these z, then it must fail to hold at all labor types in some interval containing this z.

12. This argument rests on the assumption that each individual's utility-maximizing commodity vector under W is unique. The proposition remains true under the much weaker assumption that for each j there exists an interval of labor types which are provided only by j-citizens who possess no other utility-maximizing labor types. By slightly increasing the net wages paid to j-citizens for supplying these labor types, we can distribute the excess output in a way that makes some j-citizens better off without making anyone worse off. Thus we still conclude that the original CR allocation could not have been optimal.

13. More accurately this statement holds for all n and j other than those where, for some i, z^{nji} fails to satisfy the continuity assumptions in note 11.

14. We assume here that if an individual possesses more than one utility-maximizing commodity vector, then the one he or she chooses does not depend on residence.

15. To illustrate his approach, Lancaster (1966, 1971) presents a model in which consumption and labor produce two characteristics.

16. One might suppose that each characteristic is produced using a portion of the total amount of the commodity available and a portion of the total time available. It is then reasonable to suppose that different efficient characteristics vectors can be obtained from the same commodity vector by varying these portions. A model of this type is presented by Becker (1965) and Michael and Becker (1973). But Pollack and Wachter (1975) argue that it contains very restrictive assumptions.

17. This assumption is used in the proofs of lemma 1 and proposition 2'.

18. We also assume that $u(c_1, c_2, n)$ is continuously differentiable in (c_1, c_2, n).

19. It would be significantly more realistic to allow the prestige that individuals obtain from a given z to also depend on how many of their fellow residents and citizens supply each z. The characteristics model ignores these externalities.

20. See Samuelson 1954, 1955.

21. Note 13 applies here.

22. The assumption referred to in note 17 is used here.

23. For simplicity we assume here that each individual's utility-maximizing commodity vector under W is unique when he or she resides in the country assigned by the second CR allocation. This assumption can be greatly weakened in the manner suggested by note 12.

24. This conclusion relies critically on the assumption that the LDC treats the net wages in the DC as fixed. We are also assuming that the LDC owns none of the DC's fixed factors of production. Finally, the qualification given in note 11 applies throughout this section.

25. As in the text we suppose that where there are multiple equilibria for a given world tax system, the best one can be made to prevail.

26. The proof uses the argument employed by Hahn (1973) and Sadka (1977) to show that aggregate production efficiency is desirable when commodity taxes are optimal and the profits from each firm can be taxed at separate rates.

References

Becker, G. 1965. A theory of the allocation of time. *Economic Journal* 75: 493–517.

Bhagwati, J., ed. 1976. *The Brain Drain and Taxation: Theory and Empirical Analysis.* Amsterdam: North-Holland.

Bhagwati, J., and M. Partington, eds. 1976. *Taxing the Brain Drain: A Proposal.* Amsterdam: North-Holland.

Hahn, F. 1973. On optimal taxation. *Journal of Economic Theory* 6: 96–106.

Hamada, K. 1978. Taxing the brain drain: A global point of view. Ch. 5. In: *The New International Economic Order: The North South Debate,* ed. J. Bhagwati. Cambridge, Mass.: MIT Press.

Lancaster, K. 1966. A new approach to consumer theory. *Journal of Political Economy* 81: 132–157.

Lancaster, K. 1971. *Consumer Demand: A New Approach.* New York: Columbia University Press.

Michael, R., and G. Becker. 1973. On the new theory of consumer behavior. *Swedish Journal of Economics* 75: 378–396.

Mirrlees, J. 1971. An exploration in the theory of optimal income taxation. *Review of Economic Studies* 38: 175–208.

Mirrlees, J. 1976a. The optimal structure of incentives and authority within an organization. *The Bell Journal of Economics* 7: 105–131.

Mirrlees, J. 1976b. Optimal tax theory: A synthesis. *Journal of Public Economics* 6: 327–358.

Oldman, O., and R. Pomp. 1975. The brain drain: A tax analysis of the Bhagwati proposal. *World Development* 3: 751–763.

Pollack, R., and M. Wachter. 1975. The relevance of the household production function and its implications for the allocation of time. *Journal of Political Economy* 83: 255–277.

Pomp, R., and O. Oldman. 1979. Tax measures in response to the brain drain. *Harvard International Law Journal* 20: 2–60.

Sadka, E. 1977. A note on producer taxation and public taxation. *Review of Economic Studies* 44: 385–387.

Samuelson, P. 1954. The pure theory of public expenditure. *Review of Economics and Statistics* 36: 387–389.

Samuelson, P. 1955. Diagrammatic exposition of a theory of public expenditure. *Review of Economics and Statistics* 37: 350–356.

Stern, N. 1976. On the specification of models of optimum income taxation. *Journal of Public Economics* 6: 123–162.

Index